The Reeves-Cook Debate on Baptism

by

Bruce Reeves and Gene Cook

ISBN 1-58427-166-3

Guardian of Truth Foundation
P.O. Box 9670
Bowling Green, Kentucky 42102

Table of Contents

Dedication

For Her Unfailing Love and Support
of the Defense of the Gospel of Christ,
Myself and Our Son Connor
This Book Is Lovingly Dedicated To
My Wife:

Rachel Korin Reeves

Introduction

Does baptism in water for the remission of sins nullify the gift of God's grace or proclaim the gift of God's grace? Is the gospel for all? Must one obey the gospel as spoken by Jesus? As you begin to examine the content of this debate be prepared to come face to face with the god of Calvinism. The propositions of this debate have been easily defined; however, the heart of the discussion reveals the distinction between the God of the Bible and the god of Calvinistic theology.

More than 350 people assembled four evenings to hear two disputants respond to the propositions. There have been no less than six baptisms as a result of the power of the truth of the gospel preached during this discussion. Why? The gospel is the power of God unto salvation to everyone who believes. This truth is clearly defined, while the darkness of the false doctrine of unconditional election is deafeated.

I do not believe the six baptisms will be the final number of conversions resulting from this debate. If you possess an open and honest heart, and have yet to obey the gospel of our Lord Jesus—the Lord will add you to his church as you receive with meekness the engrafted word.

— Dennis Carrow

Propositions

Resolved: "The Scriptures teach that the alien sinner receives the forgiveness of his past sins by faith only, before and without water baptism."

Affirm: Gene Cook
Deny: Bruce Reeves

Resolved: "The Scriptures teach that water baptism is essential in order for the alien sinner to obtain the forgiveness of his past sins."

Affirm: Bruce Reeves
Deny: Gene Cook

Rules of the Discussion

1. Each disputant will deliver two thirty-minute speeches alternately each evening.
2. Each disputant may have a moderator of his own choosing.
3. Five written questions will be exchanged fifteen minutes prior to the beginning session of each evening to be addressed by each debater at the beginning of his first speech.
4. No new material is to be presented in the last negative speech of each evening.
5. Each debater will follow Hedge's Rules of Honorable Controversy.
6. Each disputant will provide new charts to his opponent.

Introduction to the Reeves-Cook Debate

Keith Sharp

Gene Cook, Jr., "founding pastor of Covenant Baptist Church" in San Diego, California met Bruce Reeves, evangelist of the Highway 65 church of Christ in Conway, Arkansas, in public, oral debate on the subject of water baptism in Reynolds Auditorium on the campus of the University of Central Arkansas June 20, 21, 23, and 24, 2005. Mr. Cook hosts the weekly radio broadcast, "The Narrow Mind," is the author of *The Baptism Cult*, a critique of the International Church of Christ, and is the co-founder of the Tanzania School of Missions in East Africa. He is a Calvinistic Baptist and strongly believes and firmly defended all five points of Calvinism. He has engaged previously in 15 formal public debates, one with a gospel preacher on baptism, and has had numerous, informal radio debates. Cook was endorsed by the Foothills Fellowship Bible Church in Central Arkansas. Bruce Reeves had one previous formal, public debate. There were about 300 people present each night of the debate.

On Monday and Tuesday nights Gene Cook, Jr. affirmed and Bruce Reeves denied, "The Scriptures teach that the alien sinner is forgiven of his past sins by faith only, before and without water baptism." On Thursday and Friday nights Bruce Reeves affirmed and Gene Cook, Jr. denied, "The Scriptures teach that water baptism is essential in order for the alien sinner to obtain the forgiveness of his past sins."

This debate was not the usual exchange with a Baptist preacher on the purpose of water baptism. Most Baptists don't believe Calvinism, accepting only inherent depravity and perseverance of the saints (once saved—always saved) of the five points. Missionary Baptist preachers make arguments based on Calvinism, but they don't believe the Calvinism underlying the arguments. Thus, when pressed to be consistent, their error becomes apparent. Gene Cook, Jr. firmly believes and defends all of Calvinism and based his defense on Calvinistic theology throughout the debate.

When Bruce Reeves pressed him, instead of retreating from Calvinism, Mr. Cook made some bold statements in defense of such unpopular doctrines as infant damnation. These quotes are valuable to show the horrid consequences of Calvinism. Brethren, study the debate, get the quotes, and use them. They are dynamite!

Both men were capable and well prepared. The debate was of the highest quality in both content and demeanor. This was reflected by the audience, who listened quietly, intently, and respectfully throughout.

Only one incident marred this overall quality. In the last speech of the debate Mr. Cook, unable to come to grips with Reeves' argumentation, violated the rules of the debate and fairness by spending the entire speech introducing material completely new to the debate, which Bruce had no opportunity to answer. The irony is that this material primarily dealt with Romans 9, and Bruce was well prepared on this chapter and had wanted to discuss it more thoroughly in the earlier portions of the debate.

The debaters ably discussed the Calvinistic doctrines of hereditary depravity, unconditional election, and limited atonement and some of the basic passages that pertain to these doctrines.

The debate included a particularly good exchange on Romans 4 and James 2. Cook presented standard Calvinistic arguments on these passages, and brother Reeves not only answered his errors but also did a masterful job of presenting a clear exegesis of both passages.

Bruce pointed out that the debate was not about salvation by grace through faith (Eph. 2:8, 9; John 3:16; Rom. 5:1; Heb. 11:6), since he believed this as strongly as Cook. Rather, Reeves pointed out, he was denying that salvation is unconditional (2 Pet. 3:9), that men are justified by faith only (Jas. 2:24), and that baptism is non-essential to salvation (1 Pet. 3:21). He indicated that the real, underlying issues of the debate were the nature of God (i.e. God's universal love for and desire to save all men), the nature of man (i.e., man's ability to respond to God's love by choosing saving faith), and the nature of saving faith (i.e., the faith that submits to God's sovereign will by obeying him). He showed from the classic Old Testament examples of Noah, Jericho, and Naaman that salvation by grace includes the obedience of faith.

Bruce pointed out that Cook ignored the fact that the word "works" is used in different ways in the Scriptures. It can be used to denote works of merit (Eph. 2:8; Tit. 3:5), to name a system that demands sinless perfection for justification (Rom. 3:27; 4:2-8; 11:6), and to denote works of faith (1 Thess. 1:3; Jas. 2:14-26). This third use reveals the kind of faith that saves and is the way it is properly used to include repentance, confession, and baptism.

Brother Reeves taught that the apostle presents in the book of Romans two contrasting systems of justification: a system of works (sinless perfection) versus a system of faith (the gospel which affords forgiveness—Rom. 3:27). But the system of faith, the gospel, requires obedience by faith for justification (Rom. 1:5; 6:16-18; 16:26). This contrast between a law of faith (forgiveness by grace through obedient faith) and a law of works (flawless law keeping) is stated in Romans 3:27. This is the contrast of Romans 4:2-8. Thus, "works" in Romans 4 is not obedience of faith, but sinless law keeping, trusting in our own meritorious works. "Faith" is not "faith only," but the obedience of faith, trusting in Christ and his blood sacrifice for justification (Rom. 6:16-18).

Mr. Cook denied that Romans 6:3-7, Galatians 3:27, and Colossians 2:12 refer to water baptism. In reply, Brother Reeves showed that the Samaritans were saved and "in Christ" in Acts 8:12. Yet, they had only been baptized in the name of Jesus Christ, i.e., they had received water baptism (Acts 10:47-48), they had received no miraculous measure of the Holy Spirit, thus, no Holy Spirit baptism had occurred (Acts 8:15-17). Therefore, water baptism is the baptism of Romans 6:3-6, Galatians 3:27, and 1 Corinthians 12:13 which puts one into Christ. It is amazingly ironic that Cook, a Baptist, would use these passages to show that water baptism is a burial yet deny they refer to water baptism!

Cook showed the Baptist contempt for water baptism and his willingness to confuse the issue. He claimed the debate was about whether we are justified by "taking a bath" or by faith. Of course, baptism is not about taking a bath (1 Pet. 3:21), and the Scriptures teach we are justified by faith when we are baptized (Gal. 3:26-27).

Cook's standard argument on any baptism verses that he would admit speak of water baptism (Mark 16:16; Acts 2:38; 22:16; and 1 Pet. 3:21) was to claim that baptism is a sign of salvation. Reeves pointed out that baptism is never called a sign of salvation; rather, it pictures the death, burial, and resurrection of Christ (Rom. 6:3-6). Cook contradicted his own argument here by taking the usual Baptist position that "for" in Acts 2:38 means "because of."

The two debaters ably presented their positions on the various New Testament passages dealing with the purpose of baptism. Reeves' argumentation on the case of Cornelius was particularly telling. Cornelius had to hear words from Peter to be saved (Acts 11:14). But the only thing Peter told

Cornelius that he didn't already know was that he needed to be baptized (Acts 10:36-48). Cook had no reply to this, but countered with the standard argument that, since Cornelius received the Holy Spirit before he was baptized, he was already saved. Bruce simply noted the several examples where reception of the Holy Spirit did not prove salvation (e.g., Balaam's donkey, Caiaphas).

On the last night of the debate, when Mr. Cook had the last speech, Brother Reeves presented summary arguments on each of the New Testament passages that speak of the purpose of baptism. Of course, Mr. Cook ignored these arguments and presented new material on predestination. His unwillingness to reply to Bruce's arguments was not lost on the audience. The last I heard, seven former Baptists have been baptized for the remission of sins as direct results of this debate. Yes, properly conducted debates do accomplish good.

Brother Reeves and his assistant, Don McClain, are good examples of how to properly prepare for and publicly debate an issue. They spent countless hours for months preparing for the debate by studying the Scriptures and past debates, conversing and corresponding with other debaters, preparing notes and arguments, and putting together electronic charts. There is no mental activity more difficult than properly preparing for a debate, and there is no substitute for many, weary hours of study in preparation.

This debate will be an excellent resource for many years to document the teaching of Calvinistic Baptists, the arguments they employ, the answers to these arguments, and the evidence for the truth. Brother Reeves' material on Cornelius is worth more than the price of the book. I commend Bruce for his excellent work, Don McClain for his valuable service in a helping role, and the Guardian of Truth Foundation for publishing this high quality debate.

First Affirmative

Gene Cook, Jr.

As you have heard, my name is Gene Cook, Jr. I am the pastor of Covenant Baptist Church in San Diego, California. It is my privilege to be here tonight and to visit Arkansas, Little Rock and Conway. I am looking forward to this week, and I am looking forward to fellowshipping with some of my friends whom I have not met face to face until tonight from Foothills Bible Fellowship, John McCarty's church, the man who just came and prayed.

The proposition that I am here to defend tonight is on the board behind me. I will just read it one more time for your hearing. My proposition is that *the Scriptures teach that the alien sinner has forgiveness of his past sins by faith only before and without water baptism.* I pretty much put my presentation here on PowerPoint.

Let me begin by defining my proposition so that there is no ambiguity about what I am here to defend. When I say "the alien sinner," I am talking about the sinner who is alienated from God. He is alienated from God because Adam came as the first man and served as the representative before the entire human race. And when Adam rebelled against God, God not only rejected Adam, God not only condemned Adam, God not only put a curse on Adam and his wife, but he also put a curse on all of the earth, all of Adam's posterity, from every generation that would ever exist that is tied to Adam. When I say "forgiven," I am talking about having our sins forgiven. I am talking about being justified before God. I am also talking about becoming righteous before God. Justification is a biblical term, and I am going to get into what the Bible means when it uses the term "justification." I am also going to get into what it means to be made righteous before God.

When I say "past sins," I am talking about the condemnation that Adam brought upon the whole human race that, as a result of Adam's actions, the whole human race is said to be condemned before God according to the book of Romans 5:18 for example, "By one man, sin entered the world, and by one man, one act of righteousness, salvation entered the world," speaking of Jesus Christ. When I talk about past sins, I am not only talking about the sin of Adam, our first father, but I am also talking about our own personal transgressions of God's law. The Bible itself defines what sin is. "Sin is the transgression of God's law."

When I say "before," I am talking about in relationship to time, that is before water baptism. I believe that water baptism is something that our Lord Jesus Christ commands in Scripture, so I am not going to underplay the importance of water baptism, but when I talk about "being forgiven by faith before water baptism," I am talking about in relationship to time, and when I am talking about "without," I am talking about, once again, in relationship to the moment of faith. I am not saying that we are just forgiven and then we can do whatever we want to do. Once we have been forgiven by faith, once we have been justified, once we have been reconciled to God by faith, then we have been born into the kingdom of God, and we now have a responsibility to do all that the King commands even, *even* baptism, and so I think baptism is very important.

Now, part of the way that the debate is structured is that we were to submit questions to one another fifteen minutes before the debate begins, and you can see that the debate really is going to center around the subject of water baptism. But let me just give you a heads up. This is the first time I have met Mr. Bruce Reeves tonight when I walked in this auditorium, but let me just give you a heads up about what's about to happen. I agreed to come here and debate baptism, but since Mr. Reeves knows that I am a Calvinist, he would rather ask me questions about Calvinism. I would have been more than happy to come have a debate about Calvinism, but I really came to have a debate about baptism. However, since I consider myself a man of God and since I consider myself someone who is concerned about the truth of God's word, I do not have any questions answering anything. You can ask me, you know, what my children's names are if you want. It does not matter to me, so I am going to go ahead and answer the questions even though they have nothing to do with baptism except for the last question.

There are five questions. The first question is, "True or False? God unconditionally chooses who will be saved, and this leads to the logical conclusion that as a result of his not choosing others, he creates them and never gives them an opportunity to be saved." Well, I would have to say false because that is not what the logical conclusion leads us to at all. In fact, Jesus says in John 3:18, "He who believes in him is not judged, but he who does not believe has been judged already because he has not believed in the name of the only begotten Son of God." Therefore, the condition of man is that he is under the condemnation of both Adam and his own sins to begin with. So to say, that man does not somehow have an opportunity, or that it is a logical conclusion that man is not given an opportunity, is false.

Number 2, "If unconditional election is true, what is God's motivation for not saving the majority of mankind?" Moreover, my opponent was kind enough to make this a multiple-choice question. I have two answers from which to choose. The first one, "God is not powerful enough to provide them a way of salvation." Well, we clearly know that God is all-powerful, so that is not an option. "B: God does not love them enough to provide them a way of salvation." Well, the Bible does not tell us that either. What the Bible says in Ephesians chapter 1 concerning God's motivation, and by the way, when it comes to commenting or asking questions about God's motivation, I can only speak as far as the Scriptures speak. I cannot get inside the mind of God unless he has revealed it to me in his word, and he says in Ephesians 1:5, "He predestined us to adoption as sons through Jesus Christ to himself according to the kind intention of His will." Therefore, the only thing that God tells us about his motivation and predestination is that it is tied to the kind intention of his will, and that is good enough for me.

Number 3: "True or False? Jesus Christ died for the sins of every human being." As a Calvinist, of course, I would say false. I believe that only those who are saved have their sins paid for. The sacrifice of Jesus was for the purpose of atoning for sins, and so if somebody rejects Christ, obviously if he dies in that state, then he doesn't benefit from the death that Jesus Christ died, so in effect, Jesus Christ's death did not benefit him at all. Jesus did not die for his sins. That is why he goes to hell because he has to pay for his own sins for all of eternity.

Number 4: "True or false? An elect infant who dies in his infancy will be saved." Well, every elect person who dies will be saved. Maybe you do not like the word election, but it is in the Bible. Election is something that is synonymous with being a believer. God is the one that chose those words, not me. So yeah, anybody who is elect, no matter how old he is, will be saved.

In addition, the last question, which I said is remotely tied to water baptism, is this: "Is the baptism of Romans 6:3-6, Galatians 3:27, and Colossians 2:12 necessary for the forgiveness of past sins?" And I would say "yes," of course, because none of those passages speaks of water baptism. They speak of being baptized into Christ. They speak of regeneration. They speak of the point in which a believing sinner is immersed in Christ, which is what baptism is supposed to symbolize to begin with. So those are the answers to my questions that I have been given.

Now, let me go on with the material that I brought to present tonight. The debate tonight will center around the issue of justification, namely "How does God justify a sinner?" "How is a sinner made acceptable in God's sight?" That is the focus of this whole debate. When we start talking about the necessity of baptism, we have to ask, "Is water baptism a requirement for salvation?" Immediately we are asking the question, How is it that a sinner who is alienated from God and how is it that a sinner can be reconciled to a God who is said to be completely holy, completely without sin, completely unstained, unspotted with the sin with which men are so familiar? How is it that a man can come into close fellowship with a God who has been untouched and unspotted by sin? That is really the question. How is a man justified? If heaven is a perfect place and sinners are invited into heaven, if heaven is going to remain a perfect place, those sinners have to somehow be made perfect. That is the question here. Are sinners made perfect by taking a bath, by washing themselves with water, or are sinners made perfect by faith in Jesus Christ?

In order for me to answer that question, in order to thoroughly answer that question, I am going to have to address the following subjects. First, we are going to have to talk about the subject of faith. We are going to have to talk about salvation or the term saved. How does the Bible use these terms? What do they mean? We are going to have to talk about righteousness. What does it mean when the Bible uses the terminology "God's righteousness,"—it is not talking about man's righteousness, but God's righteousness? What does it mean when the Bible uses the term justification and how are these terms: faith, salvation, righteousness, and justification, how do these terms, how do these doctrines fit in with the doctrine of water baptism? That is what I want to talk to you about tonight.

First, let us talk about faith. Faith is a gift from God. We read here in Romans 12:3, "For through the grace given to me, I say to everyone among you, do not think more highly of yourself, or himself, than he ought to think, but to think as to have sound judgment, and God has allotted to each a measure of faith." You see, it is God who gives faith. That is why the disciples said, "Lord, increase our faith." Faith is also the antithesis of works we read in Ephesians 2:8-9. "For by grace you have been saved through faith, and that not of yourselves, it is the gift of God, not a result of works lest any man boast." So, you have faith, which is an antithesis to works. And we are told in this verse that we are saved by grace through faith. In other words, it is not about works. What are works? Works are the performance of whatever God commands in his word.

By default, because God is God, no matter what God commands, man is obligated to keep that law. And when God commands something, as soon as it comes out of his very mouth, it is by default a law. When God says through the apostle Paul for example in Acts 17, God is commanding all men everywhere to repent, it is now a law that all men everywhere repent at the pronunciation of the gospel of Jesus Christ. Faith, once again, is the antithesis of works we are told in John 6:28 when Jesus is asked by the Pharisees, "Therefore they said to Him, 'What shall we do so that we may work the works of God?'" They wanted to know, what works can we do that will make us acceptable before God? In addition, what was Jesus' response? "Jesus answered and said to them, 'This is the work of God that you believe in Him whom he has sent.'" Is Jesus now saying that belief is a work? No! Jesus is saying there are no works that man can do to make himself acceptable before God. That is why Jesus Christ had to die. He not only died that he might pay for our sins, but he also died that he might give us his perfect life.

I have been doing a study on the life of Elijah, and yesterday I was preaching about the text in Mt. Carmel when Elijah comes to King Ahab. King Ahab immediately says, "Oh, it's you, the troubler of Israel, the one who has been troubling Israel," because Elijah had pronounced that there would be a famine in the land, that it wouldn't rain until he gave the word because he was the prophet of God, and the king of Israel had been given over to idolatry. Therefore, when Elijah shows up, immediately Ahab says, "There is the troubler of Israel." And Elijah says, "No! I am not the one who has troubled Israel. You are the one that has troubled Israel by giving the nation over to idols, you and your father." Some of you might have come to this debate, and you may see me as a troubler. In fact, many of you may view me as the enemy, the bad guy, the one with the false gospel, but let me tell you something, I am not the troubler. I am the one who has been sent, I believe, by God to come and not be a trouble to you but to be a blessing to you, and as long as I stand here and I faithfully read the Scriptures, and I faithfully take you back to what the Scriptures say comparing Scripture by Scripture, I will be a blessing to you. So please do not view me as an enemy. View me as a man who is concerned not only about truth, but about the souls of people who have been given over to a system of works righteousness when the Bible itself says there are no works that will justify a man.

There is no flesh that will be justified by works. It is all of grace or it is none of grace. This is the gospel of Jesus Christ. We must come before God stripped of our own righteousness. If we stand in Christ, it is not because we are smarter than our neighbor. It is not because we have been able to figure out the doctrine of baptism. It is because God has been gracious to us, and he has blessed us, and he has shed his grace in our lives. I come as a naked, poor, wretched sinner before God. I have nothing to offer him, and yet in that state, he came, and he loved me more than anyone ever loved me, and he not only loved me, but he forgave me of my transgressions, and he not only forgave me of my transgressions, but he gave me his own Son's righteousness. And in the midst of that, he taught me from his word that it was not I who was seeking him, but he sought me. It was not I who was worthy of salvation; rather I was worthy of condemnation. And it was in the midst of that that God came and shed his grace on my heart. This is why I have such distaste, and that is a mild word it, for any system of doctrine that purports to bring man into a right standing by man's own actions.

Moreover, you say, "Well, what about faith? What about the believer's prayer, the sinner's prayer?" Faith is a gift from God. I have just given you three passages here. Faith is a gift from God. Let us talk about the term "saved." I hope that I will get this thing working by the time we are done here tonight. Saved. Saved can be spoken of, the term as it is used in the Bible, can be spoken of in the past tense as something that is already accomplished. Very important! Luke 7:50: "And he said to the woman," this is Jesus speaking; "Your faith has saved you. Go in peace." Ephesians 2:4-5: "But God being rich in mercy because of His great love with which He loved us even when we were dead in our transgressions, made us alive together with Christ, by grace you have been saved." Past tense. Titus 3:5: "He saved us," past tense, "not on the basis of deeds which we have done in righteousness, but according to His mercy by the washing of regeneration and renewing by the Holy Spirit."

But, saved can also be spoken of in the present tense as something that is now being accomplished. It says, for example in 1 Corinthians 1:18: "For the word of the cross is foolishness to those who are perishing, but to us who are being saved, it is the power of God." Who is speaking in this text? The apostle Paul is speaking. But, he speaks of salvation in the present tense. He says, "We [Christians, Saints, he addresses the letter to] are being saved." Present tense. 1 Peter 3:21, which I am sure we will talk about more, "Corresponding to that, baptism now saves you." "Now saves you," is saving you, in the present tense.

However, saved can also be spoken of in the future tense. For example, Romans 5:9: "Much more then, having now been justified by His blood, we shall be saved from the wrath of God through Him." You see that. Paul is the same one that speaks of saved past tense, the same one that speaks of saved present tense and he is the one who also speaks of saved future tense. 1 Corinthians 3:15: "If any man's work is burned up, he will suffer loss, but he himself will be saved yet as through fire." Future tense.

"What about righteousness?" We must not only understand what the Bible says about faith, that it is a gift, we must also understand that the word "saved" is used in different ways. Sometimes it points us back to regeneration or what the Bible calls the new birth, being born again. No man will see the kingdom of God unless he is born again. Sometimes it speaks to the time of sanctification whereby the Christian is working out his salvation with fear and trembling. He is being saved as he obeys God and as he wrestles with his sinful nature, but the Bible also talks about, once again, a future time in which we will be saved. But, what about the word "righteousness"? What does the word "righteousness" mean? How does somebody become righteous? Romans 10:1-4, Paul, speaking of his Jewish brethren, the ones who had rejected the gospel, says this about them: "Brethren, my heart's desire and my prayer to God for them is for their salvation. For I testify about them that they have a zeal for God but not in accordance with knowledge. For not knowing about God's righteousness and seeking to establish their own, they did not subject themselves to the righteousness of God, for Christ is the end of the law for righteousness to everyone who believes."

You see, really, there are only two religions in the world. There are only two religions in the world. There is the religion that contains those subjects, those people who have submitted themselves to what Paul calls here in verse 3 "God's righteousness," and then there are those who are seeking to establish their own righteousness. The Bible is very clear, as we shall see; man's righteousness is not good enough. Man must have God's righteousness. What does this mean? "For not knowing about God's righteousness. . . ." What do you mean, not knowing about God's righteousness? These were the Jews. These were the Pharisees. They had the Scriptures. They could quote them from heart. They challenged Jesus from the Scriptures, and you are telling me that they are not familiar with the term God's righteousness. That is right, because the Bible means something very specific when it talks about God's righteousness as juxtaposed to man's righteousness.

Man cannot be righteous enough in and of himself to be acceptable to God. Romans 9:30, Paul, before he gets to that passage that I just read, says, "What shall we say then? That the Gentiles who did not pursue righteousness attained righteousness. Even the righteousness, which is by faith, but

Israel, pursuing a law of righteousness, did not arrive at that law. Why? Because they did not pursue it by faith but as though it were by works. They stumbled over the stumbling stone. Just as it is written, 'Behold I lay in Zion a stone of stumbling and a rock of offense, and he who believes in Him will not be disappointed.'" What is Paul saying here? Paul says you know it is really a strange thing. Here the Jews were given the oracles of God. Here the Jews, of all people, were trying to keep God's law, but now something radically different has happened. The Gentiles are coming into the family of God; the very ones who were not initially pursuing the righteousness of God, now possess the righteousness of God. That is what he says. He says, "The Gentiles who did not pursue the righteousness attained righteousness." How could that be? How could somebody attain righteousness without pursuing it by the law? Well, Paul gives us the answer here. He says, "Even the righteousness which is by faith." Man becomes righteous before God by faith.

If God wanted all of us in this auditorium to understand tonight that man can only possess God's righteousness, and he could only possess God's righteousness by faith, what kind of language might he use to communicate that to us? Could he use anything clearer than this passage? Could we sit here together and come up with a formula, with a sentence that would somehow more clearly communicate that man is not made righteous by keeping God's laws, but man is made righteous by faith? No, we could not. We cannot improve upon the word of God. But how many of us have come into this auditorium tonight, how many of us like those two men that came into the temple? The one man approached the altar thinking that he had comfort and ease with God, thinking that he was acceptable before God, saying, "Oh Lord, I am glad I am not like this tax collector, the one over there who is a sinner. I am glad I pay my tithes. I am glad I come to the temple. I am glad I do almost everything you command." And the other man, we are told, was not comfortable, was not at ease with the altar of God, so he stayed in the back, and he beat upon his breast, and he said before God, "Oh God, have mercy on me, a sinner." And Jesus said as he was telling that story, "Which one do you think went home justified before God?" The sinner who had come face to face with God's holiness, with his own inability, with God's righteousness, with his own sin, and as a result, he was naked there before God, just with nothing left but to ask for mercy.

That is the only way you come into the kingdom of God, and if you have not come in that way, then you haven't come in, and I say that not as your enemy, I say that as your friend, as somebody whom, I believe, God has sent to be a blessing to you. You will not stand before a Holy God, one who, we are told, has eyes of fire in the book of Revelation so that as he looks into your heart, he sees every sin. Everyone in this auditorium has sinned today. You say, "What? How do you know?" It is because you have not loved God with all of your heart. You have not loved your neighbor as yourself. If you think you have, that is another sin. And yet, God calls us as sinners to come and dine at his table, not with anything in our hands. Isaiah says, "Come and buy food. Come and buy bread and milk without money." That is the message of the gospel. That is how man is made righteous before God. I am going to ask you as the audience here tonight. I am going to ask you to pay very close attention to what takes place in this debate, and the reason that I am asking you that is because I think that what you are going to hear is not just two radically different opinions about what the Bible is teaching. I think what you are going to hear tonight and throughout this week are two different religions, the religion of God, the only religion whereby man is saved, the gospel of grace, and the feeble attempts of man to obey and somehow attain an acceptable position before the almighty Creator, our judge. It is a dangerous thing to be here tonight and throughout this week, should you reject God's grace.

In fact, you will be made more accountable as a result of what you hear. The reason why I have come to Conway is that I am going to tell many of you things that you would just never hear in the churches that you are currently attending. I am not saying that because, you know, I think I am some prophet of God. I am saying that because the gospel preaching found in Scripture is so sparse, I can say that with confidence. God is calling us, blind, naked, wretched, death, dumb, dead, all synonyms for the condition of man outside of Christ; God is calling us to be able to see, to be able to hear, to be able to walk, and most importantly to be able to live. There are eternal consequences at hand, so I do not take this privilege lightly, and I tell you this with great conviction. I am not here to play games. I am not here to show you cartoons. I am here to show you the word of God and ask that God would persuade you of the truth. Thank you!

Monday Night

First Negative

Bruce Reeves

Good evening ladies and gentlemen. It certainly is a pleasure to be with you. I would feel remiss if I did not take a brief few moments to express my deep amount of appreciation for your presence, for the fact that you are here and that you are interested in the word of God, whatever your convictions may be. I would also like to express my deep appreciation to Mr. Gene Cook for his willingness to come all the way from San Diego, California. A congregation in this area that shares his convictions has endorsed him, and Lord willing, I believe that we can receive a great deal of benefit and profit because of being here.

Mr. Cook said several things I want to address, of course. One of the things that he told us was that you were going to see that there were two radically different religions. I will tell you as this debate progresses, I believe that you will see, and have already seen as we even get into tonight's discussion, that our views of God, and the nature of God, and who God is, and what the gospel is all about are radically different. So, I want you to keep that in mind as we progress.

Now, as we deal with this subject, I want to make sure I clarify in your mind what I am denying and what I am not denying. You may not have realized as you listened to Mr. Cook speak, but I am not denying that God is the one who saves. There is no doubt about that truth. I agree that if any of us is going to be saved, it is by the grace, and the mercy, and the favor of God. We agree on that point. I agree that salvation is by grace through faith, and that is an important phrase for you to understand as we look at some of these things. I believe Ephesians 2:8-9 with all of my heart, as well as any other passage that he will cite in this discussion regarding faith.

Here is what I am denying—I am denying that salvation is unconditional. Now, I asked him some questions, we are going to get to that in just a moment, and we were told that these questions had absolutely nothing to do with this particular debate. That his views, as he has called himself a Calvinist, his views as a Calvinist have no bearing on his view of faith only and the proposition under consideration, and yet the rest of his speech he argued exactly the opposite. He argued that salvation was unconditional. And so he told me in the questions, "Well, this has nothing to do with what we are talking about," and then in the rest of his speech he tells us there is nothing that we must do. So, that was interesting to me.

I am also denying that men are justified by faith only. I agree we are justified by faith, but the Bible does not teach that we are justified by faith only, and of course, I am denying that baptism is a non-essential to salvation.

Again, I want you to understand what this discussion is really about: (1) I am affirming to you God's universal love. We heard about the love of God and the sacrifice of Jesus Christ. I believe with all of my heart that God loves each and every human being, and he desires for each and every human being to be saved, but we must respond in faith. This debate is also about whether or not man has the ability to respond to God by choosing faith. Are we able? Can anybody choose faith and come to God? That question needs to be resolved. And he has talked about faith, grace, and works and we are going to talk about that tonight. We are dealing with the nature of a saving faith; the faith that submits to God's sovereign will by obeying him is the only faith that will save.

Now again, I believe all of these passages about faith, every time he quotes a passage about faith, I want you to understand, I believe that passage. I believe each and every one of them. We will put any of them on here that he wants me to put on here. I accept every one of them. Hebrews 11:6 says, "Without faith it is impossible to please him, for he that cometh to God," note that we must come to God, "he that cometh to God must believe that He is and that He is a rewarder of them that diligently seek him."

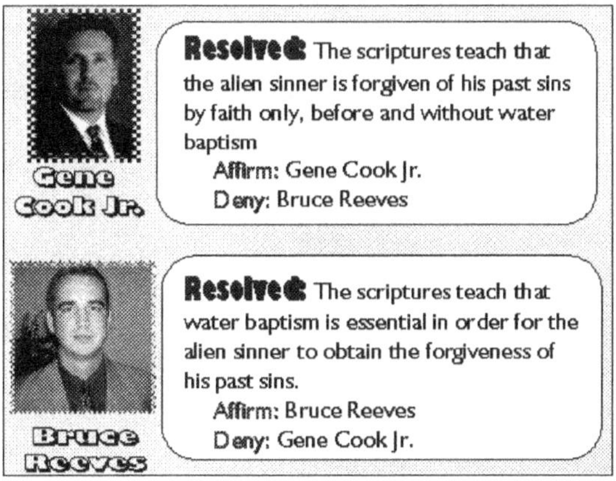
Gene Cook Jr.
Resolved: The scriptures teach that the alien sinner is forgiven of his past sins by faith only, before and without water baptism
Affirm: Gene Cook Jr.
Deny: Bruce Reeves
Bruce Reeves
Resolved: The scriptures teach that water baptism is essential in order for the alien sinner to obtain the forgiveness of his past sins.
Affirm: Bruce Reeves
Deny: Gene Cook Jr.

Now let me get to the questions that he gave to me as we consider some of these things. He said, "Please explain the meaning of Romans 10:3." And that was a chart; I did not catch the number. But, that was the chart that he put up here with Romans 10:3. Turn your Bibles to Romans the 10th chap-

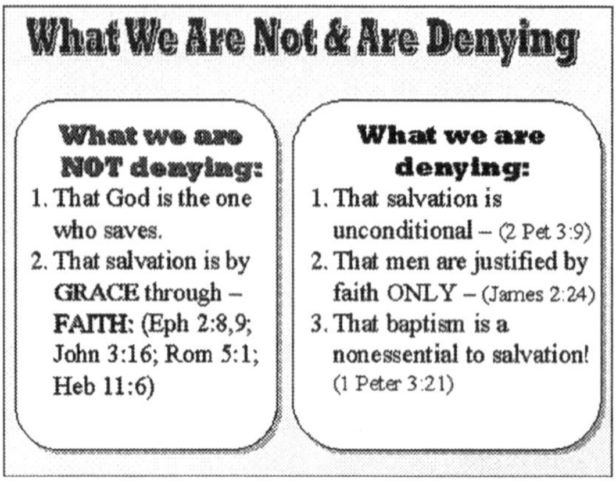
What We Are Not & Are Denying
What we are NOT denying:
1. That God is the one who saves.
2. That salvation is by GRACE through – FAITH: (Eph 2:8,9; John 3:16; Rom 5:1; Heb 11:6)
What we are denying:
1. That salvation is unconditional – (2 Pet 3:9)
2. That men are justified by faith ONLY – (James 2:24)
3. That baptism is a nonessential to salvation! (1 Peter 3:21)

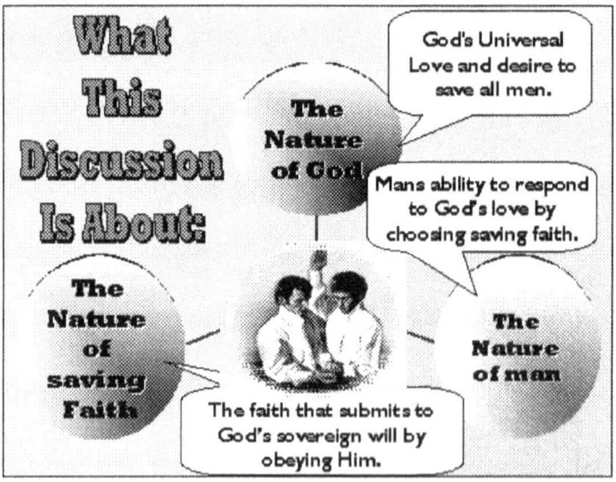
What This Discussion Is About:
God's Universal Love and desire to save all men.
The Nature of God
Mans ability to respond to God's love by choosing saving faith.
The Nature of saving Faith
The Nature of man
The faith that submits to God's sovereign will by obeying Him.

ter. Paul says, "Brethren, my heart's desire and my prayer to God for Israel is that they might be saved, for I bear them record that they have a zeal of God, but not according to knowledge, for they being ignorant of God's righteousness." Now that is what we are talking about in this debate. What is God's righteousness? They were not ignorant of the fact that God was a righteous being. "For they being ignorant of God's righteousness and going about to establish their own righteousness have not **submitted** themselves unto the righteousness of God." So, the answer to number 1, "Please explain the meaning of Romans 10:3" is that those who refuse to submit to the conditions of the gospel are not submitting themselves to God's righteousness, and that is central to this issue of baptism. It is simply choosing faith and expressing that faith in order to receive the forgiveness of my sins. Number 2: He says, "Is faith a work according to Ephesians 2:8-9?" It is not the kind of works mentioned in Ephesians 2:9. That would be a work in which one would boast. He asked me number 3: "Please define the term grace as it is used in Ephesians 2:8." It is the unmerited favor of God. Number 4: "Is baptism a work of righteousness according to Matthew 4:15?" And I think you meant, Gene, Matthew 3:15. I want to give you the benefit of the doubt here. I am sure that is what you were talking about. "Is baptism a work of righteousness according to Matthew 3:15?" It is a working of God's righteousness, not man's righteousness. And number 5: He asked me, "Please explain how Abraham became righteous according to Romans 4:3." And that was by faith. It was not by faith only, but indeed, it was by faith.

I want to get to something else as we consider the questions that I asked him and we are going to look at some of the ramifications of his answers. I am going to go in reverse here a little bit, but on number 5, the last question I asked him, "Was the baptism of Romans 6, Colossians 2, and Galatians 3 essential to receiving the forgiveness of past sins?" He said, "Yes, but it wasn't talking about water baptism." That was his answer to the question. But we have a problem here in Acts 8 if that is the argument that he was making. I want you to look at Acts the 8th chapter with me and I want you to notice verse 12. In Acts 8:12 we read, "When they believed Philip preaching the things concerning the kingdom of God in the name of Jesus Christ, they were baptized, both men and women." I think, and I believe that Mr. Cook and I will agree that those Samaritans were saved in Acts 8:12 and that they were in Christ. And yet, the passage goes on to say when we move down to verse 14, "Now when the apostles which were in Jerusalem heard that Samaria had received the word of God, they sent unto them Peter and John who when they were come down prayed for them that they might receive the Holy Ghost, for as yet he was fallen upon none of them only...," now I really want you to pay attention here, "only they were baptized in the name of the Lord Jesus." Not only does he say the Holy Spirit had not fallen upon them, even though we know they were saved up in verse 12, but he says the only baptism they had received was baptism in the name of the Lord Jesus, and we know from Acts 10, that is water baptism. Baptism in the name of the Lord Jesus is water baptism. So, the only baptism they received up in verse 12 was water baptism. The Holy Spirit had not even fallen upon them miraculously. And so clearly, water baptism is the baptism that put them into Christ.

Now as I asked Mr. Cook about some of these questions, Mr. Cook told us that they did not have anything to do with what we are talking about, and then argued that human activity in response to the gospel is non-essential. We want to know, "Does God desire for every man to be saved?" And this does have a bearing on what we will be talking about this week. In Matthew 23:37 Jesus said, "Oh Jerusalem, Jerusalem, the one who kills the prophets and stones those who are sent to her, how often I wanted to gather your children together as a hen gathers her chicks under her wings, but you were not willing." Now pay attention here. The Lord wanted them to be saved, but they had to respond to him. He wanted them to be saved, but they were not willing. Jesus wants us all to come to him. Again, God is not partial. He does not pick some and refuse others outside of this idea of those who respond in faith. Is it unconditional? Is that what we are dealing with? Is that what his first speech was about, that it has nothing to do with whether or not we respond. God is not partial: Acts 10:34-35 says, "Then Peter opened his mouth, 'In truth I perceive that God shows no partiality but in every nation whoever fears him,'" and does what? "Works righteousness." Works righteousness. We must respond in faith in order to be accepted of him. Acts 17:30 says, "Truly these times of ignorance God overlooked but now commands all men everywhere to repent." "All men everywhere to repent!" I must respond. I would like to know if repentance necessary in order to become a Christian? 1 Timothy 2 teaches us that God desires all men to be saved, "Who desires all men to be saved and to come to the knowledge of the truth."

Now we were also told that Jesus did not die for every human being. In the midst of telling us that he has firm conviction in the grace of God and in the unmerited favor of God and the love of God, we were told that Jesus did not die for every human being. 1 John chapter 2 says, "And he himself is the propitiation for our sins, and not for ours only," not just for those of us who have obeyed the gospel, but also for the whole world. Of course, not all men are saved, but it is because they refuse what has been made available to them.

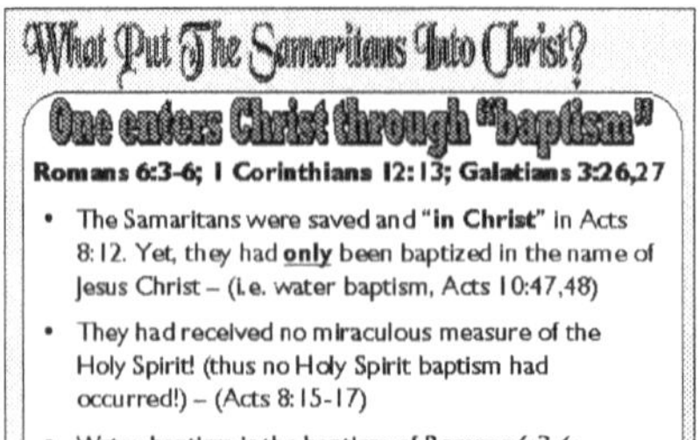
What Put The Samaritans Into Christ?
One enters Christ through "baptism"
Romans 6:3-6; I Corinthians 12:13; Galatians 3:26,27
• The Samaritans were saved and "in Christ" in Acts 8:12. Yet, they had only been baptized in the name of Jesus Christ – (i.e. water baptism, Acts 10:47,48)
• They had received no miraculous measure of the Holy Spirit! (thus no Holy Spirit baptism had occurred!) – (Acts 8:15-17)
• Water baptism is the baptism of Romans 6:3-6; Galatians 3:27; & I Corinthians 12:13 which PUTS one INTO Christ!

God's Will, Love, & Desire
Jesus "Wants" All To Come To Him!
BUT - We Must Be Willing!
Matthew 23:37 (NKJV)
"O Jerusalem, Jerusalem, the one who kills the prophets and stones those who are sent to her! How often I wanted to gather your children together, as a hen gathers her chicks under her wings, but you were not willing!

God's Will, Love, & Desire
God Is NOT Partial!
Man MUST respond to God's love & grace!
Acts 10:34-35 (NKJV)
Then Peter opened his mouth and said: "In truth I perceive that God shows no partiality.
[35] But in every nation whoever fears Him and works righteousness is accepted by Him.

God's Will, Love, & Desire
God Is NOT Partial!
Man MUST respond to God's love & grace!
Acts 17:30 (NKJV)
Truly, these times of ignorance God overlooked, but now commands all men everywhere to repent,

God's Will, Love, & Desire
God Is NOT Partial!
Man MUST respond to God's love & grace!
1 Tim. 2:4-6 (NKJV)
who desires all men to be saved and to come to the knowledge of the truth. [5] For there is one God and one Mediator between God and men, the Man Christ Jesus, [6] who gave Himself a ransom for all, to be testified in due time,

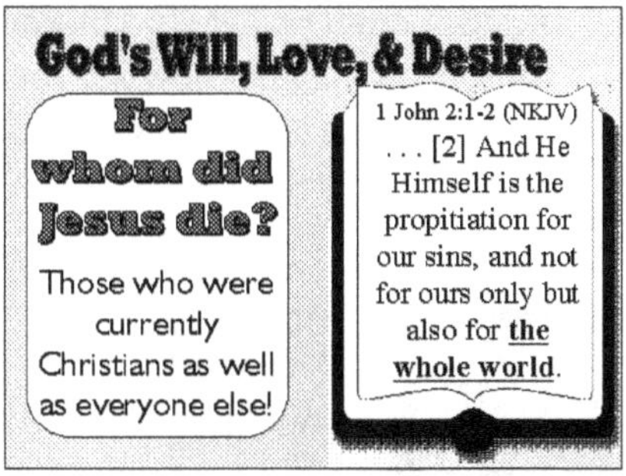
God's Will, Love, & Desire
For whom did Jesus die?
Those who were currently Christians as well as everyone else!
1 John 2:1-2 (NKJV)
. . . [2] And He Himself is the propitiation for our sins, and not for ours only but also for the whole world.

I want to go to Ephesians chapter 2 because he spent a good deal of his time on that verse. Let us talk about this idea of works, grace and faith, because that is at the heart of what we are discussing. It is really important that we understand contextually what is being discussed. Ephesians 2:8. "For by grace you have been saved through faith, and not of yourselves, it is the gift of God, not of works lest anyone should boast." So, we are talking about works in which one would boast. "For we are His workmanship created in Christ Jesus for good works which God hath prepared beforehand that we should walk in them." Again, I told you what is at the heart of this issue? Are there any conditions that the alien sinner must meet in order to be saved by God's grace? It is either unconditional or it is conditional. Must I respond in obedience is the question.

Now we need to talk about this idea of works. You know, the term works as you look into the word of God is defined in different ways as you look at different passages. Sometimes it is defined as that which is meritorious. Sometimes we are talking about something by which you would attempt to earn a thing of God, and I agree that none of us earns our salvation. We do not deserve our salvation. We cannot merit our salvation and that is what Paul is talking about in Ephesians 2:8 and Titus 3:5. Sometimes as you look at a book, such as the book of Romans, you need to recognize that there is a contrast between two systems. Paul talks about in Romans 3:27 the idea of the law of works versus the law of faith and in that context, he is talking about the gospel of Christ versus the Law of Moses. The law of works would have been a law that would have demanded sinlessness. The Law of Moses demanded sinlessness in order to justify a person. Certainly, we understand that we are under a system that provides us with grace and mercy, but that does not nullify the idea of obedience to the gospel of Jesus Christ.

In other contexts, such as in James the second chapter, we find that the term works refers to the activity of our faith, certainly, those actions are necessary in order to become a Christian, and that is where baptism would fall. Baptism is not up here in a meritorious work by which somebody would earn his salvation. That is what you heard, but that is not the case. It is a matter of our faith acting. It is a matter of us obeying the Lord.

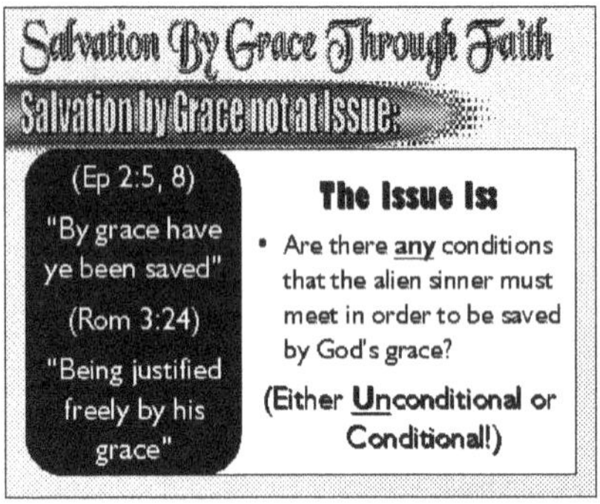
Salvation By Grace Through Faith
Salvation by Grace not at Issue:
(Ep 2:5, 8)
"By grace have ye been saved"
(Rom 3:24)
"Being justified freely by his grace"
The Issue Is:
• Are there any conditions that the alien sinner must meet in order to be saved by God's grace?
(Either Unconditional or Conditional!)

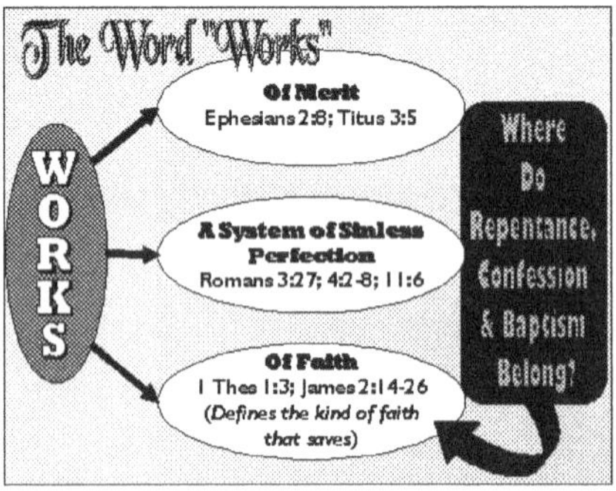
The Word "Works"
WORKS
Of Merit
Ephesians 2:8; Titus 3:5
A System of Sinless Perfection
Romans 3:27; 4:2-8; 11:6
Of Faith
1 Thes 1:3; James 2:14-26
(Defines the kind of faith that saves)
Where Do Repentance, Confession & Baptism Belong?

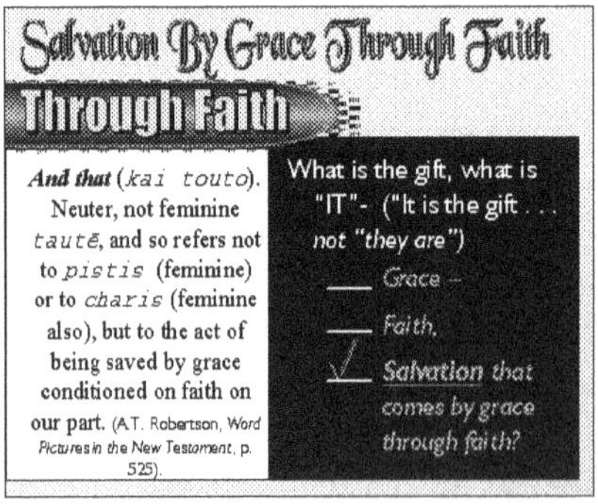
Salvation By Grace Through Faith
Through Faith
And that (kai touto). Neuter, not feminine tautē, and so refers not to pistis (feminine) or to charis (feminine also), but to the act of being saved by grace conditioned on faith on our part. (A.T. Robertson, Word Pictures in the New Testament, p. 525).
What is the gift, what is "IT"- ("It is the gift . . . not "they are")
___ Grace -
___ Faith,
√ Salvation that comes by grace through faith?

Salvation By Grace Through Faith
Joshua 6:2 (NKJV)
And the Lord said to Joshua: "See!
I have given Jericho into your hand,
its king, and the mighty men of valor.
to the camp. So they did six
days.
GRACE

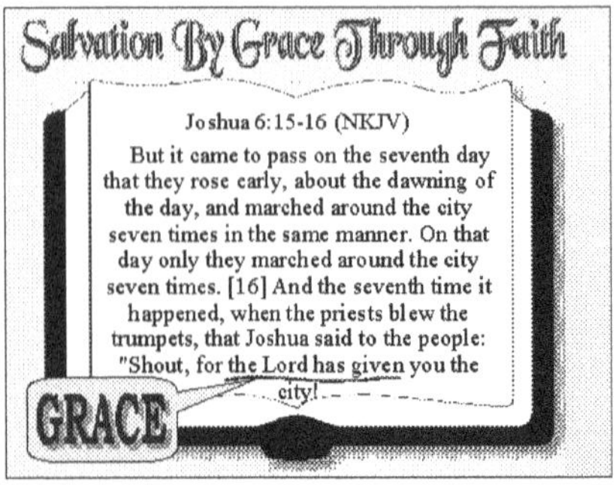
Salvation By Grace Through Faith
Joshua 6:15-16 (NKJV)
But it came to pass on the seventh day that they rose early, about the dawning of the day, and marched around the city seven times in the same manner. On that day only they marched around the city seven times. [16] And the seventh time it happened, when the priests blew the trumpets, that Joshua said to the people: "Shout, for the Lord has given you the city!
GRACE

I

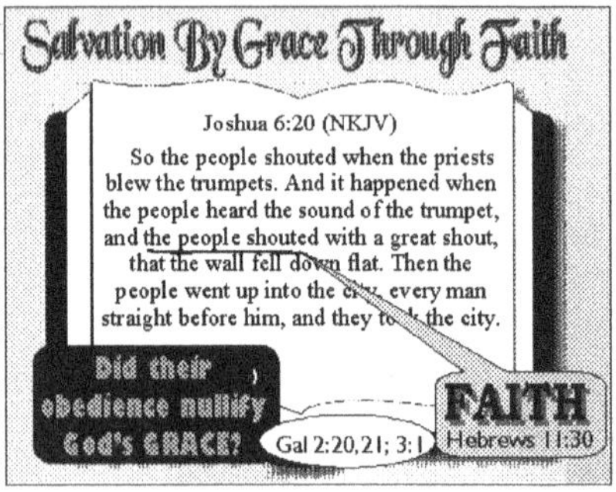
Salvation By Grace Through Faith
Joshua 6:20 (NKJV)
So the people shouted when the priests blew the trumpets. And it happened when the people heard the sound of the trumpet, and the people shouted with a great shout, that the wall fell down flat. Then the
Did their obedience nullify God's GRACE?
Gal 2:20,21; 3:1
FAITH
Hebrews 11:30

want to mention a few things that I was a little disappointed to hear from Mr. Cook. We heard that faith is a gift and the consequence of Mr. Cook's reasoning would be that God miraculously gives some people faith, but he does not miraculously give other people faith. I want you to notice what A.T. Robertson said about Ephesians 2:8-9. He says the gift is not faith, but

"Salvation By Grace Through Faith"
The Walls of Jericho Fell By?
A) Grace Only?
B) Faith Only?
C) Works Only?
D) By Grace Through a Faith that obeyed?
?
D

it is salvation. He says, "…this refers to the act of being saved by grace **conditioned** upon faith on our part." Faith is something we must exercise. He cited John chapter 6, but you will notice that John chapter 6 says that faith is a work. In John chapter 6 and in verse 28, "Then said they unto Him, 'What shall we do that we might work the works of God?' And they were told, 'This is the work of God that you believe on Him whom He hath sent.'" Faith is an activity on your part. He says faith is a work of God. The question is not if faith saves as we look at Ephesians 2:8-9. The question, friends, is what kind of faith saves? Does faith only save? I agree that faith saves, but what kind of faith saves? Let us think about the walls of Jericho. "The Lord said to Joshua, 'See, I have given Jericho into your hand, its king, and the mighty men of valor, and the second day they marched," etc., but notice, "God gave them the walls of Jericho." God did that by his grace and by his mercy. They did not earn such. Again, "The Lord has given you the city." The Lord gave them the city just as surely as the Lord gives us salvation. Yet, the Bible also says that they received it as a result of their faith. The people shouted. Did their obedience nullify God's grace? Absolutely not! But they had to obey God. Now, was it grace only, was it faith only, was it works only, or was it by grace through faith in which they obeyed God? I think we can understand that we must respond in obedience.

If you have your Bibles, turn with me to Romans. Anytime somebody approaches the book of Romans from the standpoint that works should be defined as obedience to the gospel of Jesus Christ they have missed the point of the epistle, because we know at the very beginning of the book of Romans, at the very end, and in between, that obedience to the gospel is necessary. Now then, Romans 1:5: "Through Him we have received grace and apostleship," for what? "…For obedience to the faith among all nations for His name." When the Bible speaks of faith in the book of Romans, obedience is understood and necessarily implied. The only faith that justifies is the faith that obeys. Look at Romans 6 verses 16-18 and notice what Paul says, "Know ye not that to whom you yield yourselves servants to obey,

His servants you are to whom you obey, whether of sin unto to death, or of obedience unto righteousness?" Remember, he talked about being made righteous, and Paul says that obedience is unto righteousness. Obedience is necessary in order to be made righteous, and when we obey from the heart, we are freed from sin. At the end of the book of Romans we have this statement, "But now has been made manifest and by the prophetic Scriptures has been made known to all nations according to the commandment of the everlasting God." What for? "For obedience to the faith."

Now, let us look at Romans 4 by starting up in Romans 3:27-28. We heard a lot about this, so we want to talk about it. This is a contrast in systems, i.e. "the law of works" versus "the law of faith." Notice what he says, "Where is boasting then? It is excluded. By what law? Of works? No, but by the law of faith. Therefore, we conclude that a man is justified by faith apart from the deeds of the law." He is saying it is through the gospel of Jesus Christ that a man may be forgiven of his sins. It is not through the Law of Moses. Now, that is the context as we enter into a study of Romans chapter 4: "For if Abraham was justified by works, he has something to boast about, but not before God." As he uses the term "works," it refers to the law of works, which would demand sinlessness. Had Abraham been sinless, he would have had something to boast in, but he was not. He goes on to say, "For what does the Scripture say? Abraham believed God, and it was accounted unto him for righteousness." The question is what kind of faith saved Abraham? Now let us progress to verses 4 and 5. "Now to him who works," i.e. to the man who was sinless, and that's the only way somebody could merit his salvation, "the wages are not counted as grace but as debt, but to him who does not work," to the man who has sinned, "but believes on Him who justifies the ungodly, his faith is counted for righteousness." Now, let us progress to verses 6-8, Paul talks about the Romans being forgiven of their sins. The man that does not work is the man that is not sinless, and thus, he has to receive the forgiveness of God. What kind of faith causes that to happen? I believe, if I am understanding what Mr. Cook is saying to us and what his position is, his idea is that the term "works" refers to any kind of human activity. And so, when we are dealing with this idea of works, we are dealing with any kind of human activity in obedience to Christ and what I am saying to you is that is not the case. The book of Romans, as it defines the term works, does not define it as obedience to the gospel.

Mr. Cook's point seems to be that since baptism is an act on my part or confession is an act on my part, and he talked about that a little bit, that must mean that since that is an act on my part, it is not necessary in order to be justified. Romans 4:3 says, “Abraham believed God, and it was accounted to him for righteousness.” Abraham believed God. The question is, “What kind of belief did he exercise?” Then we find his “faith is counted for righteousness.” Then he says in verse 6, “God imputed righteousness apart from works.” Now here he is talking about the idea of sinlessness, that he was justified through forgiveness conditioned upon an obedient faith. Look at what Romans 6 says, it says obedience leads to righteousness. Obedience leads to righteousness. Now I know that he was counted righteous because of his belief, I know that he was counted righteous because of his faith, and I know that righteousness did not come through works, and here he is talking about sinless law keeping, but obedience was necessary in order for him to be justified.

As you look in the book of Romans, the apostle Paul and the apostles throughout the New Testament never define works, when they were talking about what Paul was talking about in the book of Romans, as submitting to the conditions of the gospel. I want you to understand that when we confine our study to the book of Romans and we think about how Romans uses the term works, it is talking about sinlessness and we all need forgiveness, but he is not saying that we are not to respond in obedience to the gospel of

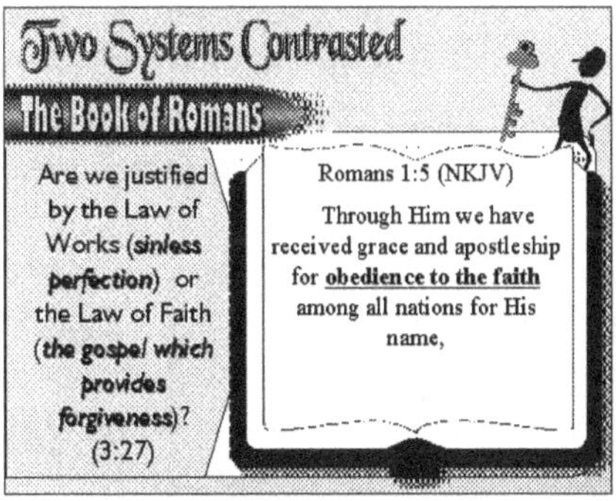
Two Systems Contrasted
The Book of Romans
Are we justified by the Law of Works (sinless perfection) or the Law of Faith (the gospel which provides forgiveness)? (3:27)
Romans 1:5 (NKJV)
Through Him we have received grace and apostleship for obedience to the faith among all nations for His name,

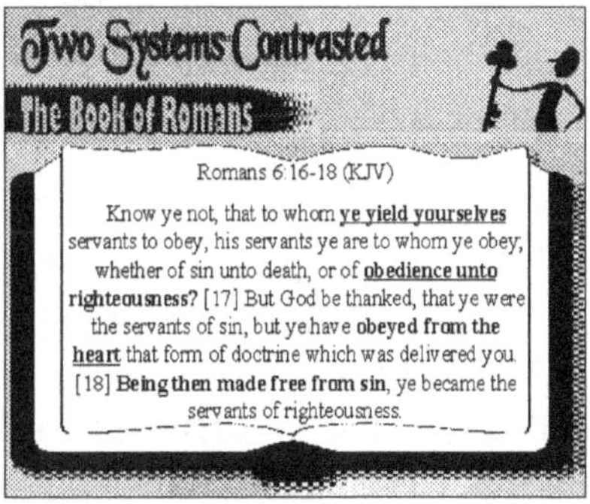
Two Systems Contrasted
The Book of Romans
Romans 6:16-18 (KJV)
Know ye not, that to whom ye yield yourselves servants to obey, his servants ye are to whom ye obey; whether of sin unto death, or of obedience unto righteousness? [17] But God be thanked, that ye were the servants of sin, but ye have obeyed from the heart that form of doctrine which was delivered you. [18] Being then made free from sin, ye became the servants of righteousness.

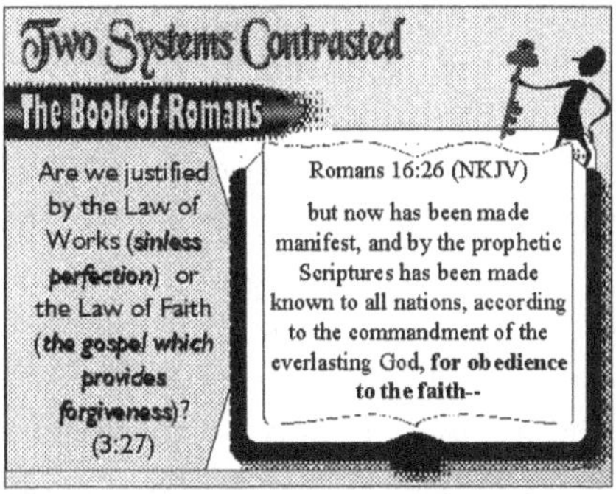
Two Systems Contrasted
The Book of Romans
Are we justified by the Law of Works (sinless perfection) or the Law of Faith (the gospel which provides forgiveness)? (3:27)
Romans 16:26 (NKJV)
but now has been made manifest, and by the prophetic Scriptures has been made known to all nations, according to the commandment of the everlasting God, for obedience to the faith--

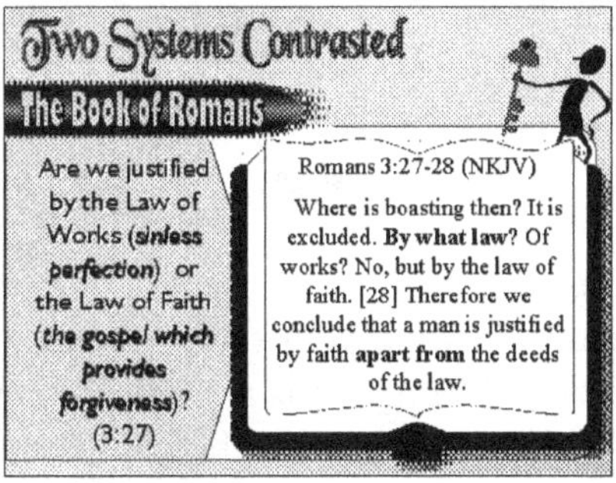
Two Systems Contrasted
The Book of Romans
Are we justified by the Law of Works (sinless perfection) or the Law of Faith (the gospel which provides forgiveness)? (3:27)
Romans 3:27-28 (NKJV)
Where is boasting then? It is excluded. By what law? Of works? No, but by the law of faith. [28] Therefore we conclude that a man is justified by faith apart from the deeds of the law.

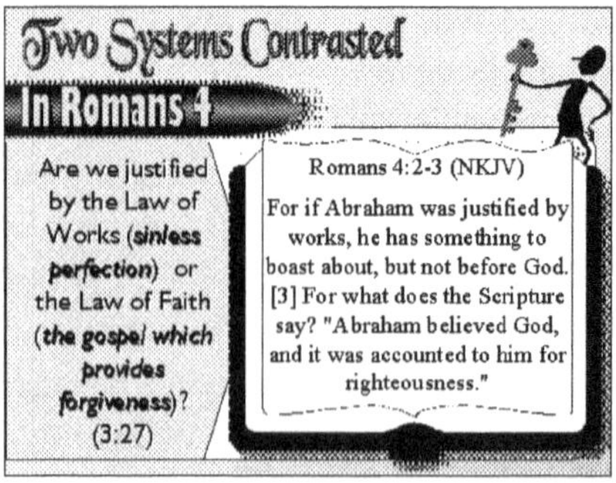
Two Systems Contrasted
In Romans 4
Are we justified by the Law of Works (sinless perfection) or the Law of Faith (the gospel which provides forgiveness)? (3:27)
Romans 4:2-3 (NKJV)
For if Abraham was justified by works, he has something to boast about, but not before God. [3] For what does the Scripture say? "Abraham believed God, and it was accounted to him for righteousness."

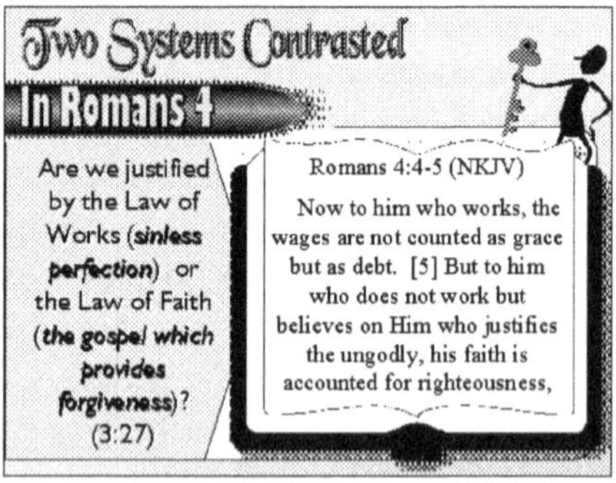
Two Systems Contrasted
In Romans 4
Are we justified by the Law of Works (sinless perfection) or the Law of Faith (the gospel which provides forgiveness)? (3:27)
Romans 4:4-5 (NKJV)
Now to him who works, the wages are not counted as grace but as debt. [5] But to him who does not work but believes on Him who justifies the ungodly, his faith is accounted for righteousness,

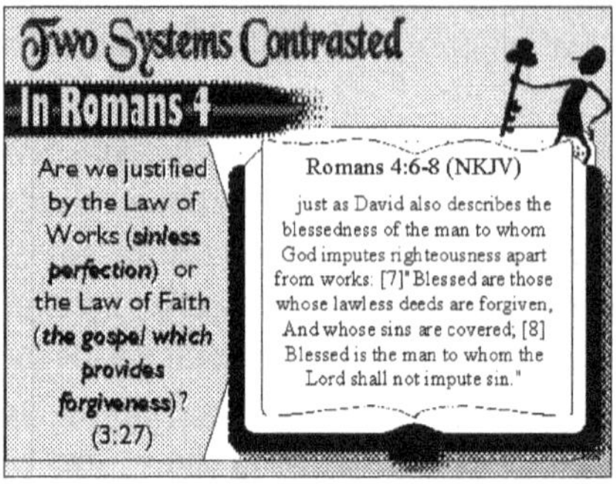
Two Systems Contrasted
In Romans 4
Are we justified by the Law of Works (sinless perfection) or the Law of Faith (the gospel which provides forgiveness)? (3:27)
Romans 4:6-8 (NKJV)
just as David also describes the blessedness of the man to whom God imputes righteousness apart from works: [7] "Blessed are those whose lawless deeds are forgiven, And whose sins are covered; [8] Blessed is the man to whom the Lord shall not impute sin."

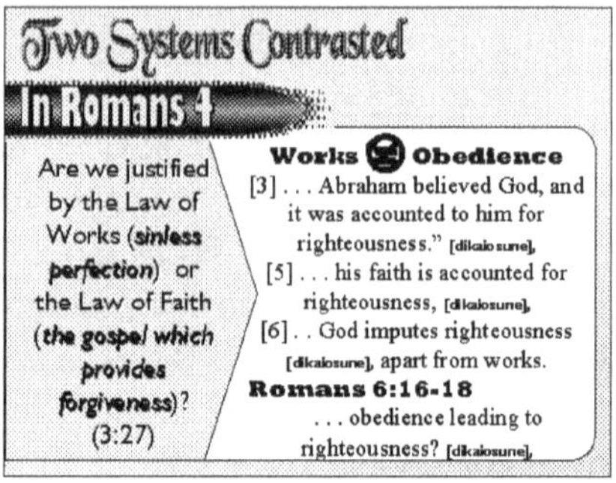
Two Systems Contrasted
In Romans 4
Are we justified by the Law of Works (sinless perfection) or the Law of Faith (the gospel which provides forgiveness)? (3:27)
Works Obedience
[3] . . . Abraham believed God, and it was accounted to him for righteousness." [dikaiosune],
[5] . . . his faith is accounted for righteousness, [dikaiosune],
[6] . . God imputes righteousness [dikaiosune], apart from works.
Romans 6:16-18
. . . obedience leading to righteousness? [dikaiosune],

Jesus Christ. Abraham is discussed in Romans chapter 4. Was he justified because he never sinned? No! Absolutely not! But did his faith, in order for that faith to justify him, have to act? That is the question. The question about baptism is about someone choosing faith and acting, obeying and doing what God said.

In James the 2nd chapter, James talks about Abraham: "But do you want to know, O foolish man, that faith without works is dead?" Now here "works" is being used from the standpoint of the activity of faith. Now think about the idea that is being advanced. James is saying we are not saved by faith only. In fact, if you look at verse 14 he says, "What does it profit, my brethren, if someone says he has faith but does not have works, can faith save him?" He is saying faith only will not save you, and when he talks about saving you, he is talking about justification. Think about this in verse 23 of this text: "The Scripture was fulfilled which says, 'Abraham believed God, and it was accounted to him for righteousness, and he was called' not the friend of man, he was called 'the friend of God.'" This is not just talking about showing your faith to somebody else. He says, "He called him the friend of God." Look at verse 24; now remember the proposition, "You see then that a man is justified by works and not by faith only." "Not by faith only." When Paul is using the term works, he is talking about someone who would be sinless, because that is what the Law of Moses demanded. And he is saying that all of us have fallen short of the glory of God. Abraham was not right because he never made a mistake, because he never sinned. He was forgiven of his sin through an obedient faith, but James is saying,

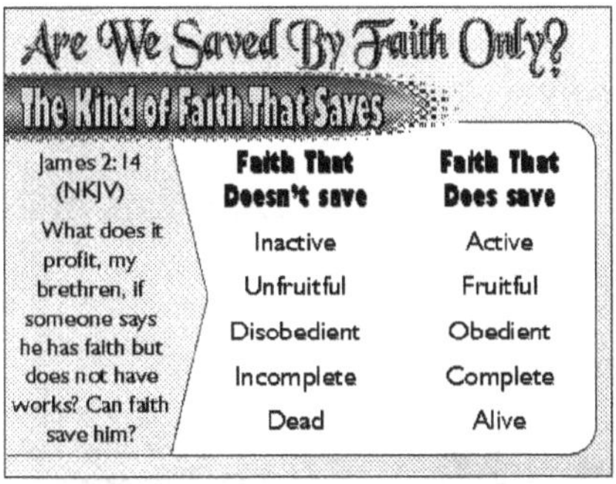
Are We Saved By Faith Only?
The Kind of Faith That Saves
James 2:14 (NKJV)
What does it profit, my brethren, if someone says he has faith but does not have works? Can faith save him?
Faith That Doesn't save
Inactive
Unfruitful
Disobedient
Incomplete
Dead
Faith That Does save
Active
Fruitful
Obedient
Complete
Alive

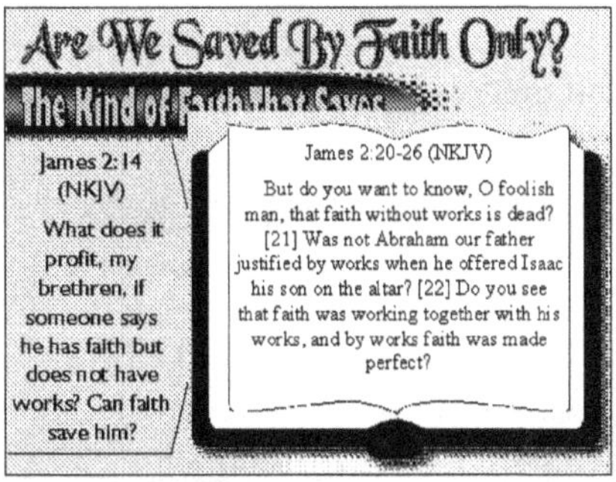
Are We Saved By Faith Only?
The Kind of
James 2:14 (NKJV)
What does it profit, my brethren, if someone says he has faith but does not have works? Can faith save him?
James 2:20-26 (NKJV)
But do you want to know, O foolish man, that faith without works is dead? [21] Was not Abraham our father justified by works when he offered Isaac his son on the altar? [22] Do you see that faith was working together with his works, and by works faith was made perfect?

Are We Saved By Faith Only?
The Kind of
James 2:14 (NKJV)
What does it profit, my brethren, if someone says he has faith but does not have works? Can faith save him?
James 2:20-26 (NKJV)
[23] And the Scripture was fulfilled which says, "Abraham believed God, and it was accounted to him for righteousness." And he was called the friend of God.
Genesis 22:5,12,16,18,19
[24] You see then that a man is justified by works, and not by faith only.

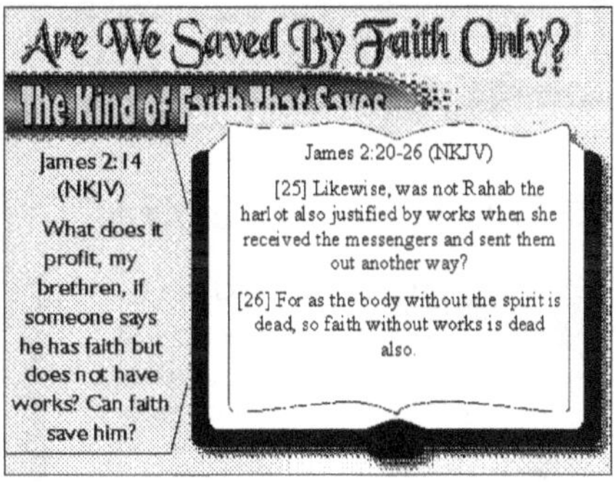
Are We Saved By Faith Only?
The Kind of
James 2:14 (NKJV)
What does it profit, my brethren, if someone says he has faith but does not have works? Can faith save him?
James 2:20-26 (NKJV)
[25] Likewise, was not Rahab the harlot also justified by works when she received the messengers and sent them out another way?
[26] For as the body without the spirit is dead, so faith without works is dead also.

"You see then that a man is justified by works and not by faith only." That faith must act, and it must submit to God. "Likewise, was Rahab the harlot not also justified by works when she received messengers and sent them out another way, for as the body without the spirit is dead, so faith without works is dead also."

Now I want to pick up some other things that he had to say. He mentioned Titus 3:5 and we are discussing the grace of God, and I agree that we are saved by grace, but this passage mentions water baptism. It says in Titus 3:5: "Not by works of righteousness which we have done, but according to His mercy He saved us, by the washing of regeneration and renewing of the Holy Ghost." We go on to 1 Peter chapter 3, which Mr. Cook introduced this evening. 1 Peter chapter 3 negates his proposition, ladies and gentlemen. His proposition says we are saved by faith only before and without water baptism, and yet this passage says here in 1 Peter 3:21 from the Old King

James, "The like figure whereunto even baptism doth also now save us, not the putting away of the filth of the flesh, but the answer of a good conscience toward God. . . ." I think we both agree it is not just taking a bath. The "appeal" in this text is not toward man, but the appeal is toward God. I am appealing to God for a good conscience. Why would I be appealing to God for something that I already have? If my conscience has already been cleansed and there is no sin on my conscience, why would I be appealing to God for

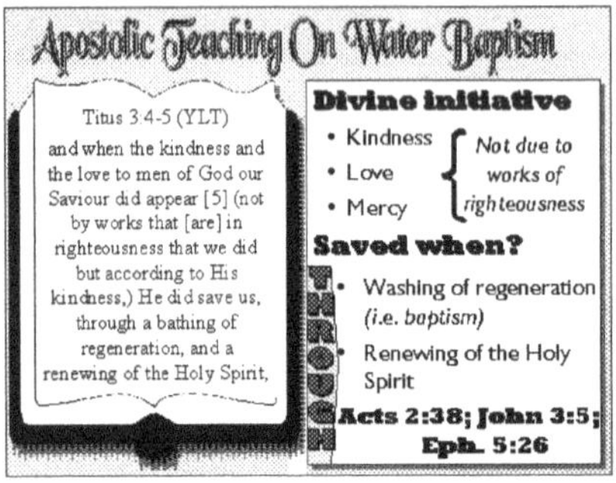
Apostolic Teaching On Water Baptism
Titus 3:4-5 (YLT)
and when the kindness and the love to men of God our Saviour did appear [5] (not by works that [are] in righteousness that we did but according to His kindness,) He did save us, through a bathing of regeneration, and a renewing of the Holy Spirit,
Divine initiative
• Kindness
• Love
• Mercy
Not due to works of righteousness
Saved when?
• Washing of regeneration (i.e. baptism)
• Renewing of the Holy Spirit
Acts 2:38; John 3:5; Eph. 5:26

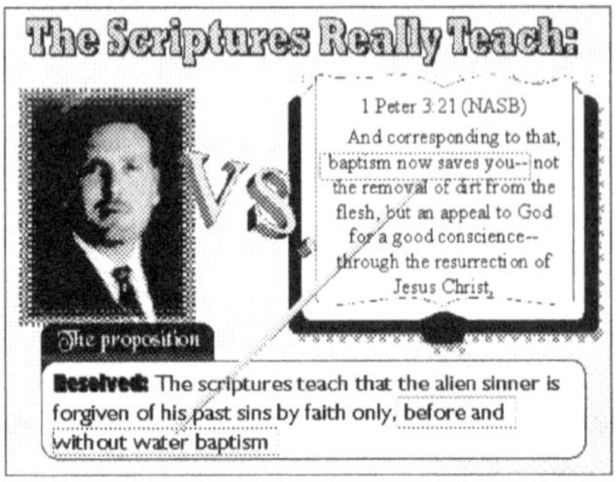
The Scriptures Really Teach:
VS.
1 Peter 3:21 (NASB)
And corresponding to that, baptism now saves you--not the removal of dirt from the flesh, but an appeal to God for a good conscience--through the resurrection of Jesus Christ,
The proposition
Resolved: The scriptures teach that the alien sinner is forgiven of his past sins by faith only, before and without water baptism

God's Purpose and Water Baptism...
Luke 7:30 (NASB)
But the Pharisees and the lawyers rejected God's purpose for themselves, not having been baptized by John.

something that I already have? The passage goes on to say, ". . .by the resurrection of Jesus Christ." That is why I have this confidence. But the passage says, "Baptism doth also now save us." And yet Mr. Cook's very proposition this evening says baptism does not save us in the sense of justification. And this passage says that it does!

Turn to Luke chapter 18. Now he brought this up as well and talked about this passage. The point of this passage is that we do not need to be self-righteous. The Pharisee stood and prayed thus with himself, "God I thank thee that I am not as other men are, extortioners and unjust. . . ." But then we read that the "Publican standing afar off would not lift up so much as his eyes unto heaven, but he smote upon his breast saying, 'God be merciful to me a sinner.'" And the Lord says, "He went down to his house justified." Did he have to do anything in that context? Did he have to act? Did he do anything there? Sure he did! That is not Mr. Cook's position.

We have looked at the book of Romans, and ladies and gentlemen, as you look in the book of Romans, remember that the term "works" cannot be used in reference to obedience to the gospel because Romans 6 says in verses 16-18 that obedience leads unto righteousness. So we know that works is not talking about meeting the conditions of the gospel. What it's talking about is a system that demanded sinlessness in order to justify you, and he says you cannot be saved that way. Why? Because we have all sinned, and we have all fallen short of the glory of God, and Jesus Christ came to this earth to suffer, to bleed, to die for every human being, for every single one of us. It is available to all of us, but we only access it through our faith acting, and James, as he talks about the activity of our faith, says, "Faith without works is dead." Baptism is simply an expression of the faith we have chosen, and the Bible says that it also now saves us. And for me to reject that, so far as justification goes, is to reject the very purpose of God. In Luke 7:30, we read that some rejected the baptism of John the Baptist. Of course, that is not the baptism that we must receive in order to be forgiven of our past sins, but in Luke 7:30, "But the Pharisees and their lawyers rejected the counsel of God," or "the purpose of God," the New American Standard says. They rejected the purpose of God. You can reject the purpose of God if you make that decision. You can! Do not do that. Accept the baptism of Jesus Christ on the basis of your faith. Thank you for your attention!

Monday Night

Second Affirmative

Gene Cook, Jr.

Okay, now I have 30 minutes to continue my presentation. Let me grab my remote control here. But I will say this by way of introduction again. If I were you, I would be thoroughly confused right now. I would be thoroughly confused for a couple of different reasons. I suppose the first reason is that you have two speakers that are both quoting Scriptures that seem to be saying opposite things. And there is a reason for that. One of the reasons is what we would call a straw man. Many of you probably know what the straw man fallacy is. The straw man fallacy is where you set your opponent's position to be something that it is not, like a straw man in a cornfield, and then you just come and plow it down. Well, many of the things that I believe were grossly, and I say grossly, misrelayed, or misunderstood, or mispresented tonight in that 30-minute speech that you just heard.

Having said that, I want to say two things. There were two things that Mr. Reeves said that really stuck in my mind. He said that Mr. Cook's position is that there is not something we must do in response of faith. Okay, I never said that. I never said there was nothing that we must do in response of faith. In fact, my position is there is much that we must do. He also said that the sinner that came into the temple, he quoted the passage, he said, "Did he have to do anything to be justified? Of course he did, but that's not Mr. Cook's position." Well, I never said that he did not have to do anything to be justified. In fact, my position is that we are justified by faith. We are justified by believing the gospel. And so, if I can, with all due respect, I want to issue a warning here. I want to issue a warning to Mr. Reeves. He can take it as he likes. I need you to listen to me very carefully because I barely have enough time to give my presentation without having to come up here and correct the things not only that I do not believe, but also that I didn't say. And, if we are going to have an honest dialogue going back and forth that is going to be of any productivity to the body of Christ, we are going to have to be very careful with what we say.

Having said that, I want to talk to you about justification. Romans chapter 3, and I am kind of glad that he went and talked a little bit about justification because that was the next slide that I was bringing up. And when I say that the believing sinner is saved by faith only, it is very important that you realize the position of the Reformed faith. When I say Reformers, I am speaking of those who broke away from the Roman Catholic Church in the 16th and 17th century, those are the Reformers, and the Reformers held the position that we are saved by faith alone, but saving faith is never alone. Okay! It was the Roman Catholic Church that taught that we were saved by faith and works. The presentation that you just heard the last 30 minutes is closer to Roman Catholicism than it is to Protestantism.

Justification! Romans 3:21: "But now apart from the law, the righteousness of God has been manifested, being witnessed by the law and by the prophets; even the righteousness of God through faith in Jesus Christ for all those who believe, for there is no distinction, for all have sinned and fallen short of the glory of God being justified as a gift by His grace through the redemption which is in Christ Jesus." Now one of the questions that I asked him, if you were paying attention, I know he was going fast, but if you were paying attention, I asked him to define grace. And his definition of grace happens to be mine also, unmerited favor. Now think about that for a moment, unmerited favor. What does it say here? It says that we are justified by grace, and so if he defines grace as unmerited favor, what does that tell us? It tells us that we are justified not by what we do, but by what God has done. God gives us the quickening. God brings us to life. And then as we have our eyes open, we respond in faith. Faith that saves is a faith that obeys, and so all of these verses about obedience to righteousness, I believe all that. I believe that is the obedience that springs from saving faith. I believe that following the gospel is obeying the gospel. I believe that, but justification is something different. That is why I said when you use the term "saved," you have to be very careful about the context in which you are using it.

Sometimes it refers to past tense usage. In fact, many of the passages I gave you refer to saved in the past tense. Those verses are speaking of justification. How can somebody who is said to be saved, past tense, still have a responsibility as a believer to obey all of God's commands? Do we not? And so if our being saved was based upon our obedience, the obedience even of faith as Mr. Reeves holds, then we could never say that we were, in fact, saved past tense. Saved would only be something future tense. And so it is important for us to know that when the Bible uses the term saved past tense, it is referring to justification, which is what I want to talk to you about right now. Romans 3:28: "For we maintain that a man is justified by faith apart from the works of the law." Mr. Reeves said that when the book of Romans uses the term "works of the law," it is talking about sinlessness. Excuse me? Where did you get that? Where does it ever say that works of the law are referring to sinlessness? We all know that no man is without sin. That is what the Bible tells us, so why does Paul belabor the contrast of faith and works of the law when he has already told us up front that none of us is perfectly sinless? That alone defeats his argument.

He said that faith, saving faith, is a faith that is accompanied by obedience, which I believe, but saving faith is also what justifies the believer. It is what allows the Bible to say that these people are, in fact, saved, past tense. It is very important for us to understand that. Romans 3:20: "Because by the works of the law no flesh will be justified in His sight, for through the law comes knowledge of sin." Now, Mr. Reeves got up and said that under the Mosaic law God demanded perfection, that God demanded sinlessness. Well, it was not just under the Mosaic law that God demanded sinlessness. What does Matthew 5:48 say? Matthew 5:48 in the midst of the Sermon on the Mount Jesus says, "Be therefore perfect even as your father in heaven is perfect."

You see, if you as an audience are going to be able to make any sense out of what we are trying to say, you have to consider something. Imagine if you will a horse pulling a cart. You are familiar with the term putting the cart before the horse. Imagine that analogy if you will. A horse is pulling a cart. The horse represents faith. The cart represents works of righteousness. We believe that we are justified by faith, and as a result, we become obedient people, okay? But what Mr. Reeves does is he puts the cart of works in front of the horse so that now you cannot be saved at a point in time, and your works are now confused with your faith. I asked him very clearly, according to Romans chapter 4, how was Abraham saved? This was the question that I gave him. Please explain how Abraham became righteous according to Romans 4:3? Well, what does Romans 4:3 say? Romans 4:3, does it say anything about baptism? Does it say anything about works? Romans 4:3, what does the Scripture say? "And Abraham believed God, and it was reckoned to him as righteousness." What was reckoned to him? His belief. Do you understand that? I am not denying that the faith that is true saving faith requires obedience. I am not denying that at all. In fact, I will affirm it to my death.

If you say that you have faith and you do not obey the law of God or you do not obey that which God commands in his word, do you really have a saving faith? James says no. We will get to that passage in just a moment. Romans chapter 4, there it is. I asked him, "How did Abraham become righteous according to Romans 4:3?" "What then shall we say about our father Abraham, our forefather according to the flesh? For if Abraham was justified by works he has something to boast about, but not before God." Very important here. Notice "not before God." I am going to come back to that in a moment. For what does the Scripture say? "Abraham believed God, and it was reckoned to him as righteousness. Now to the one who works, his wage is not reckoned as favor but what is due." Can it be any clearer? But then, one might ask, "What did Abraham believe?" When Paul says here in Romans 4:3 that Abraham believed God and it was reckoned to him as righteousness, that is a quote from Genesis 15. In fact, that is a quote from Genesis 15:4-5 where it says, "Then behold the word of the Lord came to him saying, 'This man will not be your heir,'" speaking of the one that Abraham had taken into his home, "but one will come forth from your own body. He shall be your heir.' And he took him outside and said, 'Now look toward the heavens and count the stars if you are able to count them.' And he said to him, 'So shall your descendants be.'" The next verse says, "Abraham believed God, and it was reckoned to him as righteousness." What did Abraham believe that God said? Abraham believed that he was going to have a son, which was against the natural mindset because Abraham was already an old man. God was calling Abraham to walk by faith, not by what he saw, and so he comes to him, he chooses him, out of all the Chaldeans, he sets his favor on him, and he says, "Abraham, I am going to give you a son. I am going to give you an heir, and it is not going to be Eliezer. It's going to be through your own body." And when Abraham believed that, we are told that it was reckoned to him as righteousness.

And that is important because when you get over to the book of Galatians, we are told in Galatians chapter 3 that this seed that Abraham was promised was not Isaac, but it was, in fact, Jesus Christ. Jesus Christ came through Abraham, Isaac, and Jacob, and the rest of the genealogies that are given to us in the New Testament. It was the seed, Jesus, not "seeds" plural that caused Abraham to be justified before God. But what about James? Does the Bible contradict itself? I mean, are we to believe, am I just going to throw up Romans chapter 4, and then he is going to come up and throw up James chapter 2? Well, what are we supposed to do here? What does the Bible say here in James chapter 2? "But someone may well say, 'You have faith, and I have works. Show me your faith without the works, and I will show you my faith by my works.'"

Notice this is something that has taken place between men. Show me, and I will show you, but remember moments ago when we looked at the justification of Romans chapter 4, we are talking about a justification that took place not before men, but before God. And he says, "I will show you my faith by my works." This is exactly what I believe. I believe I show forth my saving faith by my works. Verse 19: "You believe that God is one, you do well. The demons also believe and shudder. But are you willing to recognize, you foolish fellow, that faith without works is useless? Was not Abraham, our forefather, justified by works when he offered up Isaac, his son, on the altar?" And the next verse, 22: "You see that faith was working with his works."

Do you see the contrast? Faith and works. Faith was working with his works. He got up here and said faith is a work. Ephesians 2:8 says, "You are saved by grace through faith, not of works." Here he contrasts, once again, faith and works. Faith is the antithesis of works. I already pointed that out. I have already given you Scriptures to show you that. He says, "And as a result of the works, faith was perfected, and the Scripture was fulfilled which says, 'And Abraham believed God, and it was reckoned to him as righteousness, and he was called the friend of God.' You see that a man is justified by works and not by faith alone. In the same way, was not Rahab the harlot also justified by her works when she received the messengers and sent them out another way? For just as the body without the spirit is dead, so also faith without works is dead." Amen! Do not tell me you have saving faith if you do not have works because faith without works is dead. But we are talking about justification. We are talking about what causes a man to be made acceptable. And in order for us to understand that, we are going to have to use our minds here for a moment.

In Romans 4 when it says, "Abraham believed God, and it was reckoned to him as righteousness," how old was Isaac? He was not born yet. She was not even pregnant. In James 2, how old is Isaac? Well, he is a young man. He is going up the hill with his dad. His dad lays him on the altar. But Romans 4 says that when Abraham believed God, it was reckoned to him as righteousness. But then we are also told in James 2 that Abraham's faith was working with his works, therefore showing forth that he did not have a dead faith, but he had a faith that was very much alive. You as an audience are going to have to determine which position seems to take all of the facts into account and harmonize them.

How could we say that Romans 4 is talking about Abraham's works? How could we say that Abraham was justified by faith but not by faith only? Well then what else was he justified by? Isaac was not born yet. My position is the position that makes sense of this. I do not have any problem with James 2. I do not see an inconsistency there. I take Romans 4 and go back to Genesis, and I look at what he was talking about. I take James 2, and go back to Genesis, and I look at what he was talking about. I see two different periods in Abraham's life, but we are told when Paul wants to teach us something about justification, he does not take us to when Isaac was a young man. No! He takes us to the moment that Isaac was promised and Abraham believed. That is where he takes us because Isaac becomes a type of Christ later in his life when he lays him on that altar under God's command to sacrifice him and it is the showing forth of that faith in the promised son that saves a man, that is what justifies a man, and that is what makes a man righteous. You see, there are two things going on here. There is the righteousness of God that God gives us by faith, and then there is our own righteousness. If I do something God commands me to do, it is a righteous work. And so I am saved unto obedience. I am saved unto righteousness. I am saved to be a man who walks in the precepts that God has established. And that is exactly what James is teaching us here. James is teaching us that Abraham's works were shown forth to be an example of his faith.

In conclusion, faith is a gift from God. Okay? He said, "Faith isn't a gift from God. Faith is a work." I have already shown in one of my slides the passage in Romans 11, let me flip over there very fast, where it says, and "To each man is allotted a measure of faith." I'm sorry, Romans 12:3, "For through the grace given to me I say to every man among you not to think of himself more highly that he ought to think, but to think as to have sound judgment as God has allotted to each a measure of faith." Who is allotting the measure of faith? God is! To whom is he allotting it? Man! When the disciples asked God to increase their faith, are they asking to increase our ability to do good works? No! They are asking to increase their faith. Why? Because God is the one who gives faith, God is the one who increases faith, and God is the one who causes a man to be made righteous.

Now I've got a lot of time left here, so I just want to go over a few of these last points in my conclusion. Faith is not a work. I think I have made that clear. Faith is not a work. He quotes John 6, which I also quoted first. John 6:28-29 when they ask him, "What are the works that we must do? And Jesus said, 'This is the work of God: believe in the one who was sent.'" He says, "You see, it's a work." No, it is not a work! He is saying the exact opposite. You are going to have to use your common sense as an audience to try to interpret who's right on this. Jesus is using sarcasm with them. They want to know what they can do to be made righteous. They are not asking the question about sinlessness as if he thinks they are talking about in the book of Romans. They want to know, what can we do to be made acceptable before God? And Jesus says, "Believe." "Believe." "Believe, and you will be made acceptable before God." Repentance is a response to regeneration. Note that. Repentance is a response to a new birth, to a new life, to being made a new man. Dead men do not respond to anything, but we are told that the Spirit is the one who quickens us. The Spirit is the one who made us alive together with Christ when we were yet dead in our transgressions and sin. In conclusion, therefore, "saved" can be used in a very narrow sense speaking of the new birth or in the broad sense speaking of the Christian life, from the new birth until Christ's return. I do not have any problem with that at all. It fits perfect with my theology.

Righteousness is something that is received at the point of saving faith. It is something that is given by grace, which once again he defined as unmerited favor. You cannot say on the one hand that grace is unmerited favor and then read a Scripture that says we are saved by grace through faith and say, well grace is unmerited but faith is what merited it. No! That destroys the verse. Either it is unmerited or it is merited. Does faith merit grace, or is grace unmerited? If faith merits grace, then grace is not grace because grace means unmerited favor. It is that simple. You see, in the order of salvation, man must be brought to life. At the moment man is brought to life, he believes the message. "Faith comes by hearing, and hearing by the word of God." He responds in faith. He responds in repentance. He responds in good works. Why? Because, he is a new creation in Christ Jesus. It is that simple. I believe that Jesus Christ and God the Father desire all men to be saved. Once again, another straw man. Cook does not think that God wants all men to be saved. Oh yes I do! Where did you get that? The Bible says that God desires all men to be saved, does it not? That verse that he put up there about Jerusalem, but the problem is that in the very verse that he put up, he says, "But you were unwilling." You were unwilling to come on the condition of salvation. What is the condition of justification? He said, "Cook believes that salvation is unconditional." No, I do not! Justification is conditioned upon faith. I believe that with all my heart. It is on my website. It is in my confession of faith. Justification is conditioned upon belief, upon saving faith. So, if I have to get up here and correct all of the things that he says I believe that I do not really believe, then we are really not going to make much progress.

You see, when I debate somebody, and you will see this in the next Thursday and Friday nights, when he gives his 30 minute speech, I won't come up with my own material. I will come up and critique line by line what he said, because that is my job. My job is not to assume that he believes certain things. My job is not to think that because I know, you know, Joe Hypercalvinist down the street, and then Gene Cook must believe the same thing as him, because after all, they are both Baptist. No, I am to listen very carefully to what he says, then I am to base my response, my critique, upon what he says, and I will promise you I will do that. I will not, as much as humanly possible, I will not guess at what he believes. Now, I got up in my first speech, I read the questions, and I said, "You know, I don't see what any of these questions have to do with the subject at hand, except for that one." And quite frankly, I still don't. Like I said, we could have a debate on Calvinism, but I thought we were here to debate if man is saved by faith only or if man is saved by water baptism. He made a big deal about the fact that I believe in a limited atonement, and he said that God does not just choose one man to the exclusion of others. Did you ever hear of a nation called Israel? Did you ever read the Old Testament where God says that he set his favor upon them to the exclusion of the other nations? Why did he do that? Because they made good believers? No! In fact, they made better idolators than they did believers. He did that because of his grace, because of his unmerited favor toward them. He took one nation out of all the nations of the world, and not only did he do that and begin to work in their midst and set up a sacrificial system by which they could be saved in faith looking forward to the time Christ would come, but he also used them as his army on earth to go conquer other nations, and when they conquered the other nations, they were told to annihilate them. When they conquered the Amalekites, for example, God said to Joshua, "I want you to kill every last one of them. I want you to kill the men. I want you to kill the women. I want you to kill the boys. I want you to even kill the babies that are sucking on their mothers' breasts." You can go look it up in the book of Jeremiah. Is that the God that you worship? Can you somehow correlate that view of God to the view of God that you have in the New Testament? I certainly hope so because the answer is very simple. God hates sin, and unless God's favor is abiding on man, unless God's grace, unless God's unmerited favor is abiding on man, man is under the judgment of his sin.

God must judge sin, and all of those army victories of the Old Testament were just a foreshadow of the judgment that's coming, because when the judgment comes, all those who think that they're going to be saved by their own good works are going to be very disappointed according to the words of Matthew 7. "Many will come before Jesus on that day, and they will say, 'Lord, Lord, did we not cast out demons? Did we not do many good works? Did we not prophesy in your name?'" And he will say what? "I never knew you." You see, Christianity is about knowing Jesus Christ. It is about knowing his righteousness. It's about knowing the broad gap that lies between a holy God and sinful man, and when we make the same mistake that Pelagius made in the fifth century, when we start to say that no, man isn't born with any effects from Adam, no Adam did his thing, and we do ours, No! That is not what the Bible teaches. When we start to say that faith is the product of man alone, that it's not a gift of God, and not only is faith the product of man but now the good works are the product of that faith, they are motivated by that faith that man produced himself. How can you say at the end of the day that God saves us? I am the one that climbed in the water. I am the one that made the decision. I am the one that came to church. I am the one that did this. Isaiah says, "All of our righteousness is as filthy rags." Isaiah says that all of our righteousness is as filthy rags unless we first possess the righteousness of God that Paul talks about in Romans 10 and in Romans 4 and 5. We must have the righteousness of God by faith. Thank you!

Monday Night

Second Negative

Bruce Reeves

Good evening ladies and gentlemen! I appreciate your good attention this evening as we continue our discussion of some of these things, and there are some things certainly I want to pick up from the speech that you heard in your hearing. I agree that salvation is of God. The question is, must we respond in faith? And part of the problem here, certainly I do not want to misrepresent anything that Mr. Cook believes or says or anything like that, but due to his theology, he contradicts himself. He is contradicting himself in many of the statements that he has made before you. You may feel sometimes as you are hearing this that you are quite confused about exactly what he is saying about a saving faith. Is it necessary to justify us or not? And I think that is a good question. Now, I understand how somebody can just hear things wrongly, but I never said that faith merited grace. Perhaps that was just Mr. Cook overlooking that or misunderstanding or something, but I just want to make that very clear. I have said that faith is a condition of receiving salvation. Now, either we are saved by grace through faith, and faith is a condition of receiving salvation, which I think he is saying to me now that faith is a condition of salvation, therefore, he would renounce the idea that salvation is unconditional, and I am certainly glad to hear him say that. Then, we can understand that we are to respond in faith, and we are to act upon that faith.

I wrote something else down here. Mr. Cook said to us that he never said that the man did not have to do something in order to be justified. Well, I am glad to hear him say that. In Arkansas, we would say tickled pink. I am glad to hear him say that, that there is something one must do in order to be justified if that's what he meant by that statement.

He mentioned the Reformers and that kind of thing. I am not too very concerned about what the Reformers taught. Certainly, they did a great deal of good in many of their efforts. I am concerned about what the Bible teaches and what the Bible has to say to us. The reason he accuses me of misrepresenting him is his inconsistency. He said that the faith that saves is the faith that obeys. Well, that is exactly what I am saying to you. The question is at what point do we receive the forgiveness of our sins? At what point does that happen? Do I have to do anything in order to be justified? Sometimes it is yes, and sometimes it is no. We need to know that for sure.

I want to make this point because I think this is part of the problem that we are having in all of these passages about faith—I agree with every one of these passages about faith. However, because a passage affirms faith and there are many that do, it does not mean that the doctrine of faith only has been sustained. The reason is because you are not going to find a passage that teaches faith only. Now, you can quote all the faith passages you want to, but you are not going to find one that says we are saved by faith only. Because a passage explicitly mentions only faith does not exclude grace, or the work of the Holy Spirit, or confession, or repentance, or baptism, which are taught in other passages. I agree with every passage about faith. That is something we must exercise.

You heard many contradictions by Mr. Cook and this is an example of it: "We are saved by faith alone, but faith is never alone."

Please turn to Galatians 3:10 with me. I was making the point to Mr. Cook, as we were approaching our discussion of the book of Romans, that

The Law of Harmony
Because a passage explicitly mentions only FAITH, does NOT exclude grace, the work of the Holy Spirit, confession, repentance, & baptism, which are taught in other passages.
John 3:16
John 5:24
Ephes. 2:8,9
Acts 17:30
Rom. 10:9,10
1 Pet. 3:21
Matthew
Mark
Luke
John

Doctrinal Schizophrenia
"We are saved by faith alone, . . .
Sentence continued
. . . but faith is never alone."
Martin Luther
POPULAR LECTURES ON THE BOOKS OF THE NEW TESTAMENT BY AUGUSTUS H. STRONG, D. D., LL. D., LITT. D. President Emeritus of the Rochester Theological Seminary page
Calvinism Is a self contradictory theology?

in the book of Romans Paul is contrasting two systems, and the only way to be justified by the Law of Moses would be for someone to be sinless. So as Paul talks about the law of works, eventually he drops the words "law of" and just uses the idea of "works," and with the "law of faith," he drops the idea of "law of" and uses the term "faith," and so he talks about works and faith, but he is contrasting two different systems. And we were told, "No, that's not true, works really doesn't mean sinless perfection there, and where did Bruce get that idea?" "Where did Bruce get the idea that works in the book of Romans refers to sinless perfection and that it is not referring to obedience to the gospel of Jesus Christ?" Well, in Galatians

3, as you will notice this passage with me, that's exactly what Paul says in that context, and this book like unto the book of Romans is contrasting the law of works with the law of faith. In Galatians 3:10 we read this: "For as many as are of the works of the law. . . ." So, we are talking about the works of the Law of Moses. That is what Paul was talking about back there in Romans as well. "For as many as are of the works of the law are under the curse. For it is written, 'Cursed is everyone that continueth not in all things which are written in the book of the law to do them' but that no man is justified by the law." He is talking about the Law of Moses. "In the sight of God it is evident the just shall live by faith." He says the "Law is not of faith, but the men that doeth them shall live in them." The only way for the Law of Moses to justify a person would have been had that person kept that law sinlessly perfect. That is what he is talking about in the book of Romans and he is contrasting that with the faith of Jesus Christ, but that does not deny obedience to the gospel. The term "works" is not being used in a way that would apply, in the book of Romans, to obedience to the gospel. In Romans 6 we read that we "obey unto righteousness." We obey unto righteousness!

I must submit to the conditions of the gospel, and the very passage that was quoted in your hearing, i.e. in Romans 10:1-3 Paul says the reason the Jews were rejected was because they refused to submit to the righteousness of God. That is something they had to do. They had to submit to the righteousness of God. In that context, what is the righteousness of God? It is the conditions of the gospel. I must respond in faith. We can understand that, because that is exactly what Galatians 3 says, and while you are at it, in verses 26 and 27 he mentions some things you might want to take into consideration.

Now then, we heard a lot about getting the cart before the horse. Let us talk a little bit about getting the cart before the horse. We certainly do not want to do that. We do not want to get things mixed up. In Ephesians 2 we read, "For by grace you have been saved through faith," through faith, "And that not of yourselves, it is the gift of God, not of works lest any man should boast." I am not saved by meritorious works. How many times do I have to say that? We are not saved by meritorious works. We are saved by the grace of God, but that does not mean that we must not respond in obedience to the gospel in order to be justified and forgiven of our sins. "Not of works lest anyone should boast, for we are His workmanship created in Christ Jesus unto good works which God hath prepared beforehand that we should walk in them." Now, Mr. Cook has told us that we do not want to get the cart before the horse. Now we are just trying to be fair about this thing. We certainly do not want to misrepresent anybody. This is what Mr. Cook said. Let us let them hear what Mr. Cook said. "You express faith because you are alive by God, but nevertheless they happen together. You don't become alive by God because you express faith." Ladies and gentlemen, in the Scripture as we read about one who is made alive by God, and tomorrow night we would be happy to talk more about it, you will find out that this phrase has reference to the forgiveness of past sins. Colossians 2 and Ephesians 2 clearly affirm such. Notice this quotation by Mr. Cook. Mr. Cook said Bruce does not need to get the cart before the horse. He says, "You express faith because you are alive by God, but nevertheless they happen together. You do not become alive by God because you express faith." But I thought faith was a condition of receiving justification. And so, are we saying that we are alive before we exercise faith spiritually? Mr. Cook says yes, that is exactly what he believes. Romans 6:16 says we obey unto righteousness, something you might want to think about.

Let us move along here a little bit. This is the issue. Are there any conditions? Are there any conditions? And if we're both saying yes, then that

Regeneration Before or After Faith?
"You express faith because you are alive by God, but nevertheless they happen together, you do not become alive by God because you express faith."
(The Myth of the Middle Road Between Calvinism and Arminianism. Sermon delivered to Covenant Baptist Church in San Diego, California).
Ephesians 2:1-8
Colossians 2:13
1 Peter 1:22-25

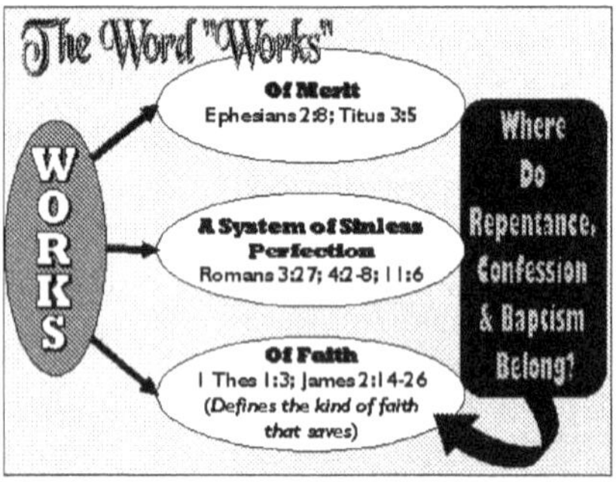
The Word "Works"
WORKS
Of Merit
Ephesians 2:8; Titus 3:5
A System of Sinless Perfection
Romans 3:27; 4:2-8; 11:6
Of Faith
1 Thes 1:3; James 2:14-26
(Defines the kind of faith that saves)
Where Do Repentance, Confession & Baptism Belong?

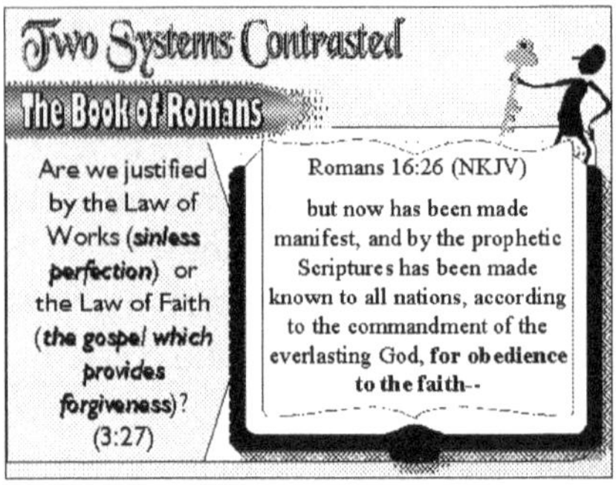
Two Systems Contrasted
The Book of Romans
Are we justified by the Law of Works (sinless perfection) or the Law of Faith (the gospel which provides forgiveness)? (3:27)
Romans 16:26 (NKJV)
but now has been made manifest, and by the prophetic Scriptures has been made known to all nations, according to the commandment of the everlasting God, for obedience to the faith--

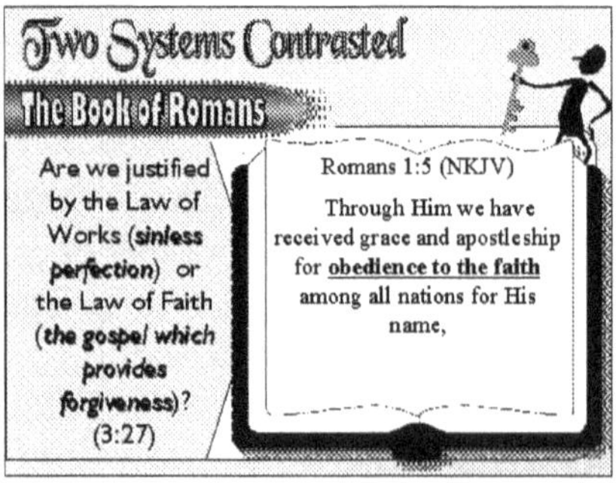
Two Systems Contrasted
The Book of Romans
Are we justified by the Law of Works (sinless perfection) or the Law of Faith (the gospel which provides forgiveness)? (3:27)
Romans 1:5 (NKJV)
Through Him we have received grace and apostleship for obedience to the faith among all nations for His name,

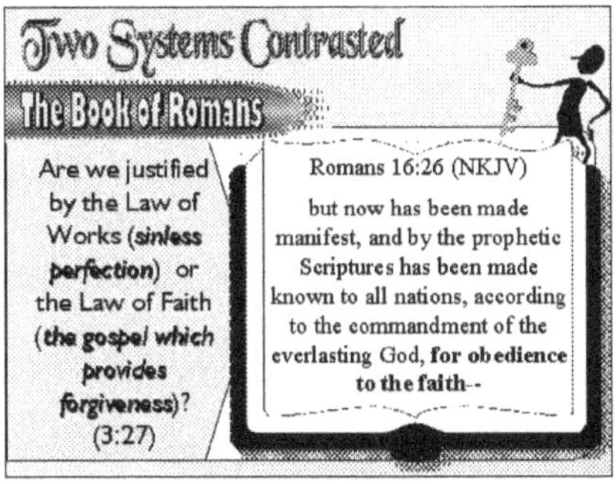
Two Systems Contrasted
The Book of Romans
Are we justified by the Law of Works (sinless perfection) or the Law of Faith (the gospel which provides forgiveness)? (3:27)
Romans 16:26 (NKJV)
but now has been made manifest, and by the prophetic Scriptures has been made known to all nations, according to the commandment of the everlasting God, for obedience to the faith--

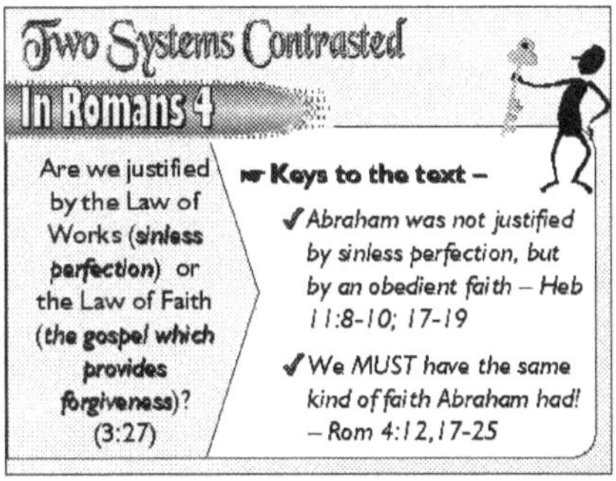
Two Systems Contrasted
In Romans 4
Are we justified by the Law of Works (sinless perfection) or the Law of Faith (the gospel which provides forgiveness)? (3:27)
Keys to the text –
✓Abraham was not justified by sinless perfection, but by an obedient faith – Heb 11:8-10; 17-19
✓We MUST have the same kind of faith Abraham had! – Rom 4:12,17-25

would mean that meeting those conditions, that is one who believes, repents of his sins, confesses his faith in Jesus, and is baptized in water for the remission of his sins is not meriting their salvation. They are simply obeying the gospel of Jesus Christ. We have made this point, but it is worthy of emphasis. The term "works" is used differently in the Scriptures.

When you have a word in the Bible that is defined differently in various contexts you have to look at the context to determine its proper meaning. Sometimes the term "works" does refer to merit, whereas, sometimes we read of the working of faith (1 Thess. 1:3 and in Jas. 2).

I want to go back to Romans 4 and James 2. Now I want to deal with something before we do that, and I am going to get there because that's where this discussion is right now, but I want you to think about Romans 12. We were told regarding Romans 12 that this text proved that this faith that justifies the sinner's soul and forgives him of past sins is given by God. We were taught that God miraculously grants faith to certain ones, and those are the ones that will be saved. Let us look at Romans 12 together. When he talks about this faith being granted, Paul is not talking about the faith that justifies the soul. Romans 12:3 is talking about the confidence in the exercising of these miraculous spiritual gifts, and just a surface reading of this context would bear that out. Romans 12:3 says, "For I say, through the grace given unto me to every man that is among you not to think of himself more highly than he ought to think, but to think soberly according as God has dealt to every man the measure of faith, for as we have many members in one body and all members have not the same office, so we being many are one body in Christ, and every one members one of another." He says in verse 6: "Having then gifts differing according to the grace that is given to us, whether prophecy, let us prophesy according to the proportion of faith, or ministry, let us await our ministering, or he that teacheth on teaching..." and so on. He goes on and mentions some other things. That is what he is talking about in the context. He is not talking about the faith that would justify man of his sins.

Now, let us go back to the book of Romans. What is the book of Romans about? It is about the fact that none of us lives sinlessly perfect—we have all sinned and we have all fallen short of the glory of God! We agree on that truth. And by the way, that is because we have all made decisions to sin against God. It is because we made the choice to sin against God that we are sinners. What is the book of Romans about? And I really want you to pay attention to this. What is this epistle about? It is encouraging people to recognize that only in Jesus Christ do they have salvation. That salvation is through the power of the gospel. It is made available to all those who will believe, both Jew and Greek, and since we have all sinned, we need the grace of God. We need the blood of Jesus. The question is how do we receive that forgiveness? In Romans 1:5, "Through whom we have received grace and apostleship for obedience to the faith among all nations for His name." As Paul uses the term "faith" comprehensively, it would include obedience. "But now has been made manifest and by the prophetic Scriptures has been made known to all nations according to the commandment of the everlasting God for obedience to the faith." That is the issue here. I must obey what the Lord told me to do in order to be saved, in order to be forgiven of my past sins.

Now let us look at Abraham a little bit more. We have talked about some of this passage already: the fact is that Abraham had to receive the forgiveness of his sins and that he did so through an obedient faith. The question is, "What kind of faith saved Abraham?" Abraham was not justified by sinless perfection, but he was justified by an obedient faith in Hebrews chapter 11. Hebrews 11:8: "By faith Abraham when he was called to go out into a place, which he should after receive for an inheritance, obeyed," he obeyed, "and he went out not knowing whither he went. By faith, he sojourned in the land of promise. He looked for a city which had foundations whose builder and maker is God." Verse 17: "By faith Abraham, when he was tried, offered up Isaac, and he that received the promises offered up his only begotten son of whom it was said that in Isaac shall thy seed be called." Now I want you to turn to Romans chapter 4 with me tonight. That is the text presented by my opponent. What I am saying is we must walk in the footsteps of Abraham in Romans 4:12. In Romans 4:12 as he is talking about Abraham, Paul says Abraham wasn't saved by works, by a law of works, or by that which would demand him to be sinless because we know Abraham had sinned, and it was through a faith that submitted to

God that he received forgiveness of his sins. Romans 4:12: "And the father of circumcision to them who are not of the circumcision only, but also walk in the steps of that faith of our father Abraham."

Who are the children of Abraham under the New Covenant? We are the children of Abraham by faith and it is those who submit to baptism and in that put on Christ. That is what we understand from Galatians the 3rd chapter. And that is just as clear as it can be. Let us talk some more about James 2. Mr. Cook said some things about James 2 that I want you to study. Here is the question that you must answer in your heart tonight. Do the works of James 2 merely have reference to justifying one before others? That is Mr. Cook's point. That is his argument. If I can show you, and I believe with all of my heart that I will before this speech is over, if I can show you that that's simply not the case, that these works had to do with one being justified before God, then I have clearly negated the proposition of the evening.

That's the only way Mr. Cook's interpretation of Romans 4 and James 2 in the affirmation of his proposition makes any sense whatsoever, and I'm going to show you as we study the Scriptures together that these works were not simply before men, but they were before God. We understand the type of faith that does not save. James tells us it is inactive, it is unfruitful, it is disobedient, it is incomplete, it is dead. The faith that does save is active, or fruitful, obedient, complete, alive. Now let us look at the Scriptures. I hope you have your Bibles. Turn to James the 2nd chapter, and I hope you can think about some of these things with me. James chapter 2, again verse 14: "What does it profit my brethren if someone says he has faith but does not have works? Can faith save him?" Can faith save him! What is his point? If that faith does not act in obedience to God, that faith does not save anybody. It does not save anybody. James 2:20: "But do you want to know, O foolish man, that faith without works is dead." Look at what he says, "Was not Abraham, our father, justified by works when he offered Isaac, his son, on the altar? Do you see that faith was working together with his works, and by works faith was made perfect."

Now Mr. Cook told us this very evening that when we are talking about James 2:18-22 that these works are not before God, they are before men. That is what his argument was; justification in this text is only before men. Paul is talking about Abraham and Abraham offering his son. I want to know who was there. I want to know. I want to know, in Genesis the 22nd chapter, who were the men before whom Abraham's faith was justifying him? I think what we're going to find out is that this act was to justify him before God, and that's exactly what James 2 is talking about. That's exactly what it's talking about! "Was not Abraham, our father, justified by works when he offered Isaac, his son, on the altar? Do you see that faith was working together with his works and by works his faith was made perfect?" Together! Of course, we are saved by faith, but it was working together with his works, and by works was faith made perfect. Genesis 22:5: This is what is being cited: "And Abraham said to his young men, 'Stay here with the donkey; the lad and I will go yonder and worship and we will come back to you.'" So it was just Abraham and the lad. And in Genesis 22:12: "And He said, 'Do not lay your hand on the lad, or do anything to him; for now I know that you fear God, since you have not withheld your son, your only son, from Me.'" In Genesis 22:16: "And He said, 'By Myself I have sworn,' says the LORD, 'because you have done this thing, and have not withheld your son, your only son.'" So God is saying that you are justified, you are right with me, because you are willing to obey My will. Genesis 22:18-19: "In your seed all the nations of the earth shall be blessed, because you have obeyed My voice. So Abraham returned to his young men, and they rose and went together to Beersheba; and Abraham dwelt at Beersheba."

Ladies and gentlemen, look at James 2 again. Now is there any question, is there any doubt that when we read that Abraham was justified by his faith that this was not merely showing others that he had faith, for he was offering his son and the young men were at a distance? He was doing this in obedience to God, and because he did it, James says what he did in James 2. Now, of course, in Romans chapter 4, any system, which would demand sinless perfection, cannot save us because we have sinned. We are not saying that we are saved because we have never made a mistake, and Galatians 3, when you harmonize it with Romans chapter 4 makes that abundantly clear. It makes it lucid that—that is the way he is using the term "works." In James the 2nd chapter, he is using the term from the standpoint of the activity of our faith, and that certainly is necessary. Look at verse 21: "Was not Abraham, our father, justified by works when he offered Isaac, his son on the altar? Seest thou how faith wrought with his works and by works was faith made perfect. And the Scripture was fulfilled which saith, 'Abraham believed God, and it was imputed unto him for righteousness,' and he was called the friend of God." He was called the friend of God, the friend of God. We have been told, "No now that is just showing faith before others." This passage says he was called the friend of God, and then it says, "You see then how that by works a man is," there's our word, "justified," justified, "And not by faith only." Not by faith only!

(I want you to find that James 2 chart. I always hate to do this to a chart man. I want you to find the early one with James 2, remember, just James 2:24 on it.) Now ladies and gentlemen, this is not that hard if you will harmonize Scripture. I recognize we have all sinned and I recognize that we have all fallen short of the glory of God. I believe that Jesus Christ died for every one of us. Now not all of us access what is available. Not all of us do that, and I would implore you to think about what the Scripture actually says. Think about what the Bible says. I understand we are not saved by meritorious works. I will say that all this week. We are not saved by anything by which we would attempt to earn our salvation, but we must obey God, and the proposition of the evening is simply in contradiction to what the Bible says.

Now on the Day of Judgment, it is not going to be Reformed Theology that judges you. It is not going to be the 1689 London Confession of Faith. It is not going to be the Philadelphia Confession of Faith. It is not going to be any of the other Confessions of Faith. It is going to be the word of

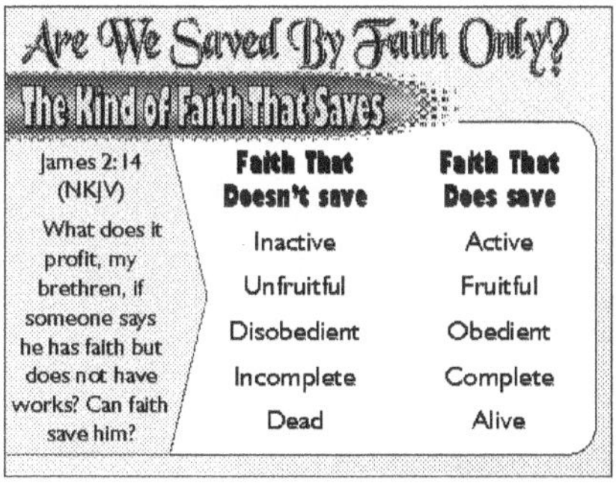
Are We Saved By Faith Only?
The Kind of Faith That Saves
James 2:14 (NKJV)
What does it profit, my brethren, if someone says he has faith but does not have works? Can faith save him?
Faith That Doesn't save
Inactive
Unfruitful
Disobedient
Incomplete
Dead
Faith That Does save
Active
Fruitful
Obedient
Complete
Alive

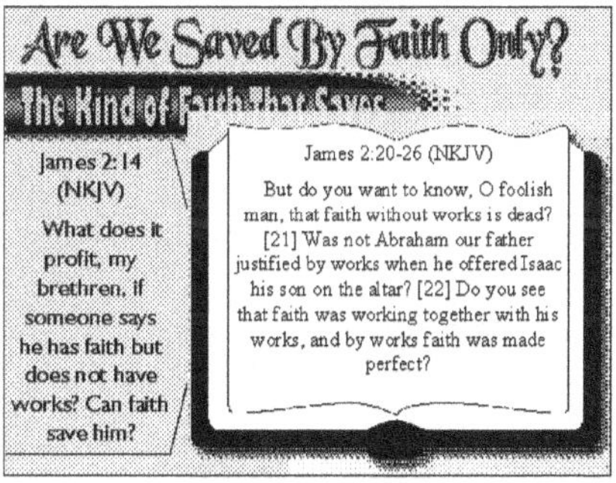
Are We Saved By Faith Only?
The Kind of
James 2:14 (NKJV)
What does it profit, my brethren, if someone says he has faith but does not have works? Can faith save him?
James 2:20-26 (NKJV)
But do you want to know, O foolish man, that faith without works is dead? [21] Was not Abraham our father justified by works when he offered Isaac his son on the altar? [22] Do you see that faith was working together with his works, and by works faith was made perfect?

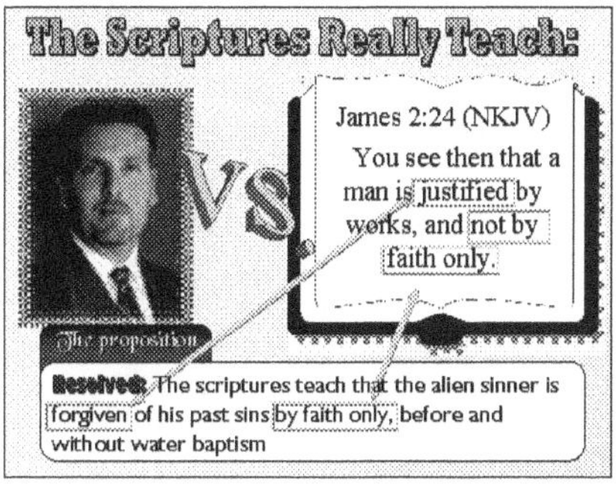
The Scriptures Really Teach:
VS
James 2:24 (NKJV)
You see then that a man is justified by works, and not by faith only.
The proposition
Resolved: The scriptures teach that the alien sinner is forgiven of his past sins by faith only, before and without water baptism

God, and Jesus said, "My word will judge you in the last day." And this passage is in direct contradiction to Mr. Cook's proposition. And we have already shown you that James 2 does apply to justification before God. Therefore, the interpretation that says this is just talking about showing your faith to others simply is not the case.

I appreciate your good attention tonight. I appreciate the opportunity to be with you. So, as you leave here tonight, and as you lay down tonight when you go to bed, you are going to have to ask yourself, "Is this a matter of trying to hang on to what men teach, or is this a matter of submitting to

God's word and to God's teaching and to the purpose of God for my life?" And so as we close this evening, I hope that you will consider these things. I hope you will come back tomorrow night. I hope you will think about the things that we have mentioned to you. And my prayer and my hope is that we may all study the Scriptures and come to a common understanding of the truth. Thank you very much!

Tuesday Night

Third Affirmative

Gene Cook

Welcome once again to the second evening of our debate on the subject of baptism and faith. Is it true that man is saved by faith alone? Is man justified by faith alone? Or, is man justified by faith plus obedience? That is the question that we will be debating not only tonight but also this coming Thursday and Friday night.

We have agreed in advance to accept questions from one another. I have given him five questions. He has given me five questions. Before I get into my presentation tonight, I want to go ahead and address his questions as best I can. Question number 1: "Does water baptism, 'taking a bath,' earn the benefit of Christ's sacrifice on the cross?" I would say, absolutely not! The answer to that question is no, an emphatic no! Number 2: "Is Genesis 15:6 the record of Abraham's initial justification?" Well, I do not know if you can describe justification by using the adjective initial. Justification is justification. Either he was justified or he was not justified. The Scriptures tell us in Romans 4:1-4 that he was justified, and so I am going to have to say that it was not his initial justification, it was his justification. Number 3: "Is the new birth unconditional?" Yes! Regeneration is unconditional. I mean, that is like asking a baby that just came out his mother's womb, did you have anything to do with being born today? That is the metaphor of regeneration, new birth. Does a baby have anything to do with being born? No! He did not choose the day, the hospital, the parents, but yet in regeneration, God is the one who sovereignly brings man to life unconditionally. Number 4: "If I am not one of the elect, is there anything that I can do about it?" Well, that is a good question, I suppose. Election is not given so that we might know who might be elect and who might not be elect. Election is given to be a comfort for those who believe. It is something that is given in God's word, which is addressed to Christians. So, if you are asking if there is anything you can do about it as far as becoming elect, I would say no! Is there anything you can do period? I would say yes. I would say that you need to humble yourself and stop preaching the gospel that you are preaching because you are actually heaping more condemnation on yourself for the Day of Judgment. Number 5: "Last night you stated that God desired that all men be saved. What is the difference between divine desire and divine will?" Well, we could spend several hours explaining this question, but just to make it simple, let me just say this: I believe that God has two aspects to his will. He has that which is his perceptive will, i.e. that which he commands. In other words, we saw last night in the book of Acts 17 Paul said, "God is now commanding all men everywhere to repent." That is God's perceptive will. That is a law of God. That is what God has commanded. Therefore, in that command is God's desire that it be obeyed no matter who hear it. However, on the other hand, we know of God's divine decrees. For example, in Isaiah 46 it says that God does whatever he pleases. God tells Job that there is nothing that can thwart his plan. We know that there is nothing that can thwart God's plan, so if there's nothing that can thwart God's plan, then God's plan must come to pass perfectly every time, every day, and it does. In addition to that, we refer to the divine decrees of God or the secret counsel of God. If you want to know more about that, you can look on John Piper's website, desiringgod.org. He has a paper there on the two wills of God.

Now to get into my presentation tonight, the first Scripture I would like us to look at, and I hope you have brought your Bibles tonight. I am privileged once again to be here defending what I believe to be the gospel of grace. I just want to go back, and I want to re-track a little bit so that we can kind of sort out some of the confusion that might have arisen out of last night's debate. I would like to talk once again about this term "saved." You remember in my presentation last night I said that saved is often spoken of in different tenses. Sometimes it is spoken of as a past tense event, sometimes it is spoken of as a present tense event, and sometimes it is spoken of in the New Testament as a future event.

Now I am going to show you tonight that sometimes saved, or salvation, refers to regeneration and sometimes saved, or salvation, refers to justification. Okay? You do not just use the term loosely. When we talk about being saved, we need to know in what sense. We can talk about a man who was a Christian and he has gone home to be with the Lord. We could say that he was a saved man. Well that is a testimony of his life. It does not mean that he was necessarily saved on a particular day. That is not what we are communicating. We are communicating something about the man's life. However, if I say that I was saved on November 25, you know whatever year, then I am talking about being born again. I am talking about regeneration. We need to be careful how we use the terms. I just want to show you. I put all my verses up on the screen tonight so that you can see them. All my Scriptures are taken from the New American Standard updated version. The first verse I would like to show you is Titus 3:5 when Paul tells us as he is writing to Titus, "He saved us." Notice the word "saved" is used in the past tense, "not on the basis of deeds which we have done in righteousness, but according to His mercy by the washing of regeneration and renewing by the Holy Spirit." Paul says, "He saved us not on the basis of deeds which we have done in righteousness."

Well, that is quite different from what we heard last night from the church of Christ side of this debate. We heard that we are saved by deeds of righteousness. He did affirm that we are not saved by keeping the law, but there is no mention here of the law. In fact, on chart 123, it says, "Water baptism is necessary for justification." That sounds like a deed of righteousness. If water baptism is something that God commands, and we perform water baptism or we submit ourselves to water baptism, then we are submitting ourselves to a deed of righteousness. On chart 126, "water baptism," again, "is necessary for justification." Now here Paul is telling us that we are not saved based on deeds, which we have done, in righteousness. If you could boil down my position to one sentence, this is it. I said repeatedly last night you are not saved by your own good works. You are not saved by doing that which God commands. You are saved by the grace of God, you are given the gift of faith, and obedience springs from faith, that is, the faith represents the horse pulling the cart of works, if you will.

I had before the debate begun a picture of me baptizing a young man in Africa. Why did I fly all the way to Africa to preach the gospel and to, you know, baptize somebody? So that I could be more righteous? No, not at all! I did that because God has so changed my heart by his unmerited favor. God has so come into my life and forgiven me of my sins, and he has revealed himself to me in such a say that I now have a desire for the nations to come to know the God who saves me, not according to my righteous deeds, as Paul says here, but by his own grace. He goes on to say, "But according to this mercy by the washing of regeneration and renewing by the Holy Spirit."

Now last night Mr. Reeves said that this verse is a proof text for water baptism. Could that be the case? Is the washing of regeneration water baptism? Well, let us substitute water baptism for washing of regeneration and see if it makes sense. He saved us not based on deeds, which we have done, in righteousness but according to his mercy by water baptism and renewing by the Holy Spirit. That would destroy the meaning of this verse. He did not save us based on deeds of righteousness that we have committed, and I tell you this, I told you this last night. If you think that you are going to stand before a holy God and point to some acts of obedience on your part, you are going to have a rude awakening on the Day of Judgment.

I did not come all the way to Little Rock, Arkansas, because I like to argue. I could stay home and do that. I have a computer. I can debate right there in the comfort of my own home. I did not come to Little Rock, Arkansas, so that I can perform some deeds of righteousness or somehow make myself think that I am an obedient Christian and thereby God is going to accept me. No! I came to Little Rock, Arkansas, because I care about the souls of people who have been deceived into believing a gospel of works righteousness. That is why I have come. My hope and my prayer is that some of you might be awakened by the Spirit of God. If you came into this debate thinking that God has accepted you on the basis of what you have done, on the basis of your response, or on the basis of your water baptism, I hope and pray that you might be awakened by the Spirit of God, that he might put his finger upon your heart as it were, and convict your heart that this is not the way that man is made acceptable before God.

I look out and I see husbands, wives, grandparents, children, and beautiful families. I think about the reality of death that has come upon this creation because of our first father's disobedience. I think about how death just converges in the lives of men and women without any notice, without any warning most of the time, and in a very tragic manner. It just tears apart our hearts and our families. It separates us from our loved ones. I think about how glad I am that I have hope of seeing my loved ones. My hope is to see those Christian family members, and my brothers and sisters with whom I worship on Sunday morning. I am so glad that my hope of seeing them is not based on me, and it is not based on them, but it is based, as Paul says, on the God who has mercy. God is a God of mercy, and he comes to us in an unconditional manner to answer one of the questions. I would use this verse. This is not based on what we have done, but based on what he has done, the washing of regeneration and renewing by the Holy Spirit.

"Saved" also refers to regeneration in 2 Timothy 1:9 where Paul says to Timothy "who has saved us and called us with a holy calling not according to our works." Once again, "not according to our works." He says to Titus "not according to works of righteousness" and here "not according to our works." Here saved is speaking of regeneration. Ephesians 2:5-6 speaks of regeneration, "Even when we were dead in our transgressions, God made us alive together with Christ. By grace you have been saved."

This is speaking of the quickening power of God's Spirit, how God takes a man, or a woman, or a child, or a human being who is formerly dead spiritually and God quickens them, he metaphorically raises them from their state of deadness just as he did Lazarus when Jesus called Lazarus out of the tomb. That is physical resurrection. Here we are told that he raises us up together. He makes us alive together. Ephesians 1 says he raises us up with him together, but here he says he makes us alive together. "By grace you have been saved." Remember grace is unmerited favor.

However, sometimes salvation refers to justification. What is justification? Justification is a forensic declaration on the part of God whereby the believing sinner is accounted as righteous. In 1 Peter 1:9, we see an example of this, "Obtaining as the outcome of your faith the salvation of your souls." See here Peter references faith and salvation. Justification comes by faith. Remember Abraham believed God, and it was accredited him, or he was accounted as righteous. However, here the word "salvation" is used. In Acts 16:30 salvation also refers to justification. "And after he brought them out he said, 'Sirs, what must I do to be saved?' And they said, 'Believe in the Lord Jesus Christ and you will be saved, you and your household.'" It is very important that we understand that here the word "saved" is in reference to justification. If you believe, you will be saved, i.e. if you believe, you will be justified.

We have to understand that the book of Acts is what we would call an historical narrative. It is a history book of the acts of the apostles. That is why it has called the book of Acts. We do not go to the history book where we see the workings of God being worked out and pull our doctrine. No! We go to those doctrinal epistles such as the book of Romans, the books of 1 and 2 Corinthians, the books of Ephesians, Philippians, and Colossians. We go to those books to get our doctrine, and let me give you an example why. Last night an argument was made from Acts chapter 8 that the Samaritans were brought into Christ by water baptism. But, if you go just two chapters over to chapter 10, you will see that Cornelius, the first Gentile convert, received the Holy Spirit before water baptism. Therefore, you cannot use Acts chapter 8 or Acts chapter 10 really, to make a case about a doctrinal position on when man receives the Spirit of God in relationship to baptism because they both seem to be teaching different things. That is because as the book of Acts is being played out, as the history of the church is being worked out before our eyes, the Holy Spirit is conquering new territories. He is first taking the Samaritans. He takes the Jews on the Day of Pentecost. Then he takes the Samaritans. Then he goes to the outer parts and begins to take Gentiles. But if you want to know what the normative order of salvation is, just look to the book of Romans or the book of Ephesians, and you will find very clear language that helps us go back and interpret the historical narratives.

Now, why is it important that I spend so much time talking about how the term "saved" is used? I mean, is this a debate about semantics? No, it is not! I wish it were only a debate about semantics, but it is not a debate about semantics. It is a debate about the difference between salvation by grace and salvation by works at its lowest common denominator. I have given an analogy here with the word "love" to try to demonstrate why I believe it is so important that we understand the way that salvation, or the word "saved," is used. Because when I use the term, I have a particular meaning in mind. I am afraid that my opponent does not have the same definitions as I do since he uses these different words. I am not just afraid; I know that to be a fact. And I'm not sure if he understands what I am trying to show you, that the word "saved" is used in different senses in different times, past, present, and future, and also of different events, justification and also glorification, but sometimes it's used of regeneration as we saw in Titus 3:5.

Let me use an analogy here using the word "love." I could say, for example, in fact, I could come all the way from San Diego, and we could be having a debate about immorality, and I could get up and I could say, "I love God, and I love my wife, and I love my neighbor, and I love my dog." Then I could sit down, and my opponent could get up and say this man is teaching adultery. Did you hear what he said? He is teaching adultery. He is not only teaching adultery, but he is teaching idolatry. He is not only teaching adultery and idolatry, but he is also teaching bestiality. Let me give you an example. I love God. Is my love for God the same as my love for my wife? No, because the Bible tells me that God is to be the one that I love with all of my heart, with all of my soul, with all of my mind, and with all of my strength. He is to be first. I am never to put anybody above him. Otherwise, I violate his very law. Therefore, if I say I love my wife, somebody could make the argument well you see, he loves his wife just as he loves God, so he is not honoring the first commandment. However, if I said I love my wife and I love my neighbor, somebody might say you see, he is having an adulterous relationship with his neighbor because I happen to know that there is a woman that lives next door to him, and he says he loves his wife and his neighbor. Therefore, since he has an intimate relationship with his wife, are we going to believe since he loves also his neighbor that he has an intimate relationship with his neighbor? However, I also love my dog. I think you get the analogy. This is what is taking place in this debate. You heard last night when a follow-up to my presentation was given, you heard Mr. Reeves saying; in fact, the chart was up on the board, that I had a schizophrenia type theology, or my doctrine is schizophrenic. Sometimes you hear him saying that salvation is unconditional, but other times you hear him saying that salvation is conditional. What was I saying once again? I was saying that regeneration is unconditional. Being born again is unconditional. Justification, however, is conditioned upon faith. But sometimes the Bible calls justification being saved. Sometimes it uses the term salvation. You see why it is so important that we understand these terms.

I am not, believe me, I am somebody that is very concerned, as a man who represents the word of God, I am somebody who is very concerned about not contradicting myself. I do not believe that the word of God contradicts itself. If somebody can demonstrate to me that I have some contradiction in my interpretation, then I will agree it is time for me to abandon that interpretation. However, when I say that a man is justified by faith, therefore faith is a condition for justification, and I say that a man is regenerated or born again unconditionally, there is no contradiction there. However, because of the explanation that you are given from my opponent, he is leading you to believe that there is a contradiction, and I am telling you there is not. Therefore, when the Scriptures say that "Abraham believed God and it was credited to him as righteousness," as we read in Romans 4:3, we would say that Abraham was saved by grace through faith, that God brought him to life spiritually because dead men don't believe anything, and that's the analogy that we're given in Scripture.

Therefore, God brings him to life, and as a response of God bringing him to life and revealing himself to him in regeneration, and then Abraham responds in faith. And as a result of responding in faith, Abraham is then justified, that is he is given the very righteousness of Christ, which is what Paul calls God' righteousness, which is the antithesis, once again, of man's righteousness. Therefore, Abraham is made acceptable because of his faith. He is made acceptable to God because in order for us to be accepted by God, we must not only have our sins forgiven, which is what justification is, but we must also have the righteousness of Christ. This is why it is important not just to view the atonement of God, or the atonement of Jesus Christ, as merely a sacrifice. It is a sacrifice. Do not get me wrong. His sacrifice takes away our sins.

He is the Lamb of God, but he also lived the righteous life. As a result of living the perfect life and obeying everything that God the Father had ever commanded, he then has the ability to transfer his righteousness to me that I might be made acceptable before the Father. Therefore, I need both things. I need forgiveness of my sins, and I need the righteousness of Christ because even as a regenerated sinner, I cannot keep God's law perfectly.

However, this verse is not speaking of being saved in the sense of regeneration. Rather, it is speaking of being saved in the sense of justification. Therefore, when I say that salvation is unconditional, I am speaking of regeneration. I would never say that justification is unconditional because the Scriptures teach that justification is conditioned on faith. How else can we say that we are saved by grace if we define grace as unmerited favor? I mean, how can we say that we are saved by grace and Mr. Reeves, this is the one of the things that we both agree on, that grace is defined as unmerited favor? You have two people sitting over here in the front row, one of them hears the gospel presentation, in fact they both hear the gospel presentation, one of them responds, and he exercises faith, and now is God's grace somehow conditioned upon his exercise of faith? Can grace be conditioned? He already said its unmerited favor. So is grace then merited by faith? No! That would undermine the definition of grace itself. That is why being saved by grace refers to the initial process, and really, the whole life of the believer, that he is brought to life by God's unmerited favor in his life.

There is one more thing that I need to clarify. Baptism of the Holy Spirit is not synonymous with regeneration. Baptism of the Holy Spirit is not synonymous with regeneration. How do I know that? Because men were regenerated in the Old Covenant but they did not receive the New Covenant gift of the Holy Spirit. Romans 2:28 says, "For he is not a Jew who is one outwardly nor is circumcision that which is outward in the flesh, but he is a Jew who is one inwardly, and circumcision is that which is of the heart by the Spirit, not by the letter, and his praise is not from men but from God." Notice circumcision of the heart is a work of the Spirit of God. It says that very clearly. I do not think that that is even disputable.

However, we go back to the Old Testament, and we look at Deuteronomy 30:6. God gives them a promise. He says in Deuteronomy 30:6, "Moreover, the Lord your God will circumcise your heart and the heart of your descendants to love the Lord your God." Now did God mean that? Did God mean that he was going to circumcise their hearts and the hearts of their children? Of course he did! However, we are told in the New Covenant, or at least in the book of Romans, that circumcision of the heart is not by hands, but it is the work of the Spirit. Therefore, this would be a proof text that I would use to prove that men in the Old Testament were regenerated by the Holy Spirit, even though they were not given the New Covenant gift of the Holy Spirit. John 7:39: "But this he spoke of the Spirit Whom those who had believed in Him were to receive, for the Spirit was not yet given because Jesus was not yet glorified." You see, the gift of the Spirit could not be given to the church until Jesus Christ ascended on high and took his seat and sent the Holy Spirit as he said he would on the day of Pentecost.

Now let us return to Abraham briefly. Romans 4:2-12: "For if Abraham is justified by works he has something to boast about, but not before God. For what does the Scripture say? Abraham believed God, and it was credited to him as righteousness. Now to the one who works, his wage is not credited as a favor but what is due, but to the one who does not work but believes in Him who justifies the ungodly, his faith is credited as righteousness just as David also speaks of the blessings on the man to whom God credits righteousness apart from works." Once again, the Bible does not contradict itself. It is very clear. God credits righteousness apart from works. Mr. Reeves clearly teaches that a man is saved by works. Let us look at his chart number 123 that we saw last night if I could get him to assist me maybe by putting this up there. Here in Romans chapter 4 it says that God credits righteousness apart from works, justification, but on chart 123, this is a different 123, this one says 123 also. Okay, we have a different chart, okay, that is okay. Therefore, here is the chart. Water baptism is necessary for justification. Now either our justification is credited to us by our works or we can go with what it says here in Romans chapter 4 that God credits righteousness apart from works.

I am out of time. Well, I have one more minute, so I am not going to go into my next chart yet, but I will say this. In a debate like this, you are literally bombarded with information, and both Mr. Reeves and I are going to put this debate up on our websites so that you can go back and listen to it again. In fact, I am also going to put my slides up, and if he would like to submit his, I will put his up as well. He can put mine on his site as well so that the people can, you know, listen to it and go through the slides at the same time. So I want to encourage you with Bibles open to take notes and to try to pay as close attention as possible.

I also want to commend, I did not get a chance to do this yet, and I want to commend Mr. Reeves. He is shoulders above the last two men that represented the church of Christ. I do not know if they were from a different sect or a different branch, but I will say this, that I am very impressed by my opponent, and I am very privileged to be here debating him.

Third Negative

Bruce Reeves

Good evening ladies and gentlemen! It certainly is a pleasure to be with you tonight. I am very grateful to be here and glad that you are here as we continue to study this most important subject. As I respond to some things that Mr. Cook had to say, I do want to express my appreciation for the opportunity to be engaged in this discussion with him and I am thankful for the kind remarks. At first, I thought he was just talking about the fact that I am 6'7" when he said I was head and shoulders above the rest, but certainly, it is a blessing to be able to come together. It is one of the freedoms that we have in our country to gather together, to study the word of God together. We can be gentlemen, and we can disagree and continue to strive toward a common understanding of the truth and act like we ought to act, and yet be able to look into the Scriptures. Therefore, I certainly share all of the sentiments that he expressed in that regard.

I want to consider a few things with you tonight that he alluded to as I was listening to his speech. I want to congratulate him for defining "salvation." Some of what he said I agree with, of course not all of it, but some of the definitions regarding the past, present, and future tense of the term "salvation" I don't have any particular objection to, but I want to mention some other things that he said. Mr. Cook talked about God's grace and God's mercy; however, I am under the firm conviction that I am the one here defending God's grace and God's mercy, the essentiality of faith, as we understand those things, etc. Mr. Cook has said to us that justification is conditioned upon faith, but he told us that regeneration is unconditional, and the idea of regeneration is being born again. Now I want you to think about some of the consequences of that position. He mentioned that regeneration brings us to life, so we are brought to spiritual life without faith if regeneration is unconditional. Justification is conditional he tells me, regeneration is not conditioned upon faith, therefore, I am born again without faith. That would have to be the conclusion to which one would come. I am born again before faith? Is that what the Bible teaches? Can one be born again without faith? Can I be born again and still be unacceptable before God? That seemed to be the logical conclusion.

In addition, he mentioned the imputed righteousness of Christ to us, and we will talk about that in just a few moments, but I would say to you that the idea of the imputed righteousness of Christ demeans the sufficiency of the death of Christ. I am the one here defending the death of Jesus Christ. In Hebrews chapter 10 and in verse 14 we read this passage: "For by one offering, He hath perfected forever them that are sanctified."

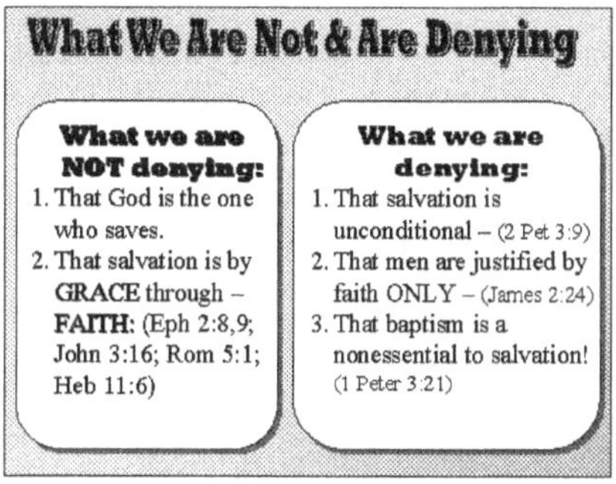
What We Are Not & Are Denying
What we are NOT denying:
1. That God is the one who saves.
2. That salvation is by GRACE through – FAITH: (Eph 2:8,9; John 3:16; Rom 5:1; Heb 11:6)
What we are denying:
1. That salvation is unconditional – (2 Pet 3:9)
2. That men are justified by faith ONLY – (James 2:24)
3. That baptism is a nonessential to salvation! (1 Peter 3:21)

Now certainly we are counted righteous through our faith. Romans 4 does not say anything about the personal life of Jesus being imputed to us. Again, I want to review what I am denying and what I am not denying. I am not denying that God is the one who saves. I am not denying that at all! Of course, God is the one who saves. If I am going to be saved, I am going to be saved by God. I am not denying that salvation is by grace through faith. No doubt about that, the Bible teaches such. Here is what I am denying: I am denying that salvation is unconditional. I am denying that one is regenerated unconditionally. I am denying that men are justified by faith only. I am denying that baptism is a non-essential to salvation. Certainly, faith is necessary.

Now one of the things Mr. Cook said that I want to pick up because I think it is important for you to recognize has to do with the statement that he did not understand why I asked him questions about unconditional election. The reason I asked him the questions that I did was that unconditional election has a bearing on why he denies water baptism as a condition of receiving salvation. Certainly, there was a connection, just him getting up here and saying, "Well there is no connection at all" does not mean that there is no connection, and as we progress, you will see that very clearly.

What This Discussion Is About:
The Nature of God
God's Universal Love and desire to save all men.
Mans ability to respond to God's love by choosing saving faith.
The Nature of saving Faith
The Nature of man
The faith that submits to God's sovereign will by obeying Him.

This debate is about the nature of God; I am defending the truth that

God loves everyone redemptively, i.e. he wants everyone to go to heaven. In order to be saved we must be willing to obey the Lord in faith. Now one of the things Mr. Cook said as you notice this third point on the nature of saving faith, which we are having some difference over, is that this debate is about whether or not we are saved by faith plus obedience. I could not have said that better. I agree whole-heartedly. That is exactly the focus of this debate. A faith that saves is a faith that obeys, and so I am affirming to you that obedience is absolutely necessary in that regard.

Questions for Tuesday Night

1. Does water baptism, ("taking a bath" G.C.Jr.) earn the benefit of Christ's sacrifice on the cross?
2. Is Genesis 15:6 the record of Abraham's initial justification?
3. Is the "new birth" unconditional?
4. If I am not one of the elect, is there anything that I can do about it?
5. Last night you stated that God desired that all men be saved. What is the difference between Divine desire & Divine will?

I want to get to his questions that he asked me. He says, number 1: "Are you a justified man?" Absolutely! Yes! He asked me, number 2 "If the answer to question number 1 is yes, then when exactly were you justified?" Well we have to understand how that term is used. I was justified when I was baptized into Jesus Christ upon the condition of my faith, I am justified as I continue to walk in Christ, and when I receive heaven, I will be justified then. He says, "On chart number 139 you stated that obedience is necessary in order to receive God's grace. Please explain how this statement fits with your definition of grace." In Luke 17:10 the Scripture says: "So likewise are you, when you shall have done all those things which are commanded you, say, we are unprofitable servants; we have done that which is our duty to do." Even when I obey God, it is still by grace and by his unmerited favor that I am saved. I never denied that principle! Conditional pardon does not negate grace. Number 4: "Please explain how much obedience is necessary to be saved." That is a good question. How much obedience is necessary to be saved? As we consider

"Salvation By Grace Through Faith"

How Much Obedience Is Enough?

- In order for Noah's family to be saved? – Gen 6:8, 22; 7:5; Heb 11:7; 1 Peter 3:21
- In order for the walls of Jericho to fall? – Josh. 6:2, 20; Heb. 11:30
- In order for Naaman to be cleansed of his leprosy? – 2 Kings 5:10-14
- In order for the 3,000 on the day of Pentecost to receive the remission of their sins? – Acts 2:38
- In order for the erring child of God to be forgiven of sin? – Acts 8:19-24; 1 John 1:7-9

this, I want you to think with me about Matthew chapter 28. In Matthew 28:20 he says, "Teaching them to observe all things whatsoever I have commanded you, and lo I am with you always, even unto the end of the world. Amen." Every commandment of God is necessary. Are there commands of God according to my opponent tonight that are not necessary? God gives a command that applies to me, but it is not necessary for me to obey that? Number 5, he asked me, and I appreciated this question: "Would you be willing to allow me to interview you for my radio show before I leave so that we can have some direct interaction?" And I would say, if he means after Friday night, absolutely. So I hope that that has taken care of his questions. Now I want to look at the questions that I asked him as we progress. I asked Mr. Cook: "Does water baptism," and I am quoting from Mr. Cook because he described that as taking a bath, "Does water baptism, or taking a bath, earn the benefit of Christ's sacrifice on the cross?" He said "no." I agree with that answer. Now if he recognizes that then we agree. I do not believe that one who has faith in the Lord, obeys him, and is baptized in water for the remission of his sins, is somehow giving an equivalent to the offering of Jesus. Why am I being charged with teaching a doctrine that says we must earn salvation? I do not believe that at all. Number 2, *(Gene, I need your chart number 21. Can you get that? Okay, you used it last night—I can tell you which one it is. It is on Abraham. Somebody hold my time, whoever is holding the time. It was, let me think for a minute here, let us see Romans 4, and it was dealing with James 2, Romans 4, Genesis 22, and Genesis 15. I am sorry; I should have told you that before. Okay! Hold that time. Thank you very much!)*

Alright! I believe on this chart that Mr. Cook is wrong on both sides of these things, and we are going to get to that in just a moment, but I believe that in James 2 the Scriptures are dealing with justification before God. In addition, I do not think that Genesis 15:6 is the first time we can read about Abraham being justified before God. We are going to talk about that more in just a moment, so you just hang on to that idea. Number 3: "Is the new birth unconditional?" He said yes, you do not have to do anything to be born again. Number 4: "If I am not one of the elect, is there anything that I can do about it?" Now I really want you to understand where the Reformed position is coming from in its view of unconditional election regarding regeneration, and why these things are being presented in the way they are, and why baptism is being denied as being essential. Now think about this for a moment. If I am on that non-elect list, there is nothing I can do about it. Now if I am on the elect list, there is nothing I can do to keep from being on the elect list. So if I do not have it, I cannot get it, and if I get it, I cannot lose it, and if I lose it, I never had it. That is the position. That is what he is affirming to you.

Number 5: "Last night you stated that God desires that all men be saved. What is the difference between divine desire and divine will?" He talked about there being two aspects of God's will, i.e. his perceptive will and his decretive will. Now last night I asked him about the verse that states that God is not willing that any should perish but that all should come to repentance. He said, of course God wants all men to be saved and even said that I had misrepresented what he had to say. Yet, he turns around and he says but God willed this, his divine decrees unconditionally foreordained before the world ever began that particular individuals were on the elect list, particular individuals were on the non-elect list, and there is nothing that can be done to change that fact. Then we are told that he is affirming the God of grace, the God of mercy, the God of love.

When you think about number 4 and number 5 keep these things in mind. I want to go back and just think briefly about some things Mr. Cook said last night about the Amalekites. I want you to consider what Mr. Cook said as he talked about those Amalekites and their little babies, the little babies that were sucking on their mothers' breasts, and the fact that God chose Israel. By the way, God chose Israel so that through them as a nation the lineage of the Messiah would be preserved. However, his idea is that when they went in there and they slaughtered all those Amalekite babies, that they were non-elect and all those babies went to hell, but he tells us that he is affirming the God of grace and the God of love. This is what the Reformed position advocates. Certainly, our hearts should pour out for our families, and we should desire to serve the Lord, but this is the position. Play that quote. That is okay. Don, I will read it. Mr. Cook said, "Non-elect infants" (this is a question that was given to him by Brother Brown), "Non-elect infants who die in their infancy will spend eternity in hell. I would answer true to that question. You have to be elect in order to be saved. If this question is false,

The Nature of God
" 'Non elect infants who die in their infancy will spend eternity in hell' – I would answer true to that question, you have to be elect in order to be saved. If this question is false, then we should perform abortion, because abortion is the greatest evangelistic act that has ever taken place since the time that Jesus walked the face of the earth, because everyone of those children are going straight to heaven according to Mr. Brown's theology"
(David P. Brown & Gene Cook, Jr. Debate, Feb 16, 2000)

then we should perform abortion because abortion is the greatest evangelistic act that has ever taken place since the time that Jesus walked the face of the earth because every one of those children is going straight to heaven according to Mr. Brown's theology." Is this the God of grace and love, and certainly God judges sin, but what sin have these little infants committed? Yet this is the God of grace and mercy that I understand the Bible to teach? Is that quote playing, Don? Okay, that is okay. Let us move on.

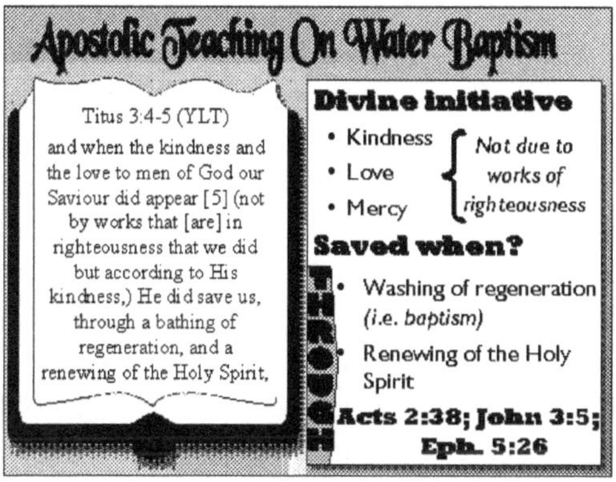
Apostolic Teaching On Water Baptism
Titus 3:4-5 (YLT)
and when the kindness and the love to men of God our Saviour did appear [5] (not by works that [are] in righteousness that we did but according to His kindness,) He did save us, through a bathing of regeneration, and a renewing of the Holy Spirit,
Divine initiative
• Kindness
• Love
• Mercy
Not due to works of righteousness
Saved when?
THROUGH
• Washing of regeneration (i.e. baptism)
• Renewing of the Holy Spirit
Acts 2:38; John 3:5; Eph. 5:26

Now, Titus 3:5 has come to our attention. I want you to notice that passage with me. I agree there is nothing we could do, have done, or will ever do that would serve as an equivalent to what Jesus did for us, but that does not mean that obedience is not necessary. Obedience to the gospel does not negate grace. Paul says to us that it was by divine initiative, the kindness, and the love, and the mercy of God, not due to works of righteousness. When are we saved? That is the issue. Here is what the passage says. This is my passage; this is not Mr. Cook's passage. The passage says that we are saved through the washing of regeneration and the renewing of the Holy Spirit, and by the way, that matches perfectly with John 3:5 that tells us we are born again. How? It is through the water and through the Spirit. That is what I am going to be affirming to you Thursday and Friday night.

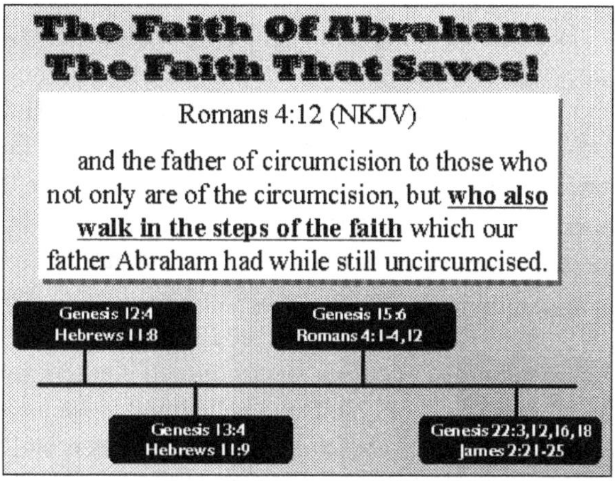
The Faith Of Abraham
The Faith That Saves!
Romans 4:12 (NKJV)
and the father of circumcision to those who not only are of the circumcision, but who also walk in the steps of the faith which our father Abraham had while still uncircumcised.
Genesis 12:4
Hebrews 11:8
Genesis 15:6
Romans 4:1-4,12
Genesis 13:4
Hebrews 11:9
Genesis 22:3,12,16,18
James 2:21-25

Now let us talk about this Abraham argument. Romans 4 tells us that we are to walk in the steps of the faith of our Father Abraham. I want you to get your Old Testament out, and I want you to turn back to Genesis 12. I believe his argument on Romans 4:3 is this: At which point was Abraham justified, and is justification a one-time event and before that, he was not justified? I want to go back to Genesis 12 because what I want to show you is that this argument regarding justification simply won't hold up. Let's look at this together in Genesis 12: "Now the Lord had said to Abram, 'Get out of your country, from your family, and from your father's house to a land that I will show you, and I will make you a great nation, and I will bless you, and I will make your name great, and you shall be a blessing, and I will bless those who bless you, and I will curse them who curse you, and in you all the families of the earth shall be blessed." The Lord is speaking to Abram, and he says I want you to go. He gives him these directions, and he says I want you to go, and Abram listened to him, and he obeyed him. "So Abram departed as the Lord had spoken to him, and Lot went with him, and Abram was seventy-five years old when he departed from Haran." I want you now to turn to Hebrews 11:8. In Hebrews 11:8, the Scripture says by what? "By faith Abraham, when he was called. . . ." When was he called? Back in Genesis 12! He was "called to go out into a place which he should after receive for an inheritance," what did he do? He "obeyed." Now listen to me, this is before Genesis the 15th chapter. This is in Genesis chapter 12, "and he obeyed." He obeyed! Did that mean that he was not saved by grace? Of course not! He did what God told him to do and he did so before Genesis chapter 15. Is this man not justified? It says by faith he did this. Let us go to Genesis chapter 13. In Genesis 13:4, we read, "There was a place with an altar which he had made there at first, and there Abram called on the name of the Lord." Abram called on the name of the Lord!

Is this man unjustified or is he justified? We would like to know. He is obeying God. He seems to have faith in God here. He does have faith in God, no doubt about it. Now let us go back to Hebrews 11:9. "By faith he sojourned in the land of promise as in a strange country dwelling in tabernacles with Isaac and Jacob." We are still before Genesis chapter 15. Now then, let us turn to Genesis 15:6. Now we are in Genesis 15, and this is what is referenced in Romans 4. So now, we are in Genesis chapter 15, and he says, "And he believed in the Lord." Listen to me! He already believed in the Lord. He had worshiped the Lord, and now in Genesis chapter 15, "He believed on the Lord, and he accounted it to him for righteousness." He was justified in Genesis 12. He was justified in Genesis 13. He was justified in Genesis 15. We go to Romans the 4th chapter, and when he is talking about some of these things, he is not saying that Abraham is not justified at all before Genesis 15; he is simply showing us that it was on the condition of his faith that he was counted righteous.

In Romans 4:12, "And the father of circumcision, to them that are not of the circumcision only, but who also walk in the steps of that faith of our father Abraham." Let us consider Genesis 22, you will remember that this is what is referenced in James 2. We need to emphasize that Abraham was justified in Genesis 12 because he believed in the Lord and he obeyed. He was justified in Genesis 13 because he believed in the Lord and he obeyed. He was justified by the Lord in Genesis 15 because he believed the Lord and he obeyed, Romans 4 says so.

In Genesis the 22nd chapter, we are not just talking about justification before men. He was not justifying himself before Isaac. Isaac was simply doing what his father told him. He was not justifying himself before the ram. He was being justified before God. As I believe in the Lord and I obey him, I am a justified man, and in Genesis 22:3: "So Abram rose early in the morning, and he saddled the donkey, and he took two of his young men with him and Isaac his son, and he split the wood for the burnt offering, arose and he went to the place which God had told him." Let us go down to verse 12. We'd be happy to read more of this context, "And he said, 'Do not lay your hand on the lad or do anything to him for now I know that you fear God since you have not withheld your son, your only son from me.'" Let us look at verse 16, "By myself I have sworn, says the Lord, because you have done this thing and have not withheld your son, your only son." Now look with me at verse 18: "In your seed all the nations of the earth shall be blessed, because you have obeyed my voice."

This debate is about faith and obedience, no doubt about it. It is about faith and obedience. Must I obey the Lord? Of course, I must. Now let us go back and let us look some other things. Mr. Cook talked about how I was teaching a works system. Again, we have to define our topic. If you are talking about a working of faith, that is exactly what I believe and that is what James is affirming. If you are talking about meritorious works, no they do not save the sinner! If you are talking about sinless perfection, as it is being used regarding the Law of Moses, no, I do not teach that! Where do repentance, confession, and baptism belong? That is an easy question to answer as we consider the proper definition of the term "works." These things are simply works of faith.

Let us think about the book of Romans. Anytime someone construes faith in a way that would say that obedience to Christ is not essential, and I will say in order to be regenerated, if that's the word we need to use, regarding

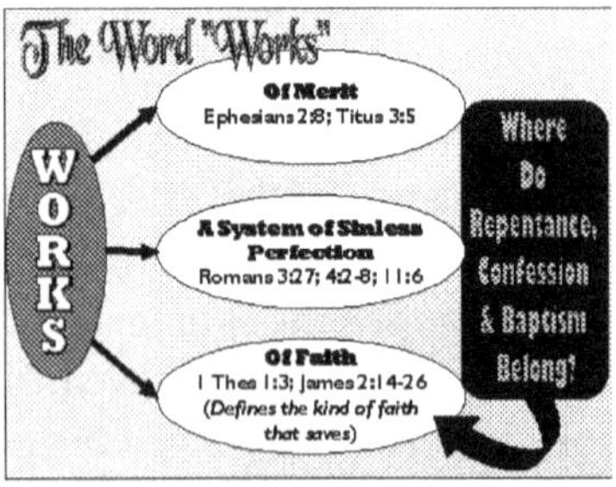
The Word "Works"
WORKS
Of Merit
Ephesians 2:8; Titus 3:5
A System of Sinless Perfection
Romans 3:27; 4:2-8; 11:6
Of Faith
1 Thes 1:3; James 2:14-26
(Defines the kind of faith that saves)
Where Do Repentance, Confession & Baptism Belong?

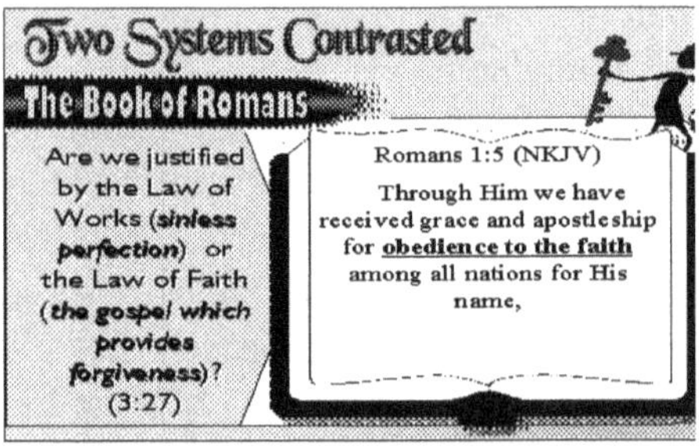
Two Systems Contrasted
The Book of Romans
Are we justified by the Law of Works (sinless perfection) or the Law of Faith (the gospel which provides forgiveness)? (3:27)
Romans 1:5 (NKJV)
Through Him we have received grace and apostleship for obedience to the faith among all nations for His name,

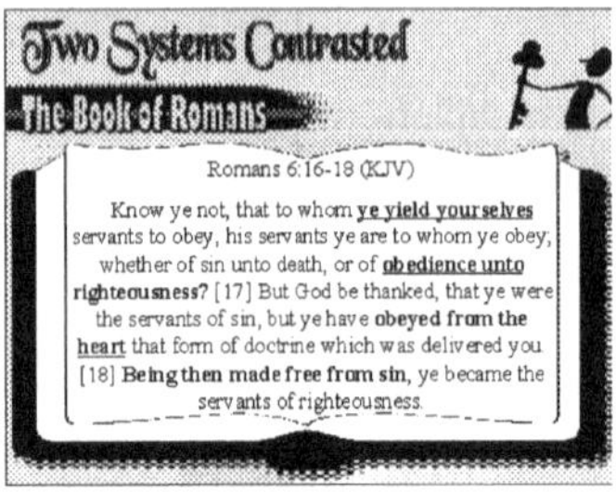
Two Systems Contrasted
The Book of Romans
Romans 6:16-18 (KJV)
Know ye not, that to whom ye yield yourselves servants to obey, his servants ye are to whom ye obey; whether of sin unto death, or of obedience unto righteousness? [17] But God be thanked, that ye were the servants of sin, but ye have obeyed from the heart that form of doctrine which was delivered you. [18] Being then made free from sin, ye became the servants of righteousness.

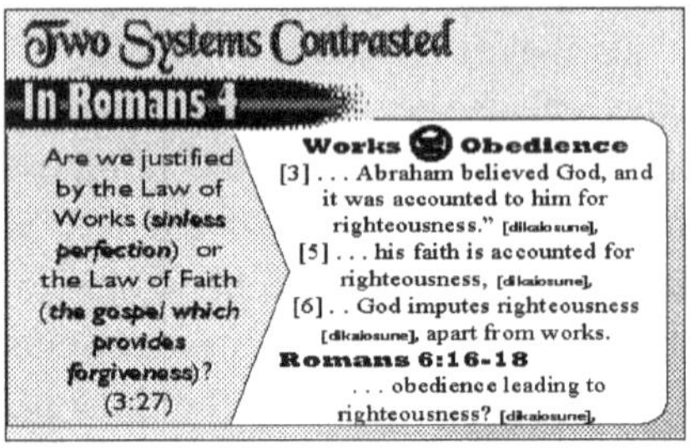
Two Systems Contrasted
In Romans 4
Are we justified by the Law of Works (sinless perfection) or the Law of Faith (the gospel which provides forgiveness)? (3:27)
Works Obedience
[3] . . . Abraham believed God, and it was accounted to him for righteousness." [dikaiosune],
[5] . . . his faith is accounted for righteousness, [dikaiosune],
[6] . . God imputes righteousness [dikaiosune], apart from works.
Romans 6:16-18
. . . obedience leading to righteousness? [dikaiosune],

what God has told us to do in order to become his children, they have missed the point of the book. Romans 1:5: "Through Him we have received grace and apostleship for obedience to the faith." That is the point of the book of Romans. Now, I really want you to pay attention to this because this makes it clear. The works that are being discussed in Romans 4 have reference to sinless perfection and that is why Paul quotes David. Paul quotes from David about receiving the forgiveness of our sins. As he uses the term "works" in Romans 4, he is talking about the sinlessness that would have been required under the Law of Moses. He is contrasting two systems. He is not saying obedience is not necessary. How do I know that, you might ask me tonight? In Romans chapter 6, "Know ye not that to which you yield yourselves servants to obey, his servants ye are to whom you obey, whether of sin unto death or of **obedience unto righteousness**." I really want you to pay attention to this, and I know you are, you are listening very well. The term "righteousness" here is the same term that we have for justification, and so Mr. Cook gets on to me and he says, "Well, Bruce is teaching works when he tells you that you have to obey in order to be born again," but this passage says we obey unto righteousness, and that's the same word for justification. Therefore, when Paul says I am "made righteous apart from works," I know he is not talking about obedience to Jesus Christ. He cannot be! He is talking about the idea that under that Law of Moses, you are not going to receive that absolute remission of sins that you need in order to be pleasing to the Lord.

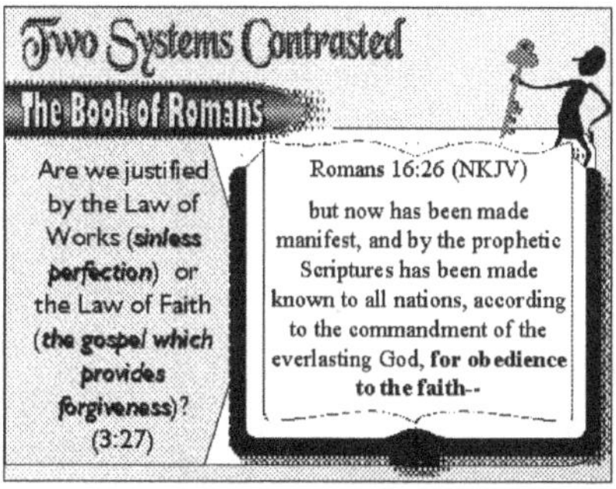
Two Systems Contrasted
The Book of Romans
Are we justified by the Law of Works (*sinless perfection*) or the Law of Faith (*the gospel which provides forgiveness*)? (3:27)
Romans 16:26 (NKJV)
but now has been made manifest, and by the prophetic Scriptures has been made known to all nations, according to the commandment of the everlasting God, **for obedience to the faith--**

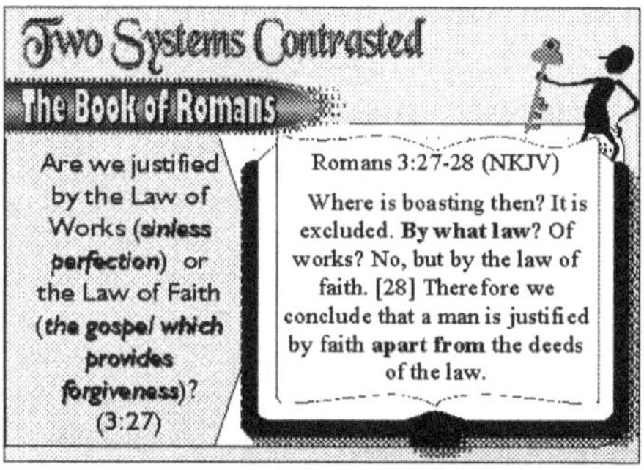
Two Systems Contrasted
The Book of Romans
Are we justified by the Law of Works (*sinless perfection*) or the Law of Faith (*the gospel which provides forgiveness*)? (3:27)
Romans 3:27-28 (NKJV)
Where is boasting then? It is excluded. **By what law?** Of works? No, but by the law of faith. [28] Therefore we conclude that a man is justified by faith **apart from** the deeds of the law.

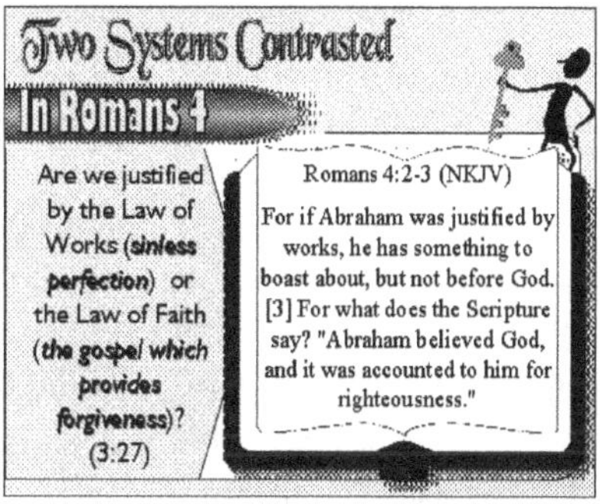
Two Systems Contrasted
In Romans 4
Are we justified by the Law of Works (*sinless perfection*) or the Law of Faith (*the gospel which provides forgiveness*)? (3:27)
Romans 4:2-3 (NKJV)
For if Abraham was justified by works, he has something to boast about, but not before God. [3] For what does the Scripture say? "Abraham believed God, and it was accounted to him for righteousness."

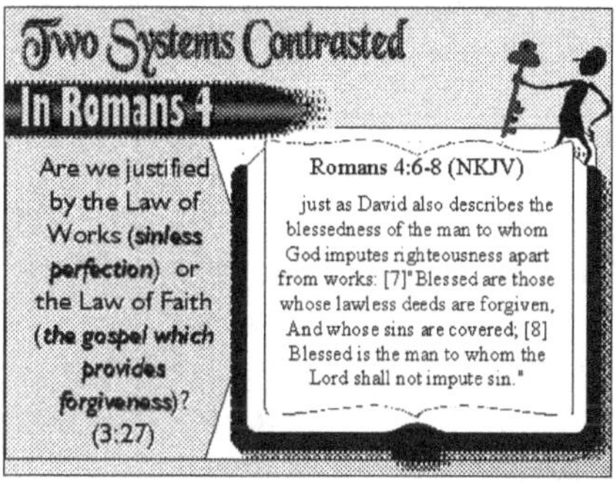
Two Systems Contrasted
In Romans 4
Are we justified by the Law of Works (*sinless perfection*) or the Law of Faith (*the gospel which provides forgiveness*)? (3:27)
Romans 4:6-8 (NKJV)
just as David also describes the blessedness of the man to whom God imputes righteousness apart from works: [7] "Blessed are those whose lawless deeds are forgiven, And whose sins are covered; [8] Blessed is the man to whom the Lord shall not impute sin."

In Romans 16, we read about "obedience to the faith." I know we are moving a little quickly here, but I want you to see that Paul is contrasting two systems. He is not saying obedience is not necessary, but he is saying the opposite. "By what law? Of works," so he is talking about the law of works that is the Law of Moses. "No! But by the law of faith." As we look at Romans 4 it is evident that this passage does not say that he was counted righteous because the personal righteousness of Christ's life was imputed to him. That is not what it says at all. He was counted righteous through his faith, and by that faith through Christ, he was forgiven of his sins. "For if Abraham was justified by works he has something to boast about, but not before God," for what does the Scripture say, "Abraham believed God, and it, (it, it) was accounted for righteousness." We are dealing with forgiveness of our past sins.

When he talks about the man that is justified apart from works, he was justified apart from his own sinlessness; he is justified through being forgiven of his sins. Now pay attention to this, Paul says Abraham "believed God, and it was accounted to him for righteousness." We read that his "faith is accounted for righteousness." We read that God "imputes righteousness apart from works," but then we read in Romans 6 "obedience leads to righteousness." Now just look at that for a minute, we are "counted righteous apart from works," i.e. apart from our own sinlessness. We have all sinned, but that

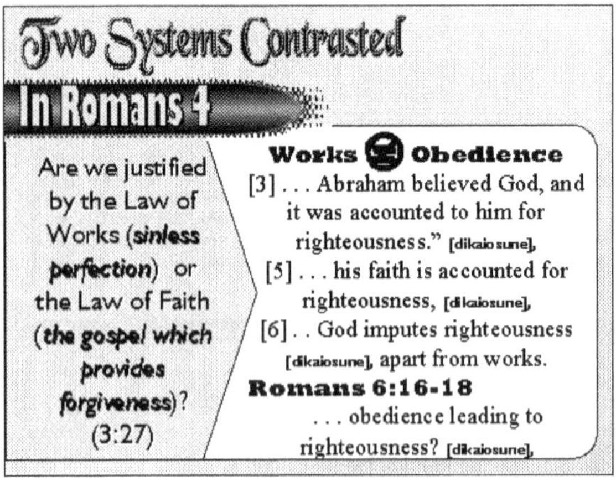
Two Systems Contrasted
In Romans 4
Are we justified by the Law of Works (*sinless perfection*) or the Law of Faith (*the gospel which provides forgiveness*)? (3:27)
Works ≠ Obedience
[3] . . . Abraham believed God, and it was accounted to him for righteousness." [dikaiosune],
[5] . . . his faith is accounted for righteousness, [dikaiosune],
[6] . . God imputes righteousness [dikaiosune], apart from works.
Romans 6:16-18
. . . obedience leading to righteousness? [dikaiosune],

does not mean that obedience is not necessary. The faith only concept is simply not true.

Now I want to look at Romans 4 some more and notice what the text teaches about Abraham. Look at verse 12, "And the father of circumcision, to them that are not of the circumcision only, but who also walk in the steps of that faith of our father Abraham, which he had being yet uncircumcised, for the promise that he would be heir of the world, was not to Abraham." I want to look at verse 20. "He staggered not at the promise of God through unbelief, but he was strong in faith giving glory to God." Abraham was justified by faith, and that faith obeyed God. This is seen in Genesis 12, Genesis 13, Genesis 15, and Genesis 22. I do not understand how somebody could get up here and tell you that obedience is not necessary in order to be born again when Hebrews 5:8-9 says "Jesus is the author of eternal salvation unto all them that obey him."

I am rushing it, but I want to get it up here. Mr. Cook brought up Acts 8. I would like to talk about Acts 8 some more. I believe he is saying that the regeneration of the Holy Spirit occurred in verse 12, but the passage said it happened before the Spirit fell on them, and it says they were only baptized in the name of the Lord Jesus. They were only baptized in the name of the Lord Jesus, and we know that was water baptism, and yes, that is the water baptism that put them into Christ. I wanted to make sure and present that as we consider these issues because that passage is a death blow to the idea that water baptism is not the baptism that puts one into Jesus Christ.

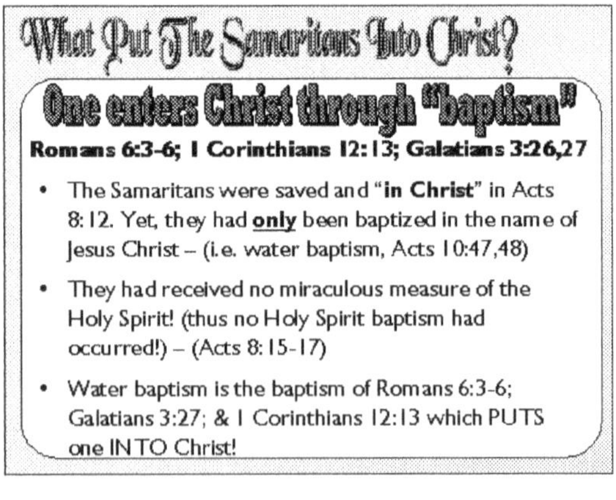
What Put The Samaritans Into Christ?
One enters Christ through "baptism"
Romans 6:3-6; I Corinthians 12:13; Galatians 3:26,27
• The Samaritans were saved and "in Christ" in Acts 8:12. Yet, they had only been baptized in the name of Jesus Christ – (i.e. water baptism, Acts 10:47,48)
• They had received no miraculous measure of the Holy Spirit! (thus no Holy Spirit baptism had occurred!) – (Acts 8:15-17)
• Water baptism is the baptism of Romans 6:3-6; Galatians 3:27; & I Corinthians 12:13 which PUTS one INTO Christ!

He brought up Acts 16 about believing. You know what Mr. Cook's problem is, and I mean this in kindness, and I think he knows that, his problem is the same problem that many denominational people have because they leave the jailhouse too quickly. Usually I do not tell people to stay in the jailhouse for very long, but he leaves the jailhouse too fast. In Acts 16 he said, "Sirs, what must I do to be saved? They said, 'Believe on the Lord Jesus Christ, and you will be saved, you and your household.'" But you know what they did? They did the very thing many denominational preachers will not do today, the same hour of the night, what did they do? They were baptized. They were baptized. Why? Because they were obeying, yes, they were obeying God, and that is what we must do. We must submit to the righteousness of God. I agree we are saved by grace through faith, and that faith does not merit salvation, but that faith is absolutely essential in order for you to be born again. Do we have a born again person without faith? Now you think about that. Do we have a born again person without faith or before, I should say, before faith? I do not believe so, you will have to consider some of these things, and I look forward to hearing from Mr. Cook.

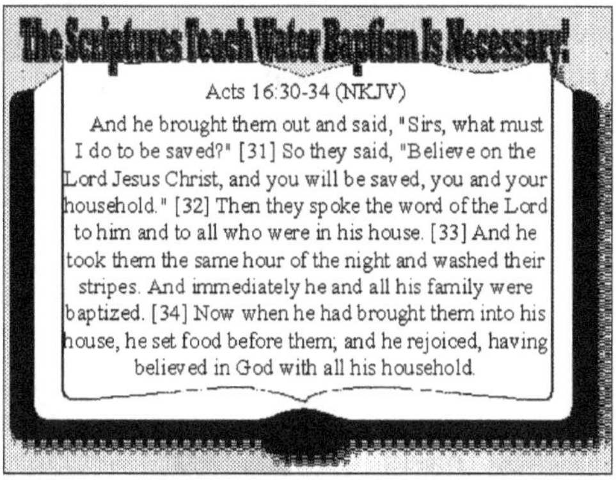
The Scriptures Teach Water Baptism Is Necessary!
Acts 16:30-34 (NKJV)
And he brought them out and said, "Sirs, what must I do to be saved?" [31] So they said, "Believe on the Lord Jesus Christ, and you will be saved, you and your household." [32] Then they spoke the word of the Lord to him and to all who were in his house. [33] And he took them the same hour of the night and washed their stripes. And immediately he and all his family were baptized. [34] Now when he had brought them into his house, he set food before them; and he rejoiced, having believed in God with all his household.

I know he is going to offer a rebuttal as he continues his affirmation, but I want you to think about these things. We are saved by faith, but we are not saved by faith only, and by the way, the chart about doctrinal schizophrenia had to do with Martin Luther's concept regarding the idea that we are saved by faith only, or faith alone, but faith is never alone. That just does not make sense, and I understand some of the different terminology, and yes, you might be confused. I do not think it is because of what I have said to you. I think Mr. Cook's distinction in terms, him moving from one term to another, to another, to another, we get to that term, he goes to another term, and that can be confusing. We do want to define things correctly and a term can mean different things, but it cannot mean two different things at the same time on the same argument on the same verse about the same issue. Therefore, we want to keep all of these things in our mind as we consider the word of God and we consider the truth.

I am not here for personal victory, and I think Mr. Cook knows that and you know that; I am here because I am concerned about your soul. I want you to go to heaven. I want all of us to go to heaven. If we open up our Bibles and study the word of God, I know that we can understand the truth and we can come closer together. However, anytime somebody gets up here, and I think that is what you are going to hear, and tells you that obedience to Christ negates grace or that I am teaching a works system, you can know that that is simply not the case. Thank you for your attention.

Fourth Affirmative

Gene Cook, Jr.

This will be my last 30 minute segment of the evening, and before I get back into what I've prepared tonight on my affirmative argument, I want to just respond to a few things that you just heard, and I want to respond to them first because they're most likely to be fresh in your mind. When we look at 2 Corinthians 5, Paul's letter to the Corinthian church, chapter 5, we read in verse 21 of the work of Christ, "He made Him who knew no sin to be sin on our behalf that we might become the righteousness of God." Therefore, you see both aspects of Christ's work in the atonement there. You see not only the sacrificial aspect of his death that takes away our sins, but also the righteousness of God being given to us in his death. Yes, in his death, his life, his righteous life is then transferred to us by faith. So, I want to make a clarification on that because Mr. Reeves believes that we are righteous by the works of our faith, we are righteous by obeying the things that God has commanded us. In fact, when I asked him how much obedience is necessary for one to be saved, his answer was, and I am quoting, "every command of God is necessary to be saved." "Every command of God is necessary to be saved." We heard a lot of talk about the law of righteousness referring to sinless perfection and how no man could be saved by the law of works, or in the Old Testament the law of righteousness, but you just heard out of his own mouth, every command of God is necessary to be saved.

Now I am going to give him the benefit of the doubt because I think he would probably, and I do not know this for sure, but I think that he would probably draw a firm line of distinction between Old Covenant and New Covenant. So, when you say every command, I'm assuming that you're probably referring to New Covenant commands, but if you notice in Romans 7:7 Paul the apostle quotes the Decalogue. He says in Romans 7:7, "What shall we say then? Is the law sin? May it never be! On the contrary, I would not have come to know sin except for the law, and I would not have known about coveting the law if it had not been said 'you shall not covet.'" And then again in Romans 13:9 he says that the law is fulfilled, he says in verse

9: "For this you shall not commit adultery, you shall not murder, you shall not steal, you shall not covet, and if there is any other commandment, it is summed up in this saying: You shall love your neighbor as yourself." Now Paul is saying that all the commandments, or namely the commandments of the Decalogue are summed up in the command to love, and so Paul is not negating the command of the Decalogue, the Ten Commandments. Paul is affirming the Ten Commandments and saying that loving your neighbor really is fulfilling the Ten Commandments. However, if I want to know how do I love my neighbor, it is not just some esoteric love. If I want to know how do I love my neighbor, I can still appeal to the Ten Commandments because the New Covenant appeals to the Ten Commandments. This is one example where they are recited, and this whole idea of drawing a sharp distinction between the moral law. The moral law of God never changes.

We saw a real cute picture of some babies, and I did not get the chart here, but I do not know if you can reference that for me, if not it is okay. The question was asked, what sin have these little infants committed, and that's a real good question because you would think that, if they stood any chance of going to hell, and by the way, let me just make a clarification on that. I believe that elect infants go to heaven, and it could be that all infants are elect, I do not know. It could be that every one of them is elect, I do not know. God has not told me which human beings are elect and which human beings are not. I was asked the question can a non-elect infant, if there is such a thing, the answer would be no, but the question was once again asked what sin have these little infants committed. In that question there is a denial of the inherent sinful nature of Adam, which is nothing more than Finneyism. I do not know if you know who Finney was. You may have heard of Charles Finney's *Systematic Theology*. He was a revivalist. He was one of the premier revivalists who denied the sinful nature, original sin.

We must understand that the Bible is a book from beginning to end, and we are told that the consequences of Adam's sin are inherited upon Adam's children. Listen very carefully, Romans 5:18. I am not making this up, believe me. "So then as through one transgression there resulted condemnation to all men." That is what the Bible teaches, that through one transgression, Romans 5:18, there results condemnation to all men or all of mankind, so much so that all of mankind is said to be under the condemnation of God. Therefore, we first and foremost are not guilty before God because of our own sin. That is a real problem, but we are guilty before God at the moment we are born because of our father's sin, Adam. Adam was put in the garden, and Adam rebelled against God. You say, "How can you be responsible for Adam's sin?" Jesus Christ, may I remind you, is called the second Adam, and if you say that you have received the forgiveness of his death as the second Adam, then I would ask you the same question. How can you deny on the one hand that you have inherited sin from the first Adam but then on the other hand affirm that you have received forgiveness from the second Adam?

That is the story that the Bible gives us. There was a first Adam that brings all of mankind into condemnation. There was a second Adam that restores that which was lost and saves men, and God would be a God of grace, and God would be a God of mercy if he even saved just one of us. That would be an act of grace and mercy in and of itself. However, when he says that every command of God is necessary to be saved, then what happens when you violate one of God's commands? Let us say that on Wednesday, tomorrow, I violate one of God's commands, and I am an adherent to his theology, does that mean I have just lost my justification? Well, logically that is exactly what it would mean. Therefore, I am justified on Tuesday but then on Wednesday I am not justified, and then what do I need to do, repent and confess my sins? However, is that enough? Should I not also be baptized again since baptism is required for justification? I can tell you right now, if I had been brought into the system of theology that I am hearing from this side of the room tonight, I would have given up a long time ago. I cannot do it. I cannot be good enough to merit God's favor and neither can you. You might be able to act well enough, let me address the men for a minute. Consider our sinful thoughts? The moment you lust after a woman, Jesus says in the Sermon on the Mount you have committed adultery. Did you just lose your justification? That is where this teaching leads. You need to think about that because, if that is the case, you have absolutely no security whatsoever, and because of your very nature, we are prone to sin. Women, what about gossip? Have you gossiped about anybody since you were baptized? Did you lose your justification?

I hope that we would be honest in answering these questions and come to the realization that we cannot make it on our obedience. That is why it is necessary to take heed to the words of Titus 3:5 that it is not based on deeds, which we have done, but it is by his mercy and the washing of regeneration and renewal of the Holy Spirit.

One of the proof texts that I found interesting here was the chart 166, if I can maybe have you put that up, chart 166. He cites Romans 4, comparing that with Genesis 12, and he says that Abraham exercised faith, or Abram exercised faith in Genesis 12, which surely he did. There is no denial here he exercised faith in Genesis 13, but I was looking very hard to find any record of justification in 12 or 13. We do not find justification until 15. Therefore, it is a presumption on his part. I would say that Abraham was not justified until the Bible says he was justified. It is very clear that when he believed that promise, because you cannot be justified without having faith in Jesus Christ, and he had not been told about Jesus Christ yet. It was not until God said I am going to bring a seed out of your body that Abraham believed God, and by believing God in that seed, which we are told in Galations 3, is none other than Jesus Christ, it was his faith in Jesus Christ that justified him. So what was happening before 15? I believe God was in the process of drawing him. Many people can obey what God commands, we would agree on that, I mean he would agree there are plenty of people who have been obedient to the command of baptism who are not saved, that are not justified. That is something on which we agree. Therefore, obedience to that which God commands does not mark justification. Even those who do not claim to be Christians sometimes obey the law of God when they are faithful to their husbands or wives.

Then he says that in James chapter 2, as he is contrasting that with Genesis chapter 22 when Isaac is taken up on the altar, he said something that I found very interesting. I believe it's Genesis 22, if I am not mistaken, Genesis 22:6, let me see if I can get the verse here. Okay, God tells Abraham to stretch out his hand against the lad and then God says in Genesis 22:12, "Do not stretch your hand out against the lad and do nothing to him, for now I know that you fear God." He wants to prop this verse up and says "see this is Abraham justifying himself before God because by Abraham's actions, now God knew that Abraham was really a man of faith." Let me ask you a question. Is God all knowing? Does an all-knowing God learn things? No, he does not. So when God says now I know, he's not speaking from the standpoint of his omniscience, no, he's talking to us in baby talk that we might understand what's going on with him and Abraham. This was all part of God's plan to begin with. Once again, this is something that happens in the life of Abraham when Isaac is already a young man, he is grown. So the question is, when actually was Abraham justified? I am going to contend that the Bible is very clear that it says he was justified in Genesis 15, but does that mean he was justified again if we are to understand James' words in James 2 of justification before God? Was Abraham justified back then and then, you know, 15 years later, he was justified again, or did he have to keep getting re-justified? No, you see, that is a confusion of the doctrines of sanctification and justification. Justification is a one-time event.

Sanctification is a process, stretching from new birth to death, whereby God conforms us to the image of Jesus Christ. He is making us holy by his Spirit and through our obedience.

Can you put up chart 146 for a second, please? I want you to notice something crucial here in chart 146. There is the statement here that obedience was from the heart, 146. See there in verse 17, "but God be thanked that ye were servants of sin but ye have obeyed from the heart." Jesus asked a question. He asks, "Can a bad tree produce good fruit?" Can you dip into a man's heart and bring something good if the man has a bad heart? The answer is no, so how does obedience come from the heart if the heart is not first changed? I do believe that they obeyed from the heart, but in order for that to happen; the heart had to be changed to a disposition toward God. A desire had to be put in that heart for obedience or else obedience never would have come.

If I could see chart 135 for a just a moment, this would be the last clarification, there is a picture of Martin Luther there. By the way, Martin Luther was not a Calvinist, never claimed to be a Calvinist. In fact, his doctrine of soteriology is not Calvinistic. You can call any Lutheran church here in Arkansas and they will confirm that, so you kind of get the impression that he might have been a Calvinist, but at the top of his page, it says doctrinal schizophrenia. Let me ask you a question. Whom was Luther arguing against when he made that statement? If you know the answer, you will know that he was arguing against the doctrine of Rome. It is quite ironic, because I said this last night, that the presentation that I heard was more kin to Roman Catholicism than it is Protestantism or biblical Christianity. You see, Martin Luther was arguing against the error of Rome. At least the priests, when they read Romans 5:18 in their Bibles, they saw that even their babies had inherited the sinful nature of Adam. So, they had enough sense to devise some doctrine of baptism for the babies to cleanse them of that original sin, but my opponent does not even have that, he just denies it altogether. And as Martin Luther argues against the doctrine of faith and works, of meriting God's grace, not by imputed righteousness but by infused righteousness through the sacraments, it all boils down to essentially the same argument. What was he saying here? He was saying that we are justified by faith alone but then he was concurring with James that a justifying faith is never a faith that is alone. That is not schizophrenia; that is biblical Christianity. It might be schizophrenic for those who are siding with Rome. Many people would be extremely angry if I told them their doctrine resembles Rome, but he is arguing against Rome.

Okay, now let me get on to my charts. I left my remote control over here. The first chart I have up here is Romans 4:9. Now Paul is going to use circumcision to teach us something about what it means to take a sign, and he says in Romans 4:9, "Is this blessing then upon the circumcised or upon the uncircumcised also, for we say faith was reckoned to Abraham as righteousness. How then was it reckoned?" Isn't that the question that we are asking tonight? How? "How was it reckoned? While he was circumcised or uncircumcised? Not while he was circumcised, but while uncircumcised, and he received the sign of circumcision, a seal of the righteousness of the faith which he had while he was uncircumcised that he might be the father of all who believe without being circumcised that righteousness might be reckoned to them also, or to them." Verse 12, "And the father of circumcision to those who not only are of the circumcision but also follow in the steps of the faith of our father Abraham, which he had while he was uncircumcised." So the argument that Paul is making is look, God commanded circumcision, but when was Abraham justified? When was he credited as righteous? Paul asked the question, when he became circumcised, after he became circumcised or before? The answer is, of course, before.

Now let me move to the subject of baptism. In the Bible, we are given something called signs. We just saw one here in Romans 4:11, "And he received the sign of circumcision." Here we know that the sign of circumcision was to signify the spiritual reality of the circumcision of the heart. That is the argument that Paul makes in Romans early on, that what really matters is circumcision of the heart, but it was to be signified by the outward act of circumcision. So we have signs and we have things that are signified by the signs. Water baptism is a sign that is given to signify something else. So, what does it signify? First, baptism signifies that believers have been made clean. It symbolizes being cleansed. Baptism signifies that believers had been made clean, it signifies being cleansed, having the guilt and condemnation before God of our sins being washed away. How does that happen? The blood of Jesus Christ, his Son, cleanses us from all sin (1 John 1:7). When we believe in him, his sacrifice on the cross is applied to us, and we are cleansed. This is why Jesus said to his disciples, "Unless I wash you, you have no part with me" (John 13:8). We are washed spiritually when we are born again and respond in faith. We should then be baptized as an outward physical sign of the spiritual reality. Baptism, therefore, is a step of obedience.

Second, baptism signifies union with Christ. As the baptized person goes under the water of baptism and surfaces again, it symbolizes union with Christ in his death and resurrection. Because he died, we have eternal life. Because he was raised from the dead, so we will also be resurrected to newness of life." Romans 6:3-5 talks about this: "For do you not know that all of us who have been baptized into Christ Jesus have been baptized into His death. Therefore, we have been buried with Him through baptism into death so that as Christ was raised from the dead through the glory of the Father, so we too might walk in newness of life. For if we have become united with Him in the likeness of His death, certainly we shall also be in the likeness of His resurrection." Baptism is a sign that points to something else. When I got off the freeway, there was a sign that said University of Central Arkansas that way, but that was not the University of Central Arkansas. That was a sign pointing me here. What I am trying to show you is that baptism is a sign that points to something else, namely these spiritual realities.

Thirdly, baptism signifies death to sin. The New Covenant sign of baptism is intimately related to the Old Covenant's sign of circumcision. In the Old Testament times, circumcision signified the removal of the sinful nature. It did not mean that the one circumcised would be saved. It was simply a sign of God's promise to cleanse those who trust in him for salvation. In New Testament times, baptism also signifies the putting off the sinful nature and is to be practiced by all of those who have trusted in the Lord. This is why we are told to repent and be baptized. It is a sign that one has died to sin and has put off the sinful nature. Let me give you an example of this from the Scripture, how circumcision is related to, that is circumcision of the heart, is related to baptism. Colossians 2:11-12, "And in Him you are also circumcised with the circumcision made without hands in the removal of the body of flesh by the circumcision of Christ, having been buried with Him in baptism in which you were also raised up with Him through faith in the working of God." So thirdly, baptism signifies death to sin.

Now the next point is very crucial to this debate. In the Bible, the sign was so closely related to the thing signified that the apostles could use the sign and the thing signified, and they could speak of them interchangeably. Before I give you an example of baptism, let me give you another example. In John 1:29 it says, "The next day he saw Jesus coming to him, and he said, 'Behold the Lamb of God who takes away the sin of the world.'" Jesus is called by John the Baptist, the Lamb of God. Does he have wool? Does he have a tail? I do not know if lambs have tails. I am from California, but I suppose you could straighten me out on that later. Was he a physical lamb? That's my point, and the answer is no, but in the Old Testament, the lamb was a sign pointing to something else, and it was pointing to Jesus Christ, the time when Jesus Christ would come, and he would be the lamb that would take away the sin of the world. Here is another example. In 1 Corinthians 11:23 it says, "For I received from the Lord that which I also delivered to you that the Lord Jesus in the night in which he was betrayed took bread and when he had given thanks he broke it and said, 'This is my body which is for you. Do this in remembrance of me.' In the same way he took the cup also after supper saying, 'This cup is the New Covenant in my blood. Do this as often as you drink it in remembrance of me.'" Now, Jesus takes the bread here in verse 23 and he says as he takes the bread in verse 24, he breaks it and he says, "This is my body." Now the Roman Catholics are all messed up on this and so they've created the doctrine of transubstantiation where they think that the bread is actually Jesus' body, and we look at that, even though we disagree on what baptism is and we laugh, we say, "Come on let's be real." But isn't that exactly what we are doing here tonight when we say that baptism is what justifies you? We are pointing to the sign and we are saying there it is. No! The sign is pointing to something else. Because the sign is so closely related to the thing that it signifies, they can be spoken of interchangeably, so much so that Jesus can say, "This bread is my body, take it." On another occasion, he said whoever eats my flesh and drinks my blood. The cup and the bread are now signs in the New Covenant that point us to something else. The cup is not the blood. The bread is not the body, but they are signs that are pointing us somewhere and to something, and I am telling you that baptism is the same thing.

Let me give you a couple of examples. Acts 22:16, "Now why do you delay? Get up and be baptized and wash away your sins calling on His name." Now I often say as a Baptist Pastor when I am about to baptize somebody, "Are you ready to have your sins washed away?" Somebody might overhear me in my church and say, "Pastor why are you saying, 'Are you ready to have your sins washed away' when you have been teaching us that we are justified by faith?" Because what is being symbolized in that water baptism is a sign, or the water baptism itself, is a sign that is pointing us to something else. It is pointing us to the reality that this is now someone who has confessed, this is somebody who has been changed, this is somebody who wants to go out now publicly and dunk himself in water in the name of the Father, the Son, and the Holy Spirit.

Galatians 3:26 is another example, "For you are all sons of God through faith in Christ Jesus. For all of you who were baptized into Christ have clothed yourselves in Christ." You know, I could argue that this is talking about the baptism of the Spirit, or I could just say, "Hey, if you want to call it baptism in water that is fine because in the mind of the apostles the two were so closely related that they could be spoken of synonymously." In fact, if I could have you put up chart 209 please; this is a perfect example of why that would be the case. As Bruce Reeves so aptly pointed out, it says there in the bottom part of verse 33, right above 34, "and immediately he and all his family were baptized." They heard the message, they responded in faith, and they were baptized immediately. So three years after that when they asked him, "When were you saved?" it would be perfectly legitimate for him to answer I was baptized on this day. Now think about this, the world in which the apostles lived was not a friendly world to Christianity. Why would anybody get up and be baptized if it meant he could lose his life? It was something that would bring persecution. They were arresting the apostles. Paul was rounding up the believers to throw into prison. In the minds of the New Testament writers, as they are inspired by the Holy Spirit, it is common for them to speak of the thing being signified and the sign interchangeably. I have given you several examples. If you are going to disagree with me, you might adopt the doctrine of Rome and say that the body and the blood are there on that table because you cannot affirm one and deny the other. If you say that that never happens, that that is an illegitimate interpretation, then you might as well go all the way and just join the Roman Catholic Church. I look forward to being back with you on Thursday night. Thank you!

Tuesday Night

Fourth Negative

Bruce Reeves

It certainly is good to be with you again. I appreciate your good patience. I know sometimes these things can wear on a little bit, but I am very happy you are here for this last speech and you have made it. It is good to be with you again. I want to thank Mr. Cook for many of the things that he introduced because it allows me to talk about some things that I want to talk about anyway in rebuttal to what you have just heard.

If you would, go ahead and turn your Bibles to 2 Corinthians 5:21. We are talking about whether or not we are made righteous through forgiveness that we are granted by God, or is the personal perfect life of Jesus imputed to us, and he introduced 2 Corinthians 5:21. I will read verse 20. He speaks of the word of reconciliation in verse 19 and then he says, "Now then we are ambassadors for Christ as though God did beseech you by us. We pray you in Christ's stead that you be reconciled to God for He hath made him to be sin for us who knew no sin that we might be made the righteousness of God in Him." From listening to what he said, I was made to wonder what about 1 Corinthians 1:30. If that verse means that the personal righteousness of Christ is imputed to us, one would wonder, as we turn our Bibles to 1 Corinthians 1:30, "But of Him are ye in Christ Jesus who of God has made unto us wisdom, and righteousness, and sanctification, and redemption" —was the wisdom of Christ, the personal wisdom of Christ, was that imputed to us also? I do not think that is what that passage means. I do not teach that we are made righteous because we earn our salvation, and if that is how he is using the term works, that is simply not what I believe. I believe we are made righteous because God forgives.

We were talking about every command of God and how much obedience is enough. Well, I want you to think about something with me. How much obedience was enough for Noah's family to be saved? How much was enough? Did they have to obey in order to be delivered? How much was enough? Well, did they not have to do what God said? They had to obey God in order to be saved. When we talk about the walls of Jericho, how much was enough for the walls of Jericho to fall? Tonight you may have the walls of sin around your heart. God gave them the city, but the Bible also says that the walls fell by faith, and they shouted because they obeyed God. It did not mean that they had earned, merited or deserved for those walls to fall down. You know, Naaman was cleansed physically. When was Naaman cleansed physically? I should ask: Why was Naaman cleansed physically? Was Naaman not cleansed physically, friends, because he obeyed what the Lord said? Does that mean that he earned it or that he deserved it in any way? Absolutely not! You know he was not cleansed physically until he did what God said.

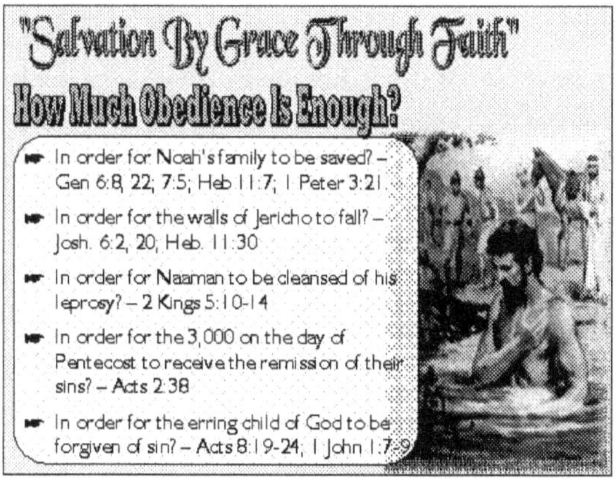
"Salvation By Grace Through Faith"
How Much Obedience Is Enough?
In order for Noah's family to be saved? – Gen 6:8, 22; 7:5; Heb 11:7; 1 Peter 3:21
In order for the walls of Jericho to fall? – Josh. 6:2, 20; Heb. 11:30
In order for Naaman to be cleansed of his leprosy? – 2 Kings 5:10-14
In order for the 3,000 on the day of Pentecost to receive the remission of their sins? – Acts 2:38
In order for the erring child of God to be forgiven of sin? – Acts 8:19-24; 1 John 1:7-9

Mr. Cook assumes that the term "law" in Romans 13 and Romans 7 is being used in the same way, and that is just not the case. By the way, in Romans chapter 8, we read about the "law of the Spirit of life in Christ Jesus" and that has reference to the gospel. Now certainly it is a law of grace, but it is still being described as a law. In James 1, we read about the "law of liberty." While we are looking at Romans let us consider chapter 5 and verse 12. Mr. Cook is telling us that every one of us is born totally depraved and I think his understanding is that we are incapable of responding to God without a miraculous operation of the Holy Spirit, thus, we cannot make a decision to respond to God. Now regarding some of the things that he said, yes I understand what Romans 5:19 says: "For as by one man's disobedience, many were made sinners, so by the obedience of one shall many be made righteous." In Romans 5:12 we have an explanation of verse 19, "Therefore, as by one man sin entered into the world." You know, before Adam sinned, there had been no sin at all, but he sinned, and as a result, "sin entered the world, and death by sin and so **death passed upon all men for that all have sinned**." We are going to talk more about that in just a moment.

Mr. Cook said to us that he hoped, I appreciate his sentiments, he hoped that all babies that die are elect and thus all of them go to heaven. What about those little babies with the Amalekites we heard about last night? What about them? I think he believes they were non-elect. I think he believes that every one of those babies as they were sucking on their mothers' breasts, and as they were slaughtered according to the divine decree of God, because remember he foreordained whatsoever shall come to pass, that those little babies, having not done anything personally good or evil, went straight to hell because God foreordained whatsoever shall come to pass.

You know in connection with these things, let us turn to Ezekiel 18. What does Ezekiel 18 say? That is a good question. Let us look at this Scripture, Ezekiel the 18th chapter, and just for sake of time, let us begin with verse 20. "The soul who sins shall die. The son shall not bear the guilt of the father nor the father bear the guilt of the son. The righteousness of the righteous shall be upon him, and the wickedness shall be upon him. But if a wicked man turns from all of his sins which he has committed, keeps all my statutes, and does what is lawful and right, he shall surely live, he shall not die." Now remember we have been told a couple of things tonight. Not only was total depravity introduced but also this idea of security. Well I believe that I have great security in God's word, in God's truth, and abiding within the doctrine of Christ. I will deal with that a little bit more in a moment, but you know, we can decide to leave the Lord. I can decide to leave God. He says here we have a "wicked man, and if he turns from all his sins he shall surely live, he shall not die, none of the transgressions which he has committed shall be remembered against him. Because of the righteousness which he has done, he shall live."

Listen to God. This is the divine will of God, "Do I have any pleasure at all that the wicked should die says the Lord God and not that he should turn from his ways and live?" Oh no, it is not according to the kindness of his good pleasure that the vast majority of people will be lost. It will be because they do not obey the Lord in faith. He says in verse 24, "But when a righteous man turns away from his righteousness," listen to that, "When a righteous man turns away from his righteousness and commits iniquity and does according to all the abominations that the wicked man does, shall he live?" Reformed theology says, "Well now, yes." Verse 24 says "all the righteousness which he has done shall not be remembered because of the unfaithfulness of which he is guilty and the sin which he has committed. Because of them, he shall die, yet you say the word of the Lord is not fair. Hear now, O house of Israel, is it not my way which is fair and your ways which are not fair?" We could go on and read some more. The Lord does not have pleasure in the death of the wicked, and yet, according to Mr.

Cook, God foreordained, God foreordained, God foreordained that those Amalekite babies should be born, and slain, and go to hell.

Turn your Bibles to Acts chapter 8. Mr. Cook introduced this idea of security, and again I believe that we are secure in God's word, in prayer, in obedience to the Lord. It is not a matter of earning anything. Mr. Cook mentioned the thoughts of our heart and that type of thing. Let us look at some passages together on that point. In Acts chapter 8, we read of Simon the sorcerer, and when you look at verse 13 it says, "Simon himself believed also, and when he was baptized he continued with Philip in wonder beholding the miracles and signs which were done." We do not want any wiggling around about whether or not Simon was really saved. It says he believed and I am going to take the book at its word. Then we progress in this context to see that Simon saw this power the apostles had to lay their hands on them and in verse 19 he says, "Give me also this power that on whomsoever I lay hands he may receive the Holy Ghost, and Peter said unto him," to this baptized believer, "thy money perish with thee because thou hast **thought** that the gift of God may be purchased with money. Thou hast neither part nor lot in this matter for thy heart is not right in the sight of God." What was he to do? "Repent therefore of this thy wickedness and pray God that perhaps the thought of thine heart may be forgiven thee."

Listen to me, Simon the sorcerer was a believer, and he had sinned against God by this action, and he was told by an inspired man, "You need to repent and pray that the thought of your heart may be forgiven," and that is exactly what we need to do today. That is exactly what we need to do today! 1 John 1:9 says, "If we confess our sins, He is faithful and just to forgive us." Peter says, "For if after they have escaped the pollutions of the world through the knowledge of our Lord and Savior Jesus Christ, they are again entangled therein and overcome, the latter end is worse with them than the beginning. For it had been better for them not to have known the way of righteousness than after they have known it to turn from the holy commandment delivered unto them, but it has happened unto them according to the true proverb 'the dog has turned to his own vomit again, and the sow that was washed to the wallowing in the mire.'" No, she never was really clean was she? The text says the opposite. Galations 5:4 says we can "fall from grace." How do you fall from something you have never been in to begin with? In 1 Corinthians, the 10th chapter we read of the example of the children of Israel falling away from God, and by the way, Paul is writing to Christians, and he says in verse 12, "Wherefore let him that thinketh he standeth take heed lest he fall. There hath no temptation taken you but such as is common to man, but God is faithful who will not suffer you to be tempted above that ye are able, but will with the temptation also make a way to escape that you may be able to bear it." Oh no, I do not sin because somehow I was created in that fashion. I do not sin because Adam corrupted my nature. I sin because I make a decision. I make a choice to transgress God's word, and every one of us has done that in our lives, every one of us has done that, and we need to repent, and we need to come to the Lord.

I want to talk about Romans 4. Turn your Bibles to Genesis 12, and certainly, I do not want to misrepresent anything Mr. Cook said. Now I want to make this clear. Mr. Cook's position, and he has brought up total depravity, is that a totally depraved person is incapable of doing that which would seek God or please God, because he is totally depraved. Now if Genesis 15:6 is this one moment in time in which Abraham was justified, does Genesis chapter 12 describe an unjustified sinner? If it is before his justification, that is quite a bit before that according to Mr. Cook, he is building altars, he is worshiping God, he is listening to God, and he is obeying God. Does that sound like somebody who is incapable of seeking God? Secondly, how could someone make such an argument in light of Hebrews 11:8? Hebrews chapter 11 is going back before Genesis 15, and it says, "by faith he did this, by faith he did this." Now did he have faith but he was not justified? I have understood that the faith that obeys God is a faith that justifies—if he was not justified until Genesis 15, but God is telling Abraham to go, and he has faith, and he goes, did he have faith and yet it did not justify him? He was not justified until Genesis chapter 15? That is problematic.

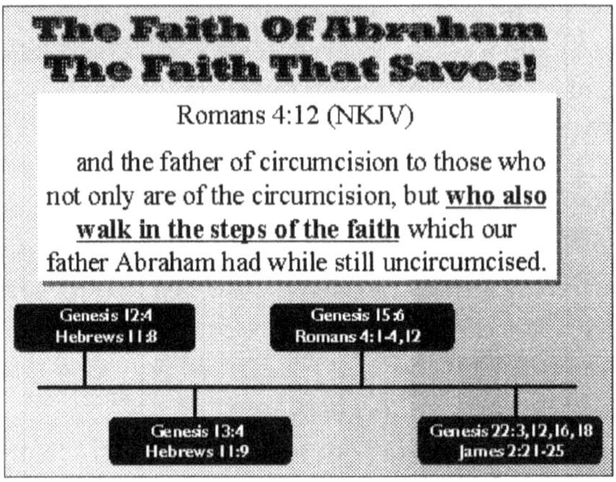
The Faith Of Abraham
The Faith That Saves!
Romans 4:12 (NKJV)
and the father of circumcision to those who not only are of the circumcision, but who also walk in the steps of the faith which our father Abraham had while still uncircumcised.
Genesis 12:4 Hebrews 11:8
Genesis 15:6 Romans 4:1-4,12
Genesis 13:4 Hebrews 11:9
Genesis 22:3,12,16,18 James 2:21-25

Now something else was presented before you, and I am glad, I really am, I am glad Gene brought this up because this is something that sometimes people are confused about as they hear us, and it is important that you make a distinction in the way the term "works" is used. We have shown you that sometimes it refers to meritorious works, Ephesians 2; sometimes we are

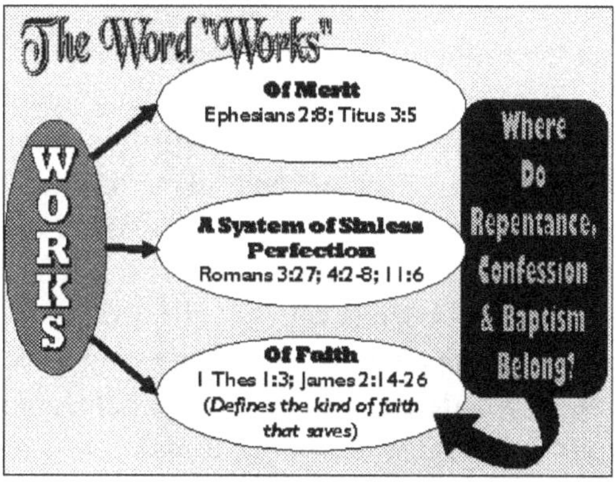
The Word "Works"
WORKS
Of Merit
Ephesians 2:8; Titus 3:5
A System of Sinless Perfection
Romans 3:27; 4:2-8; 11:6
Of Faith
I Thes 1:3; James 2:14-26
(Defines the kind of faith that saves)
Where Do Repentance, Confession & Baptism Belong?

dealing with the activity of faith, such as James 2; and certainly, we must act, and it is a faith that obeys God that will justify a person. Mr. Cook was talking about my position and he said that it was further away from the Protestant position and closer to the Roman Catholic position. I would say this to you; I just want to have the biblical position. I would also like you to know, and people that live here in Conway, I think, would know this if you have read the Log Cabin Democrat very much, I have written against the errors of Catholicism. I have Catholic friends like most of us have, and I have Baptist friends, and I have denominational friends, but I have recently written a refutation of Roman Catholicism, and I have been abundantly clear about that point. However, let me show you something worthy of note, the Protestant movement is in error, in an extreme error, just as is Roman Catholicism. They both are in error. Let me explain to you why. The Protestant movement argues for faith only, which we have heard this week. The Catholic movement, in effect, argues for works only in their teaching regarding infant baptism. The Bible, however, argues for faith and works. We have been talking about that poor old horse and cart tonight. Listen to me! If faith only is the horse, he is dead, he is lying straight out on the ground, he is dead because James says, "faith without works is dead." No, he is not going to pull anything because he is dead. (Laughter from audience.)

Mr. Cook introduced, and that is why I said I appreciate this, he introduced Romans 6 and Galatians 3. Now I want to make this point, and I am sure we will talk about it Thursday and Friday. Mr. Cook said on Monday night, and we can document this from his answers to the questions that I gave him, when I asked him if the baptism in Romans 6, in Colossians 2, and in Galatians 3 was necessary in order for the alien sinner to receive the forgiveness of his past sins, he said "yes, but it's not water baptism."

Well, I took him at his word that that was his conviction, and from things he said in the past, I understood him to be saying that it was Holy Spirit baptism. However, he told me that it was necessary, and now I have a chart, now look at the top of that chart, it says, "Baptism in the Bible, the sign was so closely related to the thing signified that the apostles would often speak of them interchangeably." Now in Acts 22:16, Galatians 3, and Romans 6, if that baptism is water baptism, even if he's saying it's just a sign but it's still water baptism, now I really want you to get this, if it is a sign and it's water baptism and he told me last night that the baptism of Colossians 2, Galatians 3, and Romans 6 is necessary, ladies and gentlemen, I don't know what we're fussing about! If the baptism in Colossians 2, Galatians 3, and Romans 6 is water baptism, and I have already been told it is necessary, then my, that is what I am going to be affirming Thursday and Friday night. I understand his argument here, but either it's not necessary and it's talking about water baptism and is just a sign, or it is necessary and it's not talking about water baptism, because if he's saying water baptism is necessary, that's what I believe. Now he can laugh about that, but that is the consequence of his position.

Now regarding Martin Luther, he mentioned that Martin Luther was not a Calvinist. Mr. Cook made the same statement Martin Luther made, and he told us he's a Calvinist, so that's why that was being brought up.

The problem with some of the things Mr. Cook has said is that it is just double talk. The reason Abraham was justified by faith before he was circumcised is that at that moment he had not been commanded to be circumcised. Additionally, I would tell you had he been commanded, as he later was, he would have done it. You know if we were not commanded to be water baptized then you might have a parallel, but we are commanded to be baptized in the name of the Lord Jesus. The reason he was an uncircumcised man when he was justified by faith was simply that he had not yet received that commandment. When he did receive that commandment, he obeyed. He can be the father of both the uncircumcised and the circumcised.

Now, he talked a lot about baptism being a sign and about how baptism symbolizes our salvation. Where is the passage that says baptism is just a sign? Now I understand in Romans the 6th chapter that baptism signifies not our salvation, you find the passage that says that and I will look at it, but is connected to the death, the burial, and the resurrection of Jesus.

Let us look at Romans the 6th chapter together if you can see your Bibles, or surely you can see this chart, notice it: "Or do you not know that as many of us," no more and no less, "as were baptized into Christ." Now I think we have been told that this verse refers to water baptism since that is what we have at the top of this chart. Paul says we are baptized into Jesus Christ, and when we are baptized into Jesus Christ, we are baptized into his death. I am baptized by faith into a relationship with God in which I enjoy the benefits of his death. I told you at the beginning of this debate, I am the one defending the death of Christ, and I am the one defending the blood of Jesus. He says we are baptized into the death of Christ. I enjoy the favors and the blessings of his death because of an obedient faith, and that does not merit my salvation. It simply is doing what God has told me to do in order to receive his grace. Paul goes on to say, "Therefore, we are buried with Him through baptism into death that just as Christ was raised from the dead by the glory of the Father, even so we also should walk in newness of life, for if we have been united together in the likeness of His death, certainly we also shall be in the likeness of His resurrection knowing this that our old man is crucified with Him, that the body of sin might be done away, that we should no longer be slaves of sin."

Now if his idea is that water baptism and Holy Spirit baptism are so close to each other we really cannot separate them, we have a problem. Now I want you to do this pretty quickly, Don. I want you to go to 111. The only baptism, the **only baptism** they had received in Acts 8:12 was water baptism, and thus they were in Christ. They could not have received any other kind of baptism, they could not have because the Holy Spirit had not fallen upon them and they had only been baptized in the name of the Lord Jesus and we know that is water baptism. The Holy Spirit had fallen upon none of them. Romans chapter 6 is speaking of water baptism, and it does not say it symbolizes salvation. Now I know many of our religious friends have taught that, but friends, that is simply not the case. It is at the point of baptism that my old man is crucified, my new man is raised to walk in "newness of life."

I want to go to Colossians 2. Let us talk about that passage, the chart is up here too, I think. Did you use Colossians 2, Gene? Okay! It is okay! It is all right, I will go with it because you and I both know you used it. Let us look at Colossians the 2nd chapter. I want you to notice this because this was introduced. Colossians 2:11 says, "In whom also ye are circumcised with the circumcision made without hands in putting off the body of the sins of the flesh by the circumcision of Christ, buried with Him in baptism wherein also you were risen with Him through the faith of the operation of God who raised Him from the dead." I want you to pay very close attention to what I am about to say. The "circumcision made without hands" is not water baptism. "The circumcision made without hands" is God forgiving us and removing our sin from us, but it is inseparably linked and related to this idea of burial with Christ in baptism. Therefore, when I am by faith buried with Christ in baptism, I am accessing the working of God. I came here tonight with all of my heart to affirm to you the working of God. This is not about us trying to earn our salvation and this is not about trying to merit our salvation. This passage says "In Him" or "In whom also you were circumcised with the circumcision made without hands," he is cutting away the sins of the body and the sins of the flesh "by the circumcision of Christ," the question is when does this occur? Verse 12, "buried with Him in baptism wherein also you were risen with Him through faith in the working of God."

You can go back if you want to Acts 22:16. Go to number 1, I want you to look at the proposition. Now Mr. Cook talked about the washing away of sins, and this shows you that this is a reality, it is a sign, it is a symbol, but that terminology regarding baptism just being a sign or a symbol of salvation cannot be found in all of the word of God, you cannot find it. "Now Saul was told to go into the city and he would be told what he must do" and "Now why are you waiting? Arise and be baptized, washing away thy sins, calling on the name of the Lord." Do you remember Romans 6 when we read that we are baptized in the death of Christ? Why would this washing away of sins be linked to water baptism? It is not holy water. It is not magical water. It is obedience. It is obedience to the grace of God and the gospel of Jesus Christ. It is in that act by faith that the blood of Christ is applied to me. If we can go to heaven without that, we can go to heaven without the blood of Jesus, and I deny it with all of my being. "And now why are you waiting? Arise and be baptized and wash away your sins, calling on the name of the Lord." He was told what he must do. He would be told the things that were appointed for him, and in Acts 22:16 he says, "Arise and be baptized washing away thy sins, calling on the name of the Lord." His sins were going to be washed away.

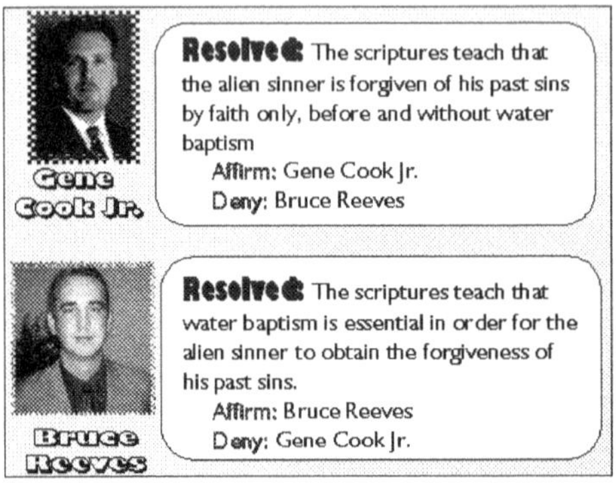
Resolved: The scriptures teach that the alien sinner is forgiven of his past sins by faith only, before and without water baptism
Affirm: Gene Cook Jr.
Deny: Bruce Reeves
Gene Cook Jr.
Resolved: The scriptures teach that water baptism is essential in order for the alien sinner to obtain the forgiveness of his past sins.
Affirm: Bruce Reeves
Deny: Gene Cook Jr.
Bruce Reeves

Now I'm telling you this thing is not that hard, friends, and with all the love in my heart and with all the compassion for every soul because I believe it is on the basis of "whosoever will may come and take of the water of life freely" you need to consider these passages. Now Mr. Cook introduced these passages, and I am showing you that what he taught you about these passages is not found in the word of God.

Now look at the proposition. Mr. Cook last night and tonight has been in the affirmative, and he has been affirming that the Scriptures teach that the alien sinner is forgiven of his past sins by faith only before and without water baptism. He brought up James 2 briefly, and we have shown you that that justification is before God, and James says that faith only will not save anybody. The idea of faith only will not save anybody. I am not teaching you a works system, but I am teaching you the working of God. We need Mr. Cook to be definitive here and we need him to be clear. We have two more nights, Thursday and Friday, I need to know clearly in a definitive way, is Romans 6, and Colossians 2, and Galatians 3:26-27 talking about water baptism? Even if Mr. Cook is going to tell me that he does not believe it's essential, if it is water baptism, he needs to make sure and tell me. If that's what he's done tonight, that's fine, and we'll go on from there, but what I'm showing you is if it is water baptism and I'm being told the baptism in these passages is necessary, now who has conceded to whom? This is the problem of the equivocation we have heard. I want you to think about it, and if your soul would like to come to the Lord, I would be happy to take your confession, and I would be happy to baptize you by the authority of Jesus Christ for the remission of your sins because the Lord has so taught. Thank you very much! Thank you, Mr. Cook!

Thursday Night

First Affirmative

Bruce Reeves

I appreciate your presence. Many of you have been here throughout the week for this discussion, and I want you to know how glad I am that you are here. I am appreciative of Mr. Gene Cook and his willingness to engage us in this debate. It is always my pleasure to have the opportunity to discuss the Scriptures. I am here with a very firm set of convictions; I am here with the conviction that the God of the universe redemptively loves every soul he has created, i.e. he desires their salvation. I am also here with the conviction that we must choose faith and that the sinner will only be saved through possessing a faith that is willing to obey God. I also have the conviction that God's word is inspired and comes from the mouth of our Father in heaven. I also want to say how much I appreciate the plane on which this discussion has taken place. It has been on a high plane, the focus has been on the issue, and that really is why we are here. I certainly hope that our time together will be productive. As you look at the proposition, we have been discussing a singular subject although the roles have reversed.

Right away, I want to get to Mr. Cook's questions that he has asked me. #1 "Did you truly think that I had changed my position on Romans 6:3, 4; Galatians 3:27, and Colossians 2:11, 12 to now be water baptism?" Yes. #2 "Can you please define the command of Deuteronomy 5:20 regarding not bearing false witness against your neighbor?" It means not to lie. #3 "Would you affirm or deny the following statement, 'Through the observance of the commandments of God and through faith cooperating with good works increase in that justice received through the grace of Christ and further justify the believer"? No, I would not affirm that statement. Either you are justified or you are not justified. #4 "When the word baptized is used in a verse how do you know if it is referring to water baptism?" This is a good question. Of course, we have to look at the context. I want you to think about this from the standpoint of simply studying the Bible. We assume a word is literal, i.e. we understand it to be literal unless the contextual evidence indicates otherwise. We cannot go to the text and assume a figurative interpretation if such is not demanded by the context. #5 "Is God pleased when a man enters the waters of baptism?" Yes. *(Would you please blank that screen out for me. Just push "B" and it should blank it out. If you will hit "B" on your computer, it will blank it out. There you go, thank you).*

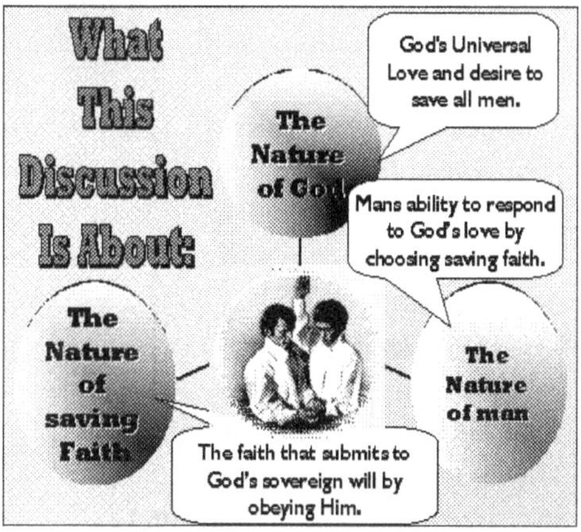
What This Discussion Is About
God's Universal Love and desire to save all men.
The Nature of God
Mans ability to respond to God's love by choosing saving faith.
The Nature of saving Faith
The Nature of man
The faith that submits to God's sovereign will by obeying Him.

I want to remind you of what this discussion is about, i.e. there are several pillars, we might say, of understanding. First, we have seen differences regarding the nature of God, i.e. his desire and will that all men be saved through an obedient faith. We have discussed man's ability to respond to God's love by choosing saving faith as we have discussed the nature of man. We also have been talking about the nature of the saving faith that submits to the sovereign will of God through obedience.

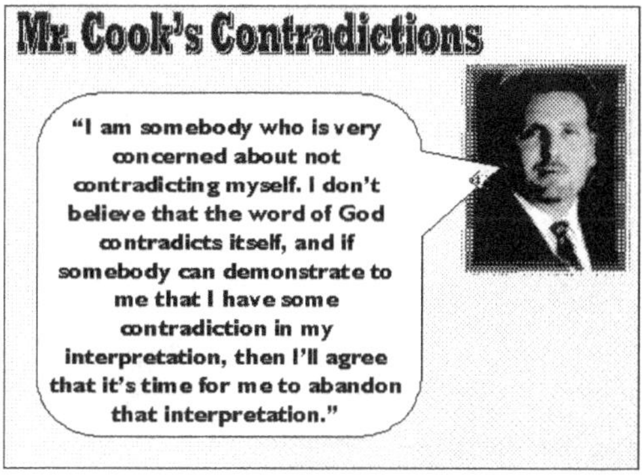
Mr. Cook's Contradictions
"I am somebody who is very concerned about not contradicting myself. I don't believe that the word of God contradicts itself, and if somebody can demonstrate to me that I have some contradiction in my interpretation, then I'll agree that it's time for me to abandon that interpretation."

There was something Mr. Cook said Tuesday evening that I would commend all of us to consider and I have the sincere belief and hope that he was speaking from his heart when he said this, *"I am somebody who is very concerned about not contradicting myself. I don't believe the word of God contradicts itself and if somebody can demonstrate to me that I have some contradiction in my interpretation, then I'll agree it is time for me to abandon that interpretation."*

I could not have said that better. I appreciate his statement. Mr. Cook said if contradiction in his interpretation of God's word were demonstrated, he would abandon that interpretation. We all ought to have that attitude. I believe we can demonstrate contradiction regarding the statements Mr. Cook has made. When we get to the heart of this issue, we will see that there are two entirely different attitudes about the Scripture. When Mr. Cook said that he does not believe God's word contradicts itself—I believe he meant every word of it. God does not contradict God. We must not contradict the Scripture in our teaching. Truth does not contradict itself. However, we have already heard several contradictions in Mr. Cook's teaching.

We have seen a failure to harmonize the Scriptures. I want you to think about what Mr. Cook said in reference to Acts 8 and 10. Mr. Cook said, *"Last night an argument was made from Acts chapter 8 that the Samaritans were brought into Christ by water baptism but if you go just two chapters over you will see that Cornelius, the first Gentile convert, received Holy Spirit baptism before water baptism. So you cannot use Acts chapter 8 or Acts chapter 10 really to make a case about a doctrinal position on when man receives the Spirit of God in relationship to baptism because they both seem to be teaching different things."*

Now, ladies and gentlemen, that quote is quite revealing about our understanding of the Scriptures. The Scriptures harmonize and the very idea that these passages are in contradiction one to the other is simply not the case. Now perhaps he did not mean that they were in contradiction one to the other, I look forward to hearing from him about that, but if that is what he was saying, then that is quite problematic. We were told that we cannot really use the book of Acts to establish doctrine, but he does so himself. He does appeal to different cases in the book of Acts, but he said we cannot establish doctrine from the book of Acts the way we would establish it from some other books in the New Testament. Play that quote: *"It's a history book of the Acts of the Apostles. That's why it's called the book of Acts. We do not go to the history book where we see the workings of God being worked out, and pull our doctrine. No, we go to those doctrinal epistles such as the book of Romans, the books of 1st and 2nd Corinthians, the books of Ephesians, Philippians, and Colossians. We go to those books to get our doctrine."*

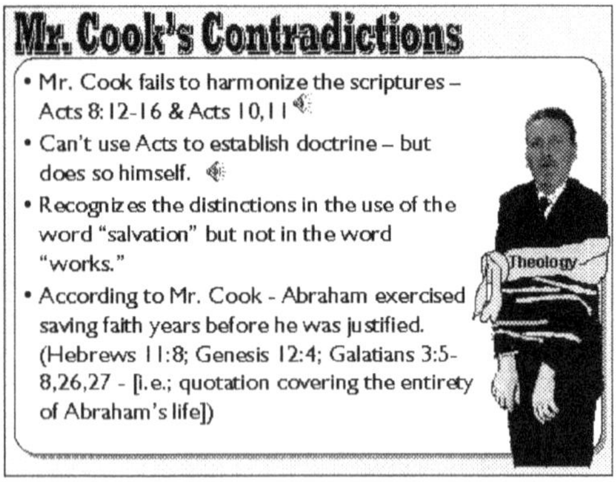
Mr. Cook's Contradictions
• Mr. Cook fails to harmonize the scriptures – Acts 8:12-16 & Acts 10,11
• Can't use Acts to establish doctrine – but does so himself.
• Recognizes the distinctions in the use of the word "salvation" but not in the word "works."
• According to Mr. Cook - Abraham exercised saving faith years before he was justified. (Hebrews 11:8; Genesis 12:4; Galatians 3:5-8,26,27 - [i.e.; quotation covering the entirety of Abraham's life])
Theology

The entire New Testament is the substance of the doctrine of Christ. The idea that, somehow, Acts is not as binding or should not be considered with the same type of authority, or whatever Mr. Cook wants to tell us from that quote, is simply not the case and I was quite surprised when I heard that statement. The book of Acts records conversions and we are going to talk about some of those conversions. When I'm talking about what one must do in order to be justified and in order to be forgiven of his past sins, and then I'm told that I can't go to the book of Acts, it's just a historical narrative, that's all that it is and therefore not quite as binding—I am concerned!

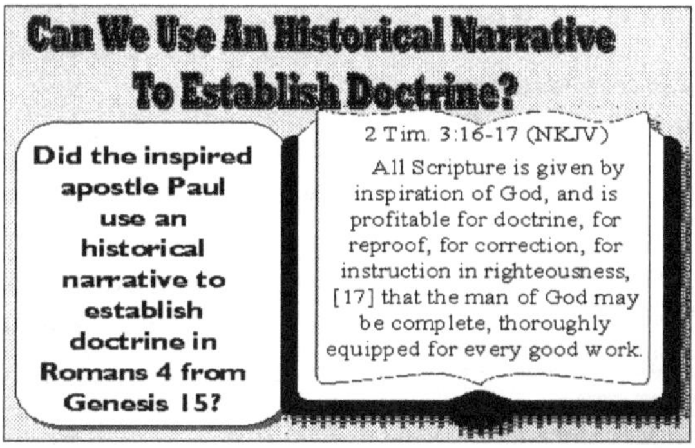
Can We Use An Historical Narrative To Establish Doctrine?
Did the inspired apostle Paul use an historical narrative to establish doctrine in Romans 4 from Genesis 15?
2 Tim. 3:16-17 (NKJV)
All Scripture is given by inspiration of God, and is profitable for doctrine, for reproof, for correction, for instruction in righteousness, [17] that the man of God may be complete, thoroughly equipped for every good work.

I would like to know, did the inspired Apostle Paul use a historical narrative to establish doctrine in Romans 4, when he appealed to Genesis, the 15th chapter? The Bible says, "All Scripture is given by inspiration of God and is profitable for doctrine, for reproof, for correction, for instruction in righteousness, that the man of God may be complete, thoroughly equipped for every good work." All Scripture is inspired. Even the historical narrative, even the book of Acts, and I know Mr. Cook knows that to be the case. Why would one say what he said Tuesday evening?

I want you to recognize that throughout this discussion, Mr. Cook has been defining "works" in one way, and we have pointed out that there is a distinction in the way that the term "works" is used. Tuesday night Mr. Cook told us that the term "salvation" was used in a past tense, a present tense, and a future tense and I agreed that such was the case. We have to understand the usage of the term in the context. But I was encouraged that he understands that a word can have different meanings depending on the context. Why doesn't he understand that about the term "works"?

Then we were told that Abraham exercised saving faith years before he was justified. I want you to turn your Bible to Hebrews, chapter 11. Now I asked about "initial justification" because Mr. Cook was affirming point justification. The Bible teaches us that God justifies us as we continue to exercise an obedient faith. From that standpoint, justification is a process. Hebrews, chapter 11 and verse 8, is a long time before Genesis chapter 15. "By faith, Abraham, when he was called to go out into a place which he should after receive for an inheritance, obeyed"—that's before Genesis 15. He possessed faith back in Genesis 12 when God called him and he obeyed the Lord. However, we were told "no, in Genesis 15 we read of justification." Well, Romans 4 does talk about Genesis 15, but you know, in Galatians 3, Paul also talks about some things that I want you to notice. You will recall as we have talked about James the 2nd chapter, we were told that, that context is restricted to justification before men, and I pointed out to you, no, that is justification before God. In Galatians 3, Paul is actually quoting from Genesis 12, Genesis chapter 15, and Genesis chapter 22.

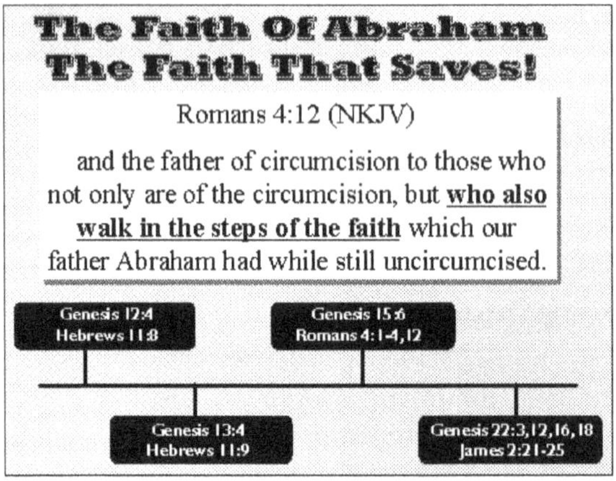
The Faith Of Abraham
The Faith That Saves!
Romans 4:12 (NKJV)
and the father of circumcision to those who not only are of the circumcision, but **who also walk in the steps of the faith** which our father Abraham had while still uncircumcised.
Genesis 12:4 Hebrews 11:8
Genesis 15:6 Romans 4:1-4,12
Genesis 13:4 Hebrews 11:9
Genesis 22:3,12,16,18 James 2:21-25

In verse 5, he contrasts the hearing of faith with the works of the Law and then he says in verse 6, "even as Abraham believed God, and it was accounted to him for righteousness. Know ye therefore, that they which are of faith, the same are the children of Abraham. And the Scripture foreseeing that God would justify the heathen through faith, preached before the gospel unto Abraham, saying, 'in these shall all nations be blessed.'" Now, one time he was told "in thee, all families of the earth shall be blessed" (Gen. 12). Later, we were told in the Scripture, in the book of Genesis, that all nations would be blessed (Gen. 15). Then as we continue in Galatians 3, we go to verses 26 and 27 and we are told that those who are heirs of this promise in verse 29, are those, who by faith, have been baptized into Christ, and thus put on Christ.

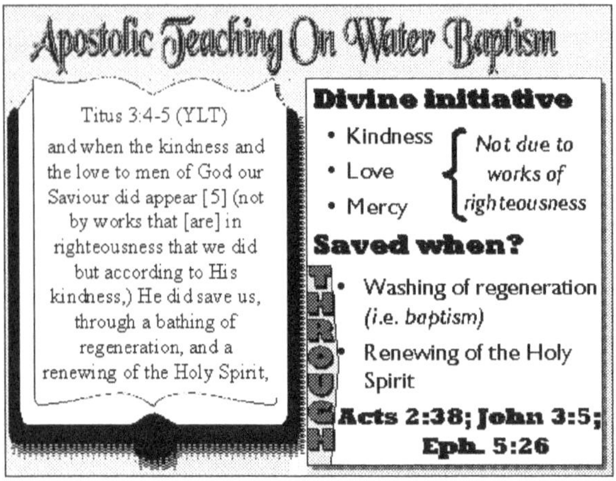
Apostolic Teaching On Water Baptism
Titus 3:4-5 (YLT)
and when the kindness and the love to men of God our Saviour did appear [5] (not by works that [are] in righteousness that we did but according to His kindness,) He did save us, through a bathing of regeneration, and a renewing of the Holy Spirit,
Divine initiative
• Kindness
• Love
• Mercy
Not due to works of righteousness
Saved when?
THROUGH
• Washing of regeneration (i.e. baptism)
• Renewing of the Holy Spirit
Acts 2:38; John 3:5; Eph. 5:26

Paul is quoting from the entirety of Abraham's life as an example of justification by faith. Such has been demonstrated clearly. The point is, that part of the problem we have had with Mr. Cook and with others, is simply understanding justification, and that as I continue to believe, God continues to justify and that is just the way it is and we would be happy to talk more about that if he so desires.

We have heard a lot about regeneration. Mr. Cook has told us that regeneration is unconditional. I deny that. That is not what the Bible teaches. Is water baptism a part of regeneration? Absolutely! I want you to look at Titus the 3rd chapter. I want you to recognize that Mr. Cook has said that water baptism does not earn salvation. I agree absolutely with that statement. Obedience to God does not earn salvation. We are saved by grace through faith. Notice Titus chapter 3, verse 4: "But after the kindness and the love of God our Savior toward man appeared, not by works of righteousness, which we have done," there's nothing we have ever done or ever will do, by which we can say, that's an equivalent to what Christ did on the cross. "But, according to His mercy, He saved us." How? "By the washing of regeneration and renewing of the Holy Ghost, which is shed on us abundantly through Jesus Christ our Savior." Christ came here, not because we deserved for him to come here, but because he loved us. Notice that he says that it was through the washing of regeneration, and the renewing of the Holy Spirit.

Now I really want you to think about some of these points. What is the washing of regeneration? That refers to water baptism. He says we are not saved by these works of righteousness, which we have done, but he tells us water baptism is essential.

Now we want to look at two passages—we need to realize that Titus 3:5 and John 3:5 are parallel. In John 3:5, Jesus said, "Most assuredly I say to you, unless one is born of" what? "Unless one is born of water and the Spirit, he cannot enter the kingdom of God." In that context, he is talking about being born again. That is the idea of regeneration. Now notice Titus 3:5, "He saved us through the washing of regeneration and renewing of the Holy Spirit." The washing of regeneration, Jesus says, is to be born of water and the renewing of the Holy Spirit is to be born of the Spirit. Is it true, is it really true that regeneration is unconditional, that baptism has nothing to

Water Baptism & The New Birth
Let Scripture Explain Scripture
REGENERATION
John 3:5 (NKJV)
Jesus answered, "Most assuredly, I say to you, unless one is born of water and the Spirit, he cannot enter the kingdom of God.
Titus 3:5 (NKJV)
He saved us, through the washing of regeneration and renewing of the Holy Spirit,

do with it? Since we have been told that regeneration is unconditional we might also ask, "Does faith, does baptism, have anything to do with being born again?" Of course it does.

Water Baptism & The New Birth
Let Scripture Explain Scripture
REGENERATION
John 3:5
Titus 3:5
Ephes. 5:26
born of water
washing of regeneration
washing of water
and the Spirit
and renewing of the Holy Spirit
by the word,

I really want to break this down because I want us to understand this very simple truth. Baptism is certainly essential! In John 3:5, He mentions being "born of water" and then in Titus 3, He mentions "the washing of regeneration." In John 3 we find the phrase "and the Spirit," whereas in Titus 3:5 we read about the "renewing of the Holy Spirit."

I want to go back to Acts 8:12-16. What baptism is it that puts us into Christ? In Acts 8, we read that the Samaritans heard the word preached and they believed the gospel in verse 12. Because of their belief, they were "baptized in the name of Jesus Christ." We know that is water baptism! They had "received the word of God." Peter and John "prayed that they might receive the Holy Spirit for He had fallen upon none of them."

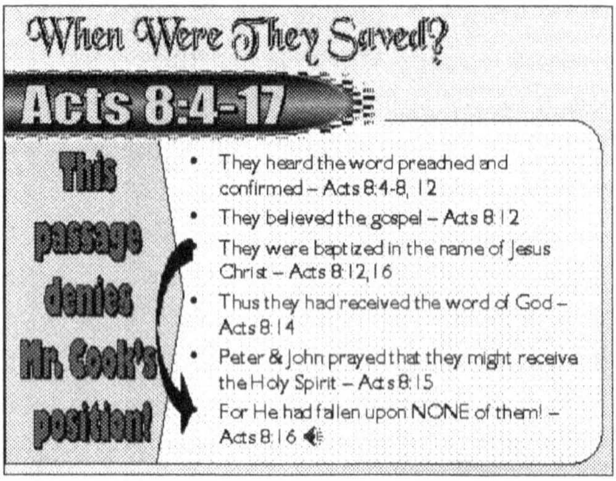
When Were They Saved?
Acts 8:4-17
This passage denies Mr. Cook's position!
They heard the word preached and confirmed – Acts 8:4-8, 12
They believed the gospel – Acts 8:12
They were baptized in the name of Jesus Christ – Acts 8:12,16
Thus they had received the word of God – Acts 8:14
Peter & John prayed that they might receive the Holy Spirit – Acts 8:15
For He had fallen upon NONE of them! – Acts 8:16

Now, was it water baptism that put them into Christ? Of course it was. That is exactly what put them into Christ. Mr. Cook recognizes that they were saved up in verse 12, and yet the Bible says that the Holy Spirit had not fallen upon them. In other words, it was not that there was a miraculous operation upon them that had caused them to come into Christ. What we are told is that they had only, they had only, only, only, only, been baptized in the name of the Lord Jesus and **that** was water baptism. Mr. Cook has said, *"I have every reason to believe that these Samaritans were saved when they professed Christ and when they were water baptized, but they* *did not receive the New Covenant gift until the Apostles laid hands on them."*

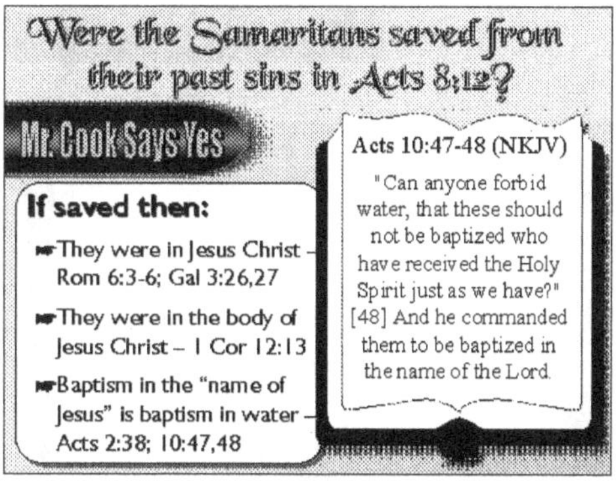
Were the Samaritans saved from their past sins in Acts 8:12?
Mr. Cook Says Yes
If saved then:
They were in Jesus Christ - Rom 6:3-6; Gal 3:26,27
They were in the body of Jesus Christ - I Cor 12:13
Baptism in the "name of Jesus" is baptism in water - Acts 2:38; 10:47,48
Acts 10:47-48 (NKJV)
"Can anyone forbid water, that these should not be baptized who have received the Holy Spirit just as we have?" [48] And he commanded them to be baptized in the name of the Lord.

So that should help us to understand that if in Acts 8 they were in Christ because they had faith and had been water baptized, which is in accordance with Titus 3, and John chapter 3 perfectly, then we know that the baptism Romans 6 and Galatians 3 is talking about is water baptism. It is not any other kind of baptism; it is water baptism. Friends, that fits perfectly with other passages such as Romans 6 and Galatians 3 and that kind of thing. Now, the baptism in the name of the Lord Jesus was water baptism and Acts 10:47-48 makes it very clear. He commanded them in Acts 10 to be baptized in the name of the Lord.

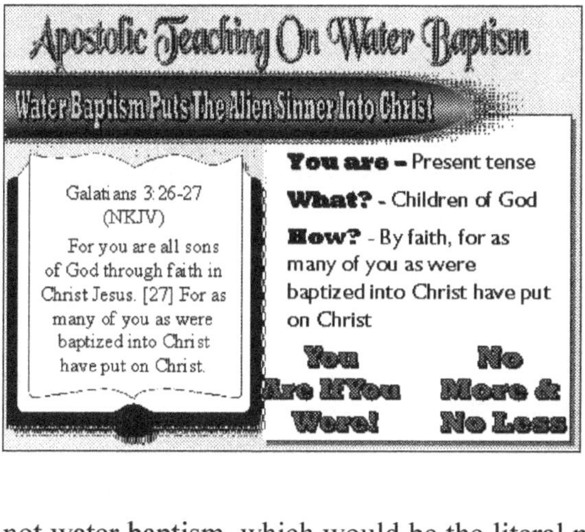
Apostolic Teaching On Water Baptism
Water Baptism Puts The Alien Sinner Into Christ
Galatians 3:26-27 (NKJV)
For you are all sons of God through faith in Christ Jesus. [27] For as many of you as were baptized into Christ have put on Christ.
You are - Present tense
What? - Children of God
How? - By faith, for as many of you as were baptized into Christ have put on Christ
You Are If You Were!
No More & No Less

Now recognizing that Acts chapter 8 teaches that water baptism is the baptism that puts us into Christ, when we go to Galatians 3:26-27, what does this passage mean? What does it mean? We read, "For you are all sons of God through faith in Christ Jesus, for as many of you as were baptized into Christ have put on Christ." Now if that is not water baptism, which would be the literal meaning here, if that is not water baptism, we need to know why it is not water baptism. I cannot come to this passage and just say well, it is not water baptism without showing proof, just asserting, or assuming that, simply does not do the job. Galatians 3 says, "You are the children of God by faith." They were presently the children of God by faith. What were they—the children of God? How? By faith, but what had they done? "For as many of you as were baptized into Christ have put on Christ."

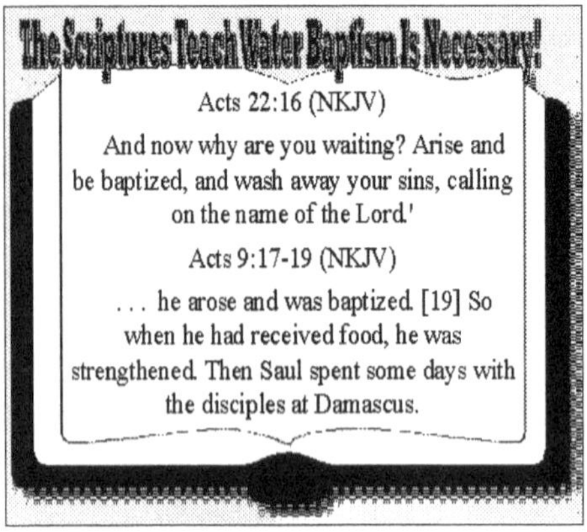
The Scriptures Teach Water Baptism Is Necessary!
Acts 22:16 (NKJV)
And now why are you waiting? Arise and be baptized, and wash away your sins, calling on the name of the Lord.'
Acts 9:17-19 (NKJV)
. . . he arose and was baptized. [19] So when he had received food, he was strengthened. Then Saul spent some days with the disciples at Damascus.

I want to think about another passage with you this evening, Acts 22:16. Saul of Tarsus was told, "And now why are you waiting, arise and be baptized and wash away your sins, calling on the name of the Lord." That does not mean that there is holy water. It does not mean that there is some magical water that washes away sins. The blood of Christ washes away our sins, but I am baptized into a relationship with him through which I receive the benefits of his sacrifice. That is extremely clear in Acts 22:16. Saul asked, "What shall I do Lord"? We have been told you cannot do anything to be regenerated. "You will be told," he said, "what you must do." Then in verse 16 of chapter 22, "Why are you waiting? Arise and be baptized and wash away your sins, calling on the name of the Lord."

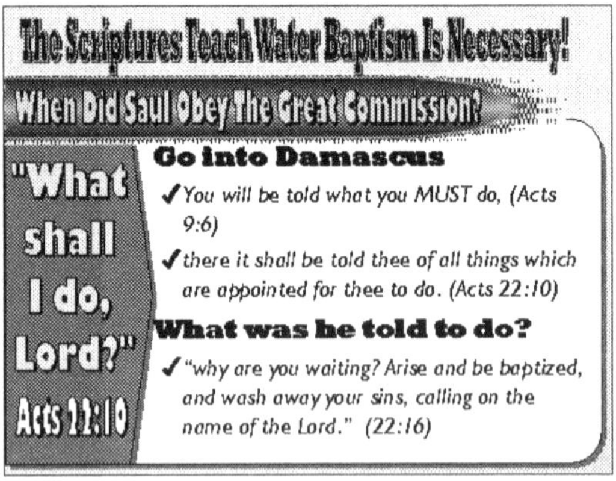
The Scriptures Teach Water Baptism Is Necessary!
When Did Saul Obey The Great Commission?
"What shall I do, Lord?" Acts 22:10
Go into Damascus
✓You will be told what you MUST do, (Acts 9:6)
✓there it shall be told thee of all things which are appointed for thee to do. (Acts 22:10)
What was he told to do?
✓"why are you waiting? Arise and be baptized, and wash away your sins, calling on the name of the Lord." (22:16)

I want to study Acts 10 with you and just think about some very simple points as we continue to affirm water baptism as being essential. In addition, there are some questions we need to ask in Acts the 10th chapter. Now remember we started out with Titus chapter 3 and John chapter 3 and we talked about being born of the water and of the Spirit, and we looked at Titus 3:5 and noticed that it mentions the washing of regen-

When was Cornelius Saved?
Act 10 & 11
While he was praying?
When the angel appeared?
When Peter BEGAN to speak?
When the Holy Spirit came?
When he obeyed the command?

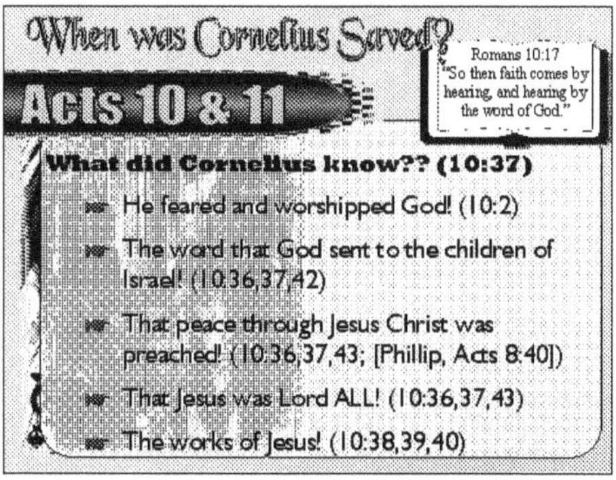
When was Cornelius Saved?
Acts 10 & 11
Romans 10:17 "So then faith comes by hearing, and hearing by the word of God."
What did Cornelius know?? (10:37)
He feared and worshipped God! (10:2)
The word that God sent to the children of Israel! (10:36,37,42)
That peace through Jesus Christ was preached! (10:36,37,43; [Phillip, Acts 8:40])
That Jesus was Lord ALL! (10:36,37,43)
The works of Jesus! (10:38,39,40)

eration and the renewing of the Holy Spirit. Here we are in Acts chapter 10 and we find that we need to ask some questions. Was Cornelius saved while he was praying? No. Was he saved when the angel appeared? No. Was he saved when Peter began to speak to him? No. Was he saved when the Holy Spirit fell? No. Was he saved when he obeyed the command of God? Absolutely! Sometimes we do not consider who Cornelius really was. Turn to Acts 10:37. We are going to find out that Cornelius entered the body of Christ the same way that the Samaritans entered the body of Christ, through faith and water baptism, by hearing the gospel, and that gospel produced faith in them. What did Cornelius know? Before his conversion, in verse 2 we read that Cornelius was a devout man. He was one that feared God with his entire house. He was a benevolent man who prayed to God always, and we even find out as we continue down to verse 4, these things were received before God as a memorial. So certainly, we can describe him as a man that would have been seeking God.

What did he know? Was he a raw pagan that did not know anything about Jesus Christ? In Acts 10:37, as Peter is preaching to Cornelius and his household, he says in verse 35, "In every nation, he that feareth Him and worketh righteousness is accepted with Him. The word which God sent unto the children of Israel, preaching peace by Jesus Christ, He is Lord of all, that word I say, ye know." He knew about that which was preached concerning Jesus being Lord of all. He says "That word I say ye know which was published throughout all Judea." If Cornelius knew these things, what did he need to be told? What did he need to know? He knew about that fact that Jesus was Lord of all as Peter preached to him Jesus Christ. Here is what he needed to know. He needed to know that God had granted repentance to life to the Gentiles as well as the Jews according to Acts 11:18. Importantly, he needed to know the word God had commanded Peter to speak to them, i.e. what they needed to do. What they needed to do to be saved? Peter taught them that they too, must be baptized in the name of Jesus Christ.

Notice this: Acts 10:6—"He will tell you what you must do." He was going to be told what to do. In Acts 10:22, he would be "divinely instructed" and he would "hear words from Peter." In Acts 10:32, "When he comes, he

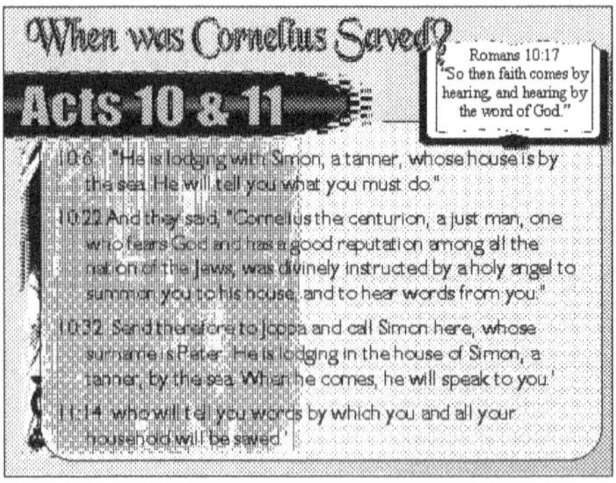
When was Cornelius Saved?
Acts 10 & 11
Romans 10:17 "So then faith comes by hearing, and hearing by the word of God."
10:6 "He is lodging with Simon, a tanner, whose house is by the sea. He will tell you what you must do."
10:22 And they said, "Cornelius the centurion, a just man, one who fears God and has a good reputation among all the nation of the Jews, was divinely instructed by a holy angel to summon you to his house, and to hear words from you."
10:32 Send therefore to Joppa and call Simon here, whose surname is Peter. He is lodging in the house of Simon, a tanner, by the sea. When he comes, he will speak to you.'
11:14 who will tell you words by which you and all your household will be saved.'

will speak to you." In Acts 11:14, "He will tell you words by which you and all your household will be saved." What did he hear? He heard that baptism in the name of Jesus Christ was a command of God. He recognized that he needed to be baptized. He was **commanded** to be baptized. When you combine Acts 10:47-48 with Acts 11:17 Peter even says that had he forbade water baptism he would have been withstanding God. Had he refused to baptize them, he would have been withstanding God. Why would he say such a thing if baptism had nothing to do with him being born again?

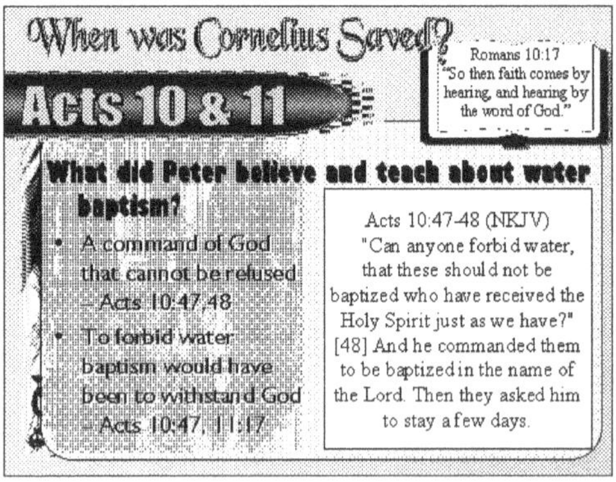
When was Cornelius Saved?
Acts 10 & 11
Romans 10:17 "So then faith comes by hearing, and hearing by the word of God."
What did Peter believe and teach about water baptism?
• A command of God that cannot be refused – Acts 10:47,48
• To forbid water baptism would have been to withstand God – Acts 10:47, 11:17
Acts 10:47-48 (NKJV) "Can anyone forbid water, that these should not be baptized who have received the Holy Spirit just as we have?" [48] And he commanded them to be baptized in the name of the Lord. Then they asked him to stay a few days.

I want to progress a little bit and introduce 1 Peter 3:21. Open your Bibles there with me. I look forward to the discussion on this point. This passage affirms my proposition. It is a clear passage.

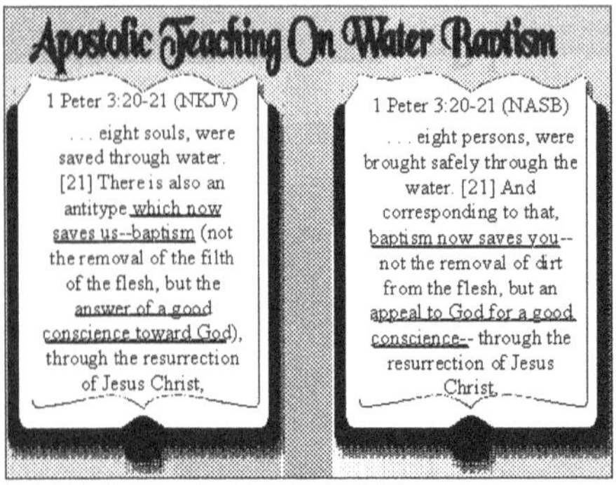
Apostolic Teaching On Water Baptism
1 Peter 3:20-21 (NKJV)
. . . eight souls, were saved through water. [21] There is also an antitype which now saves us--baptism (not the removal of the filth of the flesh, but the answer of a good conscience toward God), through the resurrection of Jesus Christ,
1 Peter 3:20-21 (NASB)
. . . eight persons, were brought safely through the water. [21] And corresponding to that, baptism now saves you--not the removal of dirt from the flesh, but an appeal to God for a good conscience-- through the resurrection of Jesus Christ,

Now notice the New American Version regarding Noah and those eight persons who were brought safely through the water "and corresponding to that, baptism now saves you." Baptism now saves you! Baptism is not just getting wet. It is not just taking a bath. He says "not the removal of the dirt from the flesh, but an appeal to God for a good conscience through the resurrection of Jesus Christ." Negatively, it is not just removing dirt from the flesh. Positively, it is making an appeal to God for a good conscience. Now I really want you to

Apostolic Teaching On Water Baptism
1 Peter 3:20-21 (NASB)
. . . eight persons, were brought safely through the water. [21] And corresponding to that, baptism now saves you-- not the removal of dirt from the flesh, but an appeal to God for a good conscience-- through the resurrection of Jesus Christ,
Negatively
"not the removal of dirt from the flesh,"
BUT
Positively
"an appeal to God for a good conscience-- through the resurrection of Jesus Christ,"

think about this. The idea of "an appeal" is an "inquiry, a question, and earnestly seeking a thing." The person in 1 Peter 3:21 is earnestly seeking something. He is appealing not toward man. The term "toward" is the term *eis*, i.e. "in order to," he is appealing to God, not to man. He is not just showing man his faith. He is appealing to God for a good conscience. Now we need to think about this verse. Why would a person be appealing for a good conscience if his conscience has already been cleansed by the blood of Jesus? He should already have a good conscience. The point is that it is in baptism that I make an appeal toward God for a good conscience.

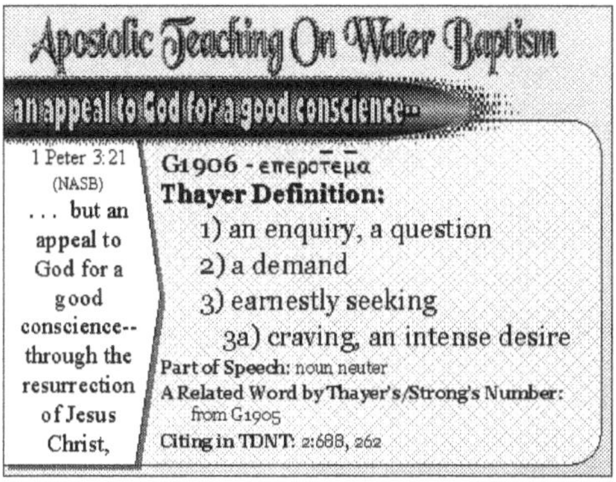
Apostolic Teaching On Water Baptism
an appeal to God for a good conscience--
1 Peter 3:21 (NASB)
. . . but an appeal to God for a good conscience-- through the resurrection of Jesus Christ,
G1906 - επεροτεμα
Thayer Definition:
1) an enquiry, a question
2) a demand
3) earnestly seeking
3a) craving, an intense desire
Part of Speech: noun neuter
A Related Word by Thayer's/Strong's Number: from G1905
Citing in TDNT: 2:688, 262

Now on the Day of Judgment, these passages will say the same thing then that they say now. The word of God will judge us. When we consider the concept of regeneration, the Bible is extremely clear. When is one regenerated? When is he born of the water and the Spirit? When is one made alive? Romans 6 says that we are baptized into Christ. The old man is crucified; the new man is raised to walk in newness of life. When does one

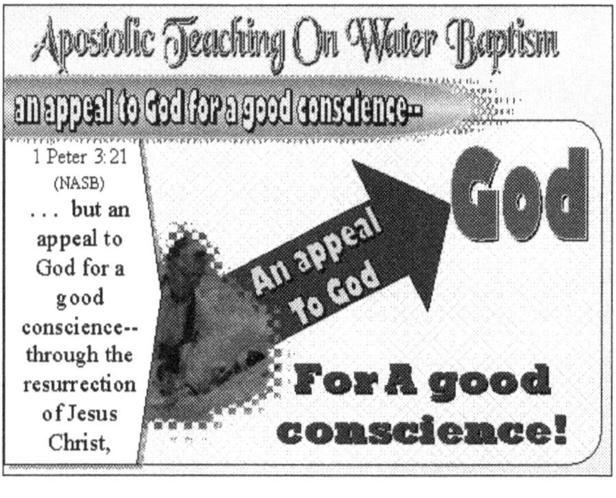
Apostolic Teaching On Water Baptism
an appeal to God for a good conscience--
1 Peter 3:21 (NASB)
. . . but an appeal to God for a good conscience-- through the resurrection of Jesus Christ,
An appeal To God
God
For A good conscience!

enter into Christ's body? 1 Corinthians 12:13 says it is when we are baptized. When does one become a child of God? We read in Galatians 3:26 -27, it is when we put on Christ though baptism. When is one forgiven of his past sins? Acts 22:16 says, "Arise and be baptized, washing away thy sins, calling on the name of the Lord." When is one saved? By saved, I am talking about having his sins forgiven. When are his sins washed away?

At the end of the way, it is not going to be what Gene Cook said or what Bruce Reeves said. What will matter is, "What did the Lord say?" Now, take your Bible in hand tonight. Look at these passages. This is not about earning salvation. You cannot earn salvation. Look at these passages and think about what God says. That is what matters. In addition, your justification, your forgiveness, your salvation must rest in the word of God, not in the philosophies and theologies of men. It is a matter of what the Lord says. Paul said, when we read the words of the Lord we can understand the truth. He said understand the will of the Lord (Eph. 5:17). These Scriptures have been read, and if these Scriptures do not mean what apparently they mean, we need to be told why. I think you can read your Bible and you can know what these verses mean. The Lord revealed these things to us for a reason. Thank you very much.

The Pieces Fit!
When is one regenerated? Titus 3:3-5; John 3:3-5
When is one made alive? Romans 6:3,4
When does one enter into Christ' body? I Corinthians 12:13
When does one become a child of God? Galatians 3:26,27
When is one forgiven of his past sins? Acts 2:38; 22:16
When is one saved? Mark 16:16; I Peter 3:21

First Negative

Gene Cook

It is a pleasure to be with you once again, and I appreciate what the moderator had to say about this audience. This audience has been delightful to engage in front of in the public exercise of debate. I have had some bad audiences in the past, but this is, I agree, a very good audience.

First, I want to address the questions that were presented to me, since we have an agreement to submit questions to one another. Question #1 from Mr. Reeves: "When the children of Israel obeyed God, did they earn any part of God causing the walls to fall down?" The answer to that question is no. As he just mentioned, salvation and grace are not something that can be earned. Romans 11:6 says, "But if it's by grace, it's no longer on the basis of works, otherwise grace would no longer be grace."

Question #2: "What baptism put the Samaritans into Jesus Christ according to Acts 8:12 and 16?" I would say regeneration was what put the Samaritans into Jesus Christ. Regeneration, that has been my argument from the beginning. That is why I argued in the last two evenings, Monday night and Tuesday night, that regeneration is distinct from the gifting of the Holy Spirit. I do want to say that when I am talking about the gifting of the Holy Spirit, I am not talking about what the Pentecostals are talking about. I am talking about the indwelling presence of the Holy Spirit that leads us and guides us through sanctification. Question #3: Is justification a one-time, unrepeatable event, or an ongoing process? Of course, my position is that it is a one-time event. Question #4: "Do we earn sanctification?" No, we do not earn sanctification. Philippians 2:12-13 says that we should "work out our salvation with fear and trembling for it is God who works in us, to will and to accomplish His good pleasure." Therefore, at the end of the day, even our active obedience, even our acts of obedience were wrought by the inward work of the Holy Spirit. Question #5: Is it just for God to hold accountable for what we are not able to do? Yes, it is. God commands us all kinds of things that we are unable to do, apart from him. He commands us, for example, to obey his law. Jesus, in Matthew 5:48, says, "therefore be perfect." The Bible commands us to be holy as Jesus is holy. Those are all things that we cannot do in and of ourselves.

Remember, it was Pelagius who first developed this line of reasoning, that God would not command man to do that which he was incapable of doing himself. However, when God does command men to do something such as be perfect, he also provides the means. I have been arguing throughout this debate that the means of perfection is to the imputed righteousness of Christ that is received by faith. I would like to move now to my first chart. Regarding a few statements that were made on Tuesday night, I am just going to spend a couple of minutes cleaning up, since my opponent spent a couple of minutes tonight addressing some things that were said on Tuesday night. I will say this—that I believe that there is a slight advantage on the part of Mr. Reeves in that he was able to go back and review the audio files. He did have the courtesy to ask me if I minded him playing the audio files during the course of the debate. I told him I did not care. He could do whatever he wanted to do. However, I believe there is a slight advantage in reviewing the things that were said on Tuesday night. I was requesting those files but I was unable to get them until tonight. Tonight I do have them. I am very grateful for that. I would have liked to review some of those statements that were made on Tuesday night as well, but unfortunately, I will not be able to do that until tomorrow.

First, did I change my position on Romans 6:3-6, Galatians 3:27, and Colossians 2:12? Absolutely not! I did not come all the way from San Diego to flip-flop my position between Monday night and Tuesday night. Now because I have not had the benefit of listening to those recordings, I am not sure if I am the one that is at fault. It could have been that I said something that came out the wrong way, or it could have been that I misspoke, and that is why I asked Mr. Reeves if he truly believed that I had changed my position, to which he said yes. Now I want you to notice something that is going on in this debate. I am a person who is very concerned about truth. In addition, the other night when Mr. Reeves made the comment, when I asked him the question, "How is a man justified?" he said, "by keeping all of the commands of God." Now this is the first time that I have met Mr. Reeves, but I had enough sense to know that he did not mean the Old Testament Law. But I could have got up here and raved for five or ten minutes that now he is teaching that, did you hear him, he said we must obey every. . . . I did not do that. I gave him the benefit of the doubt. I said that I believe what Mr. Reeves means is those things that are commanded in the New Testament. Now the reason I point this out to you is that I do not want you to get side tracked on the things that are not meant, either by me or by my opponent. I am very much concerned about getting to the truth of this matter. I am very much concerned about accuracy. I think you should be also.

I still maintain, as I did on Monday night, that these verses are speaking of the baptism of the Holy Spirit. The point that I was making was that these verses describe the things that are signified in water baptism. I did say that Acts 22:16 was water baptism. It says in verse 16, "Now why do delay, get up and be baptized, and wash away your sins, calling on His name." Remember, my argument was that the things signified by the sign are so closely related in the minds of the Apostles that they could be used interchangeably. That was my position. However, Galatians 3:27 and Romans chapter 6 are not referring to water baptism, though the term baptism is used. Galatians 3:26 and Romans 6:3 are there for you. We have already heard them tonight so it is not necessary for me to repeat them again. However, from this point forward, when I address a particular verse, I will specify if I believe that this is baptism of the Holy Spirit or baptism by water, okay? Because the last thing I want is for us to be confused.

Now I want to address something else that was said on Tuesday night. I had come up here and I made the statement, on more than one occasion, that what I was hearing from this side of the room sounded very much like the doctrines of Roman Catholicism. To that, Mr. Reeves responded that he was someone who argues against Roman Catholicism. In fact, he even wrote an article against Roman Catholicism for the newspaper. Now he went on to say that both Roman Catholics and Protestants are in error, because the Protestants are teaching that we are saved, or justified, by faith alone, and the Roman Catholics are teaching, on the other hand, that we are justified by works alone. That is just historically inaccurate. Mr. Reeves has a responsibility when he makes a statement such as that, to be historically accurate to you. Now that is why I asked him in the opening question, what does it mean to bear false witness against your neighbor? Because, although I am convinced he did not intend to misrepresent the facts, surely he did. Moreover, because he misrepresented the facts, he is guilty of bearing false witness. So I want to know if he has not repented of that sin, is he a justified man as he debates before you tonight? Because remember, his doctrine is, that once you sin, you lose your justification.

I have been maintaining all along because we are human beings, because we have a sinful nature, we are prone to sin. My sin does not negate the fact that God has given me his imputed righteousness in Jesus Christ, which I will get more into tonight. Now, this is taken from the Council of Trent, which was convened in the years 1545–1563. Chapter 10—"The increase of justification received through the observance of the commandments of God, faith cooperating with good works, increased that justice received through the grace of Christ and are further justified." You see that? That is why I was making the reference. Now tonight we have heard something that is somewhat confusing to me, and before I, you know, hit the hammer to the metal, I want to get some clarification. Therefore, I am going to hold off and just throw the question out there. We seem to have some contradictory statements in Mr. Reeves' opening remarks because I asked him the question. This was question #3: "Would you affirm or deny the following statements, that this is about, of course, faith cooperating with good works increases that justice received through the grace of Christ and further justifies the believer?" He said no, which I am glad he said no. However, he said you are either justified or you are not. Then later on, he called justification a process. Go back and rewind this tape when you get a chance. He called justification a process. He not only said that but he said quote "God continues to justify us." Okay, so I am a little bit confused. Is justification a process? Is it a one-time event? Is somebody either justified, or are they not justified? Was Abraham, when Abraham was justified, in Genesis 15, was he justified? If so, then why did he need to be justified further by his works? You see it is his argument that, that James 2 is talking about Abraham being justified by his works, but if Abraham was already justified, according to Mr. Reeves' definition, and then he was justified. He said you are either justified or you are not.

Now going on to the next chart—imputed righteousness, this is very important for us to understand. This also came up. 1 Corinthians 1:30-31: "But of Him, you are in Christ Jesus who became for us wisdom from God and righteousness and sanctification and redemption, that it is written, he who glories, let him glory in the Lord." Mr. Reeves quoted this verse, and he asked, "Have we received the wisdom from God?" What does the verse say? It says, but of him, you are in Christ who became for us, wisdom from God. Is Christ my wisdom from God, if I am a Bible-believing Christian? I certainly hope so. He said no, he is not. In the same way that Christ is my wisdom from God, Christ is my righteousness from God. In the same way that Christ is my righteousness of God, Christ is also my sanctification and my redemption. 2 Corinthians 5:21: "For He made Him who knew no sin to be sin for us, that we might become the righteousness of God in Him." You see, there is this double action taking place in the work of Christ. On the one hand, he is paying, he is making atonement for sins, and on the other hand, he has been living the perfect life so that he might give us his righteousness, so that we might be made acceptable to God. Philippians 3:8: "Yet indeed, I also count all things loss for the excellence of the knowledge of Christ Jesus my Lord, for whom I have suffered loss of all things, and count them as rubbish, that I may gain Christ, and be found in Him, not having my own righteousness which is from the Law, but that which is through faith in Christ, the righteousness which is from God, by faith." People, please, this is the word of God. Paul says, I do not want to have my own righteousness. In addition, of course, it says righteousness that is of the Law. However, if God commands you to be baptized, is it a law? Is it optional? He even said himself, which commands are negated, which commands are not necessary. Every command is necessary and every command is given by the Holy Spirit, and the Law of God that is said to be written on your heart, is the same law that was written on stones. Or rather, it is the same author. The Holy Spirit who wrote the Law on our hearts has also written the Law in the Old Testament on stones. Are we to suppose that he somehow, has changed his mind about morality or that it is unlawful to have adultery with my neighbor's wife? Of course not! But, where do we go to affirm that? We do not just say, well my heart tells me it is okay to cheat on my wife. No! We go to the objective standard of God's law and so you see, this law never changes.

Paul says, I do not want to be found having my righteousness, because Isaiah says our righteousness is as filthy rags. Romans 10:2, Romans chapter 10, verse 2. "For I bear them witness that they have a zeal for God, but not according to knowledge." This was Paul's plea for the Jews. They were very zealous people. I am sure they could pack the theater just like this; I am sure that they could have their experts in the Law, you know, recall Old Testament verses. However, what does he say about them? He says that they are seeking to establish their own righteousness because they are ignorant of God's righteousness. What is God's righteousness? We must be sure, because if we are not sure what God's righteousness is, then we will never be saved. Because they were not saved. They were ignorant of God's righteousness. Also, they were ignorant of God's righteousness and they had not submitted to the righteousness of God. What does it mean to submit to the righteousness of God? To do what Paul says, to say, I would be found that, Oh, Lord that I would be found not having my own righteousness, not that I could say, Lord, I was baptized in your name. Or Lord, I did this in your name, or I did that in your name. But that I might stand as Joshua, the High Priest, stood before God. When Satan was there accusing him, he was wearing the very garments of the King, clothed in Christ. That is the righteousness of God, to be clothed in Christ.

Man's story from the beginning has been that he has been found naked. Once he rebelled against God, once he was found in sin, Adam was found in a state of rebellion against God, what did Adam do? He started to clothe himself with fig leaves. However, God said no, Adam. Even when he was clothed, he said why did you hide? He said because I was naked. But, wait a minute, was he naked? No, he had fig leaves on. He was naked in the sight of God because, in order for Adam to be clothed, he must be clothed with righteousness. He must be clothed with Christ. That is the imputed righteousness of the gospel. That is why the gospel is the good news. Good news is not hey, here is a bunch of rules. Regeneration, repentance, faith, baptism—follow these rules and you will be fine. No, that is not good news at all. Because the moment I sin, all of that is negated.

You know that in your heart of hearts. When you are alone by yourself, and the Holy Spirit makes you aware of your sins, what are you going to do? You are going to live in a constant state of fear under this type of theology. Because there is no assurance, there is no assurance that, if I die when I am in that state of sin, I will be saved. However, what does Paul tell us? He tells us that God has not given us a spirit of fear. Fear comes from the enemy. Sure, we are to fear God but that is talking about having a holy reverence for God. That is not talking about being afraid that God is going to reach down from the sky and judge me because I have sinned today. No, Jesus is the author of salvation. He is the Prince of Peace. He is the one who makes his people have peace in their hearts because they can rest in him.

I want to talk again about faith being a gift. Philippians 1:29: "For to you it has been granted for Christ's sake, not only to believe in Him, but also to suffer for His sake." God is the one who grants faith. John 6:65: "And He was saying, 'For this reason I have said to you that no one can come to me unless it has been granted him from the Father." Acts 13:48: "When the Gentiles heard this, they began rejoicing and glorifying the word of the Lord, and as many as have been appointed to eternal life believed." You see faith is something that is granted by God.

Let us talk about these baptism verses because that is really what we are here to discuss tonight. I asked Mr. Reeves, how do you know when baptism, when the word "baptism" is being used, whether it means water baptism or not? He gave you the same answer that I would give. Contextually, contextually you will know. Okay, I am in agreement with that. Luke 12:50: "But I have a baptism to undergo, and how distressed I am until it is accomplished." There the word baptism is used in reference to the crucifixion. Acts 1:4-5, chapter 1, verses 4 and 5: "Gathering them together, He commanded them not to leave Jerusalem, but to wait for what the Father had promised, which He said, you have heard from me, for John baptized with water, but you will be baptized with the Holy Spirit not many days from now." Well here, the context is clearly teaching that there is something in the New Covenant, this is after the resurrection, and there is something in the New Covenant that is called the baptism of the Holy Spirit. Once again, when I talk about the baptism of the Holy Spirit, I am not talking about it in the same sense that the Pentecostal does.

I found it somewhat ironic that Mr. Reeves would take my words about the book of Acts, and I think that he knows my position. I do not hold the book of Romans as being more authoritative than the book of Acts. However, what I was saying is that we must understand the book of Acts in light of the clear doctrinal teaching in the book of Romans. He said, no, they are all God-given. Amen! They are all able to teach us doctrine. Amen! However, don't the Pentecostals make the argument that when you are baptized you have to speak in tongues because there it is in the book of Acts? Now how do you prove from the book of Acts that they are wrong? You do not. You go to the epistles. That is what I am trying to say. I am trying to say that there are things that are happening in the book of Acts that are unusual. These things are unusual because something very unusual is happening. The Holy Spirit, the New Covenant gift of the Holy Spirit is now given to a body of believers. Because of that, there are miraculous signs that are taking place. There are people being included in the family of God, such as Samaritans and Gentiles that have never before been drawn like this to have a relationship with God. So please, understand that I do not think that somehow the book of Romans is more authoritative than the historical narrative of Acts. I am saying that we interpret them together. Interpreting the obscure with the clear, which are the epistles, the doctrinal teachings that are found in those books. Sure, Paul quotes from the book of Genesis, an historical narrative, but Paul has apostolic authority to do so. He has apostolic authority not only to quote, but to give interpretation as he does in Galatians chapter 3 when he tells us that the seed is not Isaac but Christ. You see, Mr. Reeves and I do not possess that type of authority. Therefore, I think there was a big misunderstanding.

Now concerning my comments between Acts 8 and Acts 10, please do not think that I hold those things in tension when I stated, that Acts 8 contradicts 10. I would not do that after I have just said that I am very concerned and that I do not believe the Bible contradicts itself. I would be a fool to get up here. I wish that Mr. Reeves would give me the benefit of the doubt on some of these things, instead of taking them and running with them. However, that has not been the case so I have to spend some time explaining what I meant. I have made the argument, in my opening presentation on Monday and on Tuesday night, I showed you plenty of verses that the gift of the Holy Spirit is distinct, mark my words, distinct, from regeneration. I made it very clear. One of the reasons that I make that argument is because you have the Holy Spirit in the book of Acts, being given at different times. You have in Acts 8 for example, you have the Holy Spirit being given of, or given by, the laying on of hands. In Acts 10, as we will see in just a moment, you have the Holy Spirit given through the preaching of the word, before water baptism. Therefore, what I was saying is in Acts 8, it is after water baptism, and Acts 10, and it is before water baptism, so how are we going to know which it is? Are we going to cite these verses and say, "I'm holding on to 8 and you're holding on to 10"? No. I am saying, let us go to the epistles and weigh these verses in light of the clear doctrinal instruction that we find in the epistles. That has been my position all along.

Mark 16:16 I believe is speaking of water baptism. "And he said to them, go into all the world and preach the gospel to all creation, and he who has believed and has been baptized shall be saved, but he who has disbelieved shall be condemned." This verse does not address the man who believes and is not baptized. It does not address the man who believes and dies before he has an opportunity to be baptized, such as the thief on the cross. I mean, what happens if somebody in a church of Christ service, at the invitation of the gospel; now, I hope that I am picturing this accurately, because I have never witnessed a church of Christ, but I can imagine that, at the end of the preaching that there is probably an invitation to come forward, or an invitation, at least, to be baptized. What would happen if on the way up, or on the way into the water, the man had a heart attack? Which in our day and age, could very well happen, or a stroke? Would that man be lost eternally because he was not baptized? That is absurd. I certainly hope that is not your position, because once again, Rome is the one that says the sign is where the power is. We are saying, no, the sign points to the power.

We heard Bruce Reeves get up here and affirm baptismal regeneration, which is another doctrine of Rome. I'm amazed at all the doctrines that

I'm hearing that are taken, and I could even come back tomorrow night, if you like, and bring you a nice fat quote that shows that Rome believes that when an infant is baptized, he is regenerated. That is their position. Now his position is a little bit different. At least you have to be an adult, or you have to be cognizant, or you have to participate, but it is a correspondence there between two groups that claim authority and yet, both teach baptismal regeneration.

What about the thief on the cross in Luke 23:42? "And he was saying, 'Jesus, remember me when you come into your kingdom.' And He said to him, 'Truly, I say to you, today you will be with me in Paradise.'" Was this simply old covenant? Am I going to allow Mr. Reeves to come up and say, well, you see, Gene is confusing old covenant and new covenant because that happened prior to the cross and now we're talking about after the cross. No. John 19:31 says, "Then the Jews, because it was the day of preparation, so that the bodies would not remain on the cross on the Sabbath, for the Sabbath was a high day, asked Pilate that their legs might be broken. And that they might be taken away. So the soldiers came and broke the legs of the first man and of the other who was crucified with Him. But coming to Jesus when they saw Him, He was already dead and they did not break His legs." Why is that significant? Jesus died before the two thieves. Well because Hebrews 9:15 says, "For this reason He is the mediator," speaking of Christ, "of a new covenant so that since a death has taken place, for the redemption of the transgressions that were committed under the first covenant, those who have been called may receive the promise of the eternal inheritance. For where a covenant is, there must of necessity be the death of the one who made it, for a covenant is valid only when men are dead, for it is never enforced while the one who made it lives." So I ask you, according to these verses, was the new covenant in effect? Yes it was. Yet we have an example of a man being promised by Jesus Christ that he will be in paradise that day without water baptism. Now, I have heard some people argue that well, he was baptized in his own sweat. I do not think that is going to be Mr. Reeves' argument, I would be surprised if I heard that. However, it is amazing the things that you hear to try to get away from this type of language.

How about Acts 2:38? It says in verse 37, "Now when they heard this, they were pierced to the heart, and said to Peter and the rest of the Apostles, 'Brethren, what shall we do?' And Peter said to them, 'Repent and each of you be baptized in the name of Jesus Christ for the forgiveness of your sins, and you will receive the gift of the Holy Spirit." They were commanded to be baptized, note this, they were commanded to be baptized because they had received forgiveness of sins so, not so that they, not so that they could receive forgiveness of sins. Let me show you two examples where this word is used. The word here is *eis* in the original language. There are two examples of this that I brought with me tonight. In Matthew 3:11 for example: "As for me, I baptized you with water for repentance." This is John the Baptist. Now John the Baptist uses the same language. I baptize you with water for repentance. Was John the Baptist baptizing with water so that the people could repent? No. He was baptizing them because they had repented. The word "for" can also be translated here "because." As for me, I baptize you with water because of repentance. So what came first, repentance or water baptism? We know historically from the gospels that repentance was the requirement for John's baptism. How about Matthew 12:41? "The men of Nineveh will stand up with this generation at the judgment and will condemn it because they repented at," the word *eis*, the same word is used, "at the preaching of Jonah. And behold something greater than Jonah is here." It says they repented at the preaching of Jonah. Did they repent so that Jonah could preach? No, they repented because Jonah preached. It is not an anomaly to see that in Acts 2:38 it says, "Repent each one of you, be baptized in the name of Jesus Christ, for the forgiveness of your sins." Because of the forgiveness of your sins, because these men had been cut to the heart, they wanted to know what to do. I am going to argue that the very fact that they were asking the question, "What shall we do?" was evidence that their hearts had been changed. They were commanded to be baptized because they had received forgiveness of sins, not so they could receive forgiveness of sins.

Bruce Reeves' interpretation also denies repentance is a gift. You see, if you reject my interpretation, and you take Mr. Reeves' interpretation, then you are going to have to deny that repentance is something that God gives to men. Not only is faith a gift, but repentance is also a gift. Let us look at a few of these verses. Acts 5:31: "He is the one whom God exalted to His right hand as a Prince and a Savior, to grant repentance to Israel, and forgiveness of sins, to grant repentance." Acts 11:18: "When they heard this they were quieted down and glorified God saying, 'Well then, God has granted to the Gentiles also repentance that leads to life.'" See, it is God who grants repentance. John 6:65: "And He was saying, for this reason I have said to you that no one can come to me unless it has been granted to him from the Father." I think one of the strongest verses is 2 Timothy 2:23 or 2:24. "The Lord's bondservant must not be quarrelsome but be kind to all, able to teach, patient when wronged, with gentleness correcting those who are in opposition, if perhaps God may grant them repentance." Notice: "God may grant them repentance leading to the knowledge of truth, and they may come to their senses and escape from the snare of the Devil, having been held captive by him to do his will." Let us give honor and credit where honor and credit is due. Salvation, from beginning to end, is the gift of God. Thank you.

Thursday Night

Second Affirmative

Bruce Reeves

Good evening, ladies and gentlemen. It is my pleasure to be back before you this evening as I continue my affirmation of the proposition. Please put the proposition up, Don. The proposition reads, Resolved: "The Scriptures teach that water baptism is essential in order for the alien sinner to obtain the forgiveness of his past sins." That is what I am here to affirm. That is what Mr. Cook is here to deny. I would like to make a few observations about the speech that you have just heard. Monday night, Mr. Cook gave me a short lecture about the responsibility of the negative, that is, that the negative was to follow the affirmative. Mr. Cook did not deal with many of the arguments that I have offered in affirmation of the proposition this evening. Now, if he gets to them in the last speech of the evening, I will not have the opportunity to respond and some of you may not be back tomorrow night. Maybe this is a good reason for you to come back. I hope that you will come back tomorrow night and hear some more things that I have to say. I just wanted to point that out to you and I want you to note that fact, i.e. that he did not respond to much of the argumentation that I offered in affirmation of the proposition. This evening, I will not have the opportunity, because of the format of our discussion, to be able to respond to him and you can make your decisions upon that basis.

There were a few things Mr. Cook mentioned that I would like to note. I want to re-emphasize some of the things that I have already presented that remain untouched. I am wondering why he didn't answer much of the argumentation that I presented this very evening because I know he understands the responsibility of the negative in that regard.

We heard about the imputation of the personal righteousness of Christ. Tuesday night we talked about that subject somewhat, because I was following him. You might turn in your Bible to Romans 4:7: "Blessed are they whose iniquities are forgiven and whose sins are covered." So we are "counted righteous" because of our faith. What cleanses us of our sins?

Of course, you know it is the blood of Jesus Christ. The imputation of the personal righteousness of Christ is irrelevant to what we are talking about tonight, which is supposed to be the essentiality of water baptism, but nonetheless, that is something worthy of your consideration.

Mr. Cook accused me of sin this evening. He said I misrepresented the Roman Catholics. Well, I want to point out to you what I said. I said that ***infant baptism*** is an example of works alone being taught by our Catholic friends. Now, he also went on to say some things about baptismal regeneration and that was a misrepresentation of my position. The idea of baptismal regeneration again, is what our Catholic friends practice. It is the idea of water baptism without faith. That is not what I teach. I teach what the Lord taught, i.e. faith plus baptism.

He mentioned our lack of security and being in and out of fellowship with God. Well, what assurance does his position offer you? He told us the other night that election was not for us, but for God from the standpoint of knowledge and he did not know who was elect and who was not elect. If he does not know who is elect and who is not, does he know that he is elect? I assume that he would tell us yes he does.

We were told that I misrepresented Mr. Cook but as he was talking about the book of Acts he said, and I wrote this down, "Acts is obscure" and we were also told that we should use the epistles in the New Testament and not the book of Acts to establish doctrine. Would you turn your Bibles to 2 Peter the 3rd chapter with me tonight? You know, that is not what the Scripture says about the book of Acts. Mr. Cook says that about the book of Acts, but that is not what the Scripture says. In 2 Peter 3:16, speaking of Paul's epistle, Peter says "As also in all his epistles speaking in them of these things, and which are some things hard to be understood, which they that are unlearned and unstable wrest as they do also the other Scriptures unto their own destruction." He says some of Paul's epistles were more challenging. Yet that is not what you heard this evening.

Mr. Cook mentioned the thief on the cross in an attempt to deny the essentiality of water baptism. Let me see if I can have his chart pulled up if they can find it. Just the thief on the cross chart if you do not mind putting that up. I will go ahead and deal with this as they are attempting to do so. He made the point that the new covenant was in effect when Jesus died, but that is not what the Bible has to say to us. In Isaiah 2 we read about the word of the Lord coming forth from Jerusalem, now that has reference to Pentecost and that is when the new covenant was in effect. I want you to notice some things about the thief on the cross with me. Turn your Bibles to Luke 23:26-

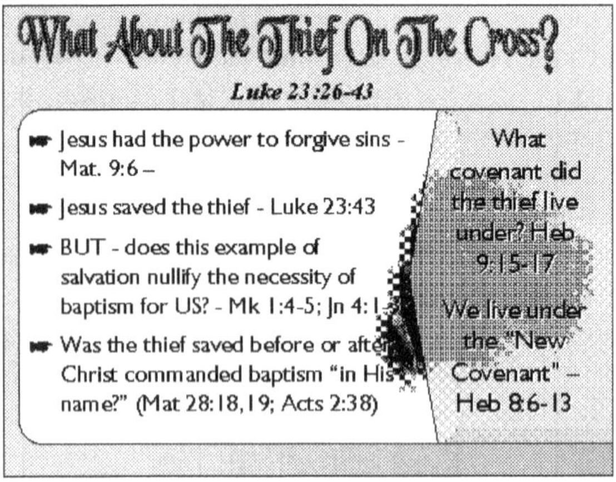
What About The Thief On The Cross?
Luke 23:26-43
Jesus had the power to forgive sins - Mat. 9:6 –
Jesus saved the thief - Luke 23:43
BUT - does this example of salvation nullify the necessity of baptism for US? - Mk 1:4-5; Jn 4: 1
Was the thief saved before or aft
Christ commanded baptism "in Hi
name?" (Mat 28:18,19; Acts 2:38)
What covenant did the thief live under? Heb 9:15-17
We live under the "New Covenant" – Heb 8:6-13

43 with me very quickly. You know, Jesus had the power to forgive sins according to Matthew 9:6. Jesus saved the thief. I do not deny that truth. That is not an issue! Look in Luke 23:43, the question is, "Does this example of salvation nullify the necessity of baptism for us?" Here is the question, here is the consideration and I want all of this audience to remember this when Mr. Cooks talks about the thief on the cross, "Was the thief saved before or after Christ commanded baptism in His name?" Matthew 28: 18-19 and Acts 2:38 make it very clear, that the command to be baptized in the name of Christ was issued after he both died and was resurrected. Baptism in the name of Christ was not preached until the day of Pentecost. Therefore, the thief on the cross does not negate the idea of water baptism being essential.

Since you heard very little in the previous speech about some of the verses that we have mentioned, and I suppose that is coming in the next speech, I want you to think about what we have said. Turn to John 3:5 and notice what the Scriptures teach.

In John, the 3rd chapter, Jesus is talking about the new birth. He is talking about regeneration. In John 3:3 here is what the Scripture says, "Jesus answered and said unto them, 'Verily, verily, I say unto you except a man be born again he cannot see the kingdom of God.' Nicodemus asked him, 'How can a man be born when he is old. Can he enter the second time into his mother's womb and be born?' Jesus said, 'Verily, verily I say unto thee, except a man be born of the water and of the Spirit, he cannot enter into the kingdom of God.'" We have been told that regeneration and being born again are unconditional,

Water Baptism & The New Birth
Let Scripture Explain Scripture
REGENERATION
John 3:5
Titus 3:5
Ephes. 5:26
born of water
washing of regeneration
washing of water
and the Spirit
and renewing of the Holy Spirit
by the word,

but that is not what the Son of God said about it. The Son of God says to us that we must be born of the water and of the Spirit. Paul indicates the same thing in Titus 3:4: “But after that the kindness and the love of God our Savior toward men appeared, not by works of righteousness which we have done, but according to His mercy He saved us, by the washing of regeneration and renewing of the Holy Ghost.” The “washing of regeneration” is very clearly having reference to the idea of being born of water in John chapter 3, i.e. it has reference to water baptism. Then Paul mentions the “renewing of the Holy Spirit.” When you just compare those you will notice that we have the phrases “born of the water” and “the washing of regeneration” being used synonymously. John 3:5 and Titus 3:5 need to be considered together.

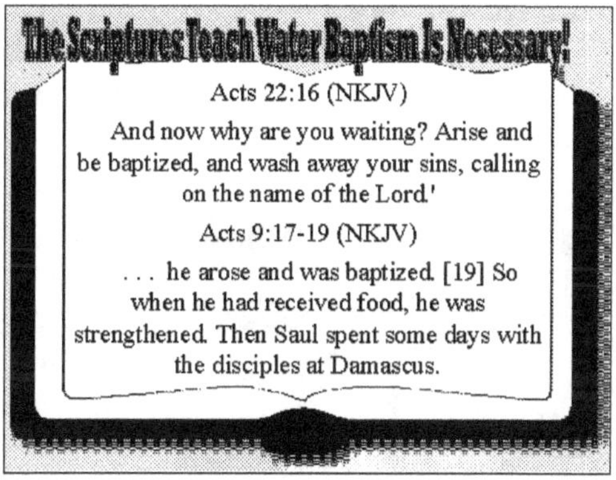
The Scriptures Teach Water Baptism Is Necessary!
Acts 22:16 (NKJV)
And now why are you waiting? Arise and be baptized, and wash away your sins, calling on the name of the Lord.'
Acts 9:17-19 (NKJV)
. . . he arose and was baptized. [19] So when he had received food, he was strengthened. Then Saul spent some days with the disciples at Damascus.

Now what does Acts 22:16 say? What does it say? Saul of Tarsus was told to go into the city. We are even told why he should go into the city, “You will be told what you must do.” What you must do for what? Look at the passage. Now let us not accept sophistry here. Let us not start cutting these texts up and trying to turn them around in order to match up with our theology. Let us make sure what we believe is in harmony with what the Book says. That is what is going to judge us on the last day. He says in this verse, “And now why are you waiting, arise and be baptized and wash away your sins, calling on the name of the Lord.”

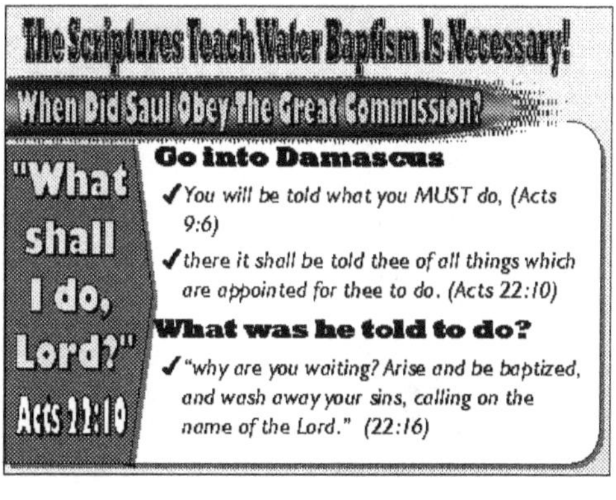
The Scriptures Teach Water Baptism Is Necessary!
When Did Saul Obey The Great Commission?
"What shall I do, Lord?" Acts 22:10
Go into Damascus
✓You will be told what you MUST do, (Acts 9:6)
✓there it shall be told thee of all things which are appointed for thee to do. (Acts 22:10)
What was he told to do?
✓"why are you waiting? Arise and be baptized, and wash away your sins, calling on the name of the Lord." (22:16)

I have already told you, it is not a matter of the water being holy. It is not that by my baptism I am earning or meriting my salvation. How many times do I have to say that in this debate? I have said that over and over repeatedly. However, the passage does teach us that it is through obedience to the gospel that our sins are washed away.

The question is not what washes my sins away. The blood of Jesus washes away sin. The means of our salvation is the offering of Christ at Calvary. We are saved by God's grace. The question for us is when does that happen? ***When*** does that happen? In Acts 22:10 Saul said, "What shall I do, Lord?" He was told to go into Damascus and he would be told what to do. The Scripture says, "There shall be told thee of all the things which are appointed for thee to do" (Acts 22:10). What was he told? Now when somebody comes to me and he says, "Listen brother Bruce, what must I do to be saved, what must I do to be born again?" Should I say, "Nothing"? "You don't have to do anything in order to be regenerated"? "You don't have to do anything to be born again?" Alternatively, must I tell him what is told us in John 3:5, what we learn in Titus chapter 3 and verse 5, what Saul of Tarsus was told by the way, in that historical narrative which we can all understand. I am going to tell them exactly what Saul was told in Acts 22:16: "Why are you waiting? Arise and be baptized and wash away your sins, calling on the name of the Lord."

The Scriptures Teach Water Baptism Is Necessary!
When Did Saul Obey The Great Commission?
Acts 22:16 (NKJV)
And now why are you waiting? Arise and be baptized, and wash away your sins, calling on the name of the Lord.'
When he arose and was baptized – Acts 9:18; 22:16
His sins were washed away –
He called on the name of the Lord
Then he ate – Acts 9:19

If Saul of Tarsus was forgiven before Acts 22:16, and I think that is what Mr. Cook is telling us, if his sins had already been washed away before Acts 22:16, why was this statement made? Why would he be told, "Arise and be baptized, washing away thy sins, calling on the name of the Lord," if his sins had already been washed away? Why in the world would that be expressed? He arose, he was baptized, and as a result, his sins were washed away.

Turn your Bibles to Acts the 10th chapter. Now we mentioned this to you. I suppose we will have the opportunity to talk about this some more tomorrow night. When was Cornelius saved? Was it while he was praying? Was it when the angel appeared to him? Was it when Peter began to speak? No. Was it when the Holy Spirit came? No. Was it when he obeyed the Lord? Absolutely!

When was Cornelius Saved?
Act 10 & 11
While he was praying?
When the angel appeared?
When Peter BEGAN to speak?
When the Holy Spirit came?
When he obeyed the command?

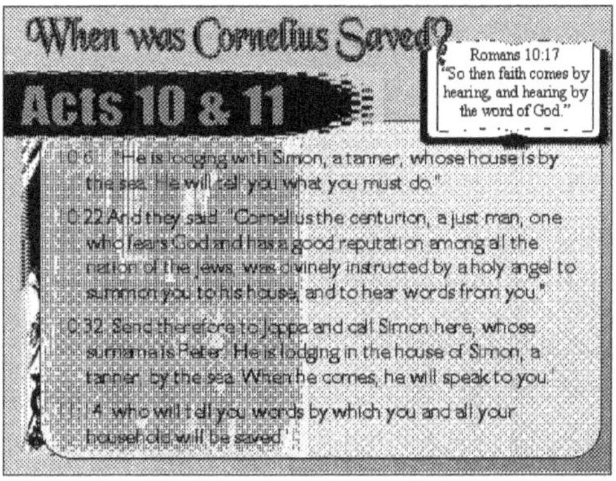
When was Cornelius Saved?
Acts 10 & 11
Romans 10:17 "So then faith comes by hearing, and hearing by the word of God."
10:6 "He is lodging with Simon, a tanner, whose house is by the sea. He will tell you what you must do."
10:22 And they said, "Cornelius the centurion, a just man, one who fears God and has a good reputation among all the nation of the Jews, was divinely instructed by a holy angel to summon you to his house, and to hear words from you."
10:32 Send therefore to Joppa and call Simon here, whose surname is Peter. He is lodging in the house of Simon, a tanner, by the sea. When he comes, he will speak to you.'
11:14 who will tell you words by which you and all your household will be saved.'

The Holy Spirit came upon Cornelius in order to show the Jews that the Gentiles could be accepted. This was the first Gentile convert. When was he saved? What caused him to have faith? Are we to believe that God miraculously causes some people to have faith and miraculously causes some people to repent? Yes, God grants repentance in the sense that he gives us time and opportunity and we have the teaching that encourages us to repent. Are we really to believe that God miraculously gives repentance and faith to some, but he will not give it to others, and these folks go to Heaven and these other folks go to Hell? I think that is what we are being told. However, you know in Acts 10, Cornelius' faith came through the preaching of the word of God. In Acts the 10th chapter, we see this preaching taking place and Cornelius hears words from Peter. How did Cornelius receive faith? Was it something miraculous that the Holy Spirit did to him? Or, was it through the preaching of the word? In Acts 10:6, we are told, "He will tell you what you must do." In Acts 10:22, "Cornelius, the centurion, a just man, one who fears God and has a good reputation among all the nation of the Jews, was divinely instructed by a holy angel to summon you to his house, and to hear words from you." Listen to that passage, "To hear words from you"! The word is what produces faith. Look at chapter 11 and verse 14: "Who will tell you words by which you and all your household will be saved." In Romans, the 10th chapter and verse 17 Paul writes, "Faith cometh by hearing and hearing by the word of God." What did Peter believe and teach about water baptism? He believed it was a command of God that cannot be refused! Peter believed that to forbid water baptism would have been to withstand God. Withstand God from doing what?

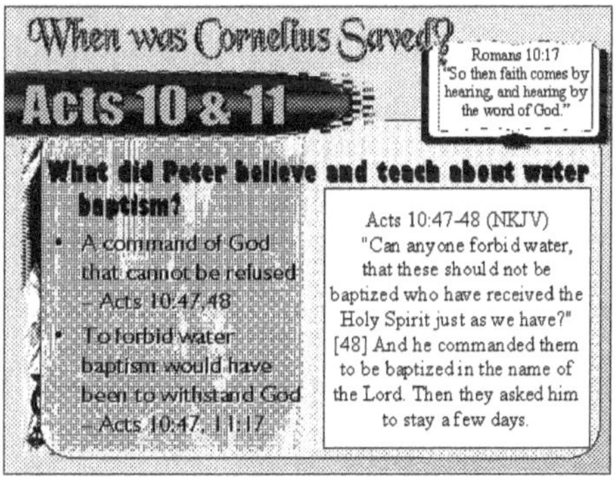
When was Cornelius Saved?
Acts 10 & 11
Romans 10:17 "So then faith comes by hearing, and hearing by the word of God."
What did Peter believe and teach about water baptism?
• A command of God that cannot be refused – Acts 10:47,48
• To forbid water baptism would have been to withstand God – Acts 10:47, 11:17
Acts 10:47-48 (NKJV) "Can anyone forbid water, that these should not be baptized who have received the Holy Spirit just as we have?" [48] And he commanded them to be baptized in the name of the Lord. Then they asked him to stay a few days.

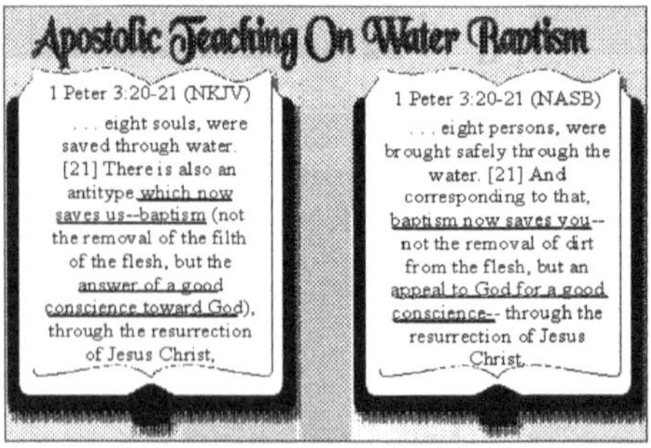
Apostolic Teaching On Water Baptism
1 Peter 3:20-21 (NKJV)
. . . eight souls, were saved through water. [21] There is also an antitype which now saves us--baptism (not the removal of the filth of the flesh, but the answer of a good conscience toward God), through the resurrection of Jesus Christ,
1 Peter 3:20-21 (NASB)
. . . eight persons, were brought safely through the water. [21] And corresponding to that, baptism now saves you-- not the removal of dirt from the flesh, but an appeal to God for a good conscience-- through the resurrection of Jesus Christ.

Turn your Bibles to 1 Peter 3:21. What did we hear about 1 Peter 3:21? Did you hear anything? I am just trying to be as fair as I can possibly be, but did you hear anything? I do not believe we did. You know, it is interesting, how few faith and baptism passages we have heard and that is what we are here to debate. Many of the passages Mr. Cook talked about had not even been introduced. I am glad he brought them up, I want to talk about them, but I did not introduce them. I really wished that we could have talked about 1 Peter 3:20-21. I am here to affirm the essentiality of water baptism. I introduced 1 Peter 3:21, which is a key passage and we did not hear a whisper. Let us read the text together. We read about Noah and his family being delivered, "Which sometimes were disobedient, when once the longsuffering of God waited in the days of Noah. While the ark was prepared, wherein few, that is, eight souls were saved by water." They were delivered from the flood. Let us consider verse 21: "There is also" the New King James says, "an antitype." The New American Standard Bible says, "and corresponding to that baptism now saves you." Now I understand that salvation can have a past, present, and future tense meaning and in order to determine how a term is being used that has a plurality of definitions we go to the context and we ask, "How is Peter using the term?" He says it is not the removal of dirt from the flesh, but an "appeal to God for a good conscience." I am forgiven of my sins because I am cleansed by the blood of Christ. Peter says in baptism, I am appealing not to man, but I am appealing to God for a good conscience through the resurrection of Jesus Christ.

Apostolic Teaching On Water Baptism
1 Peter 3:20-21 (NASB)
. . . eight persons, were brought safely through the water. [21] And corresponding to that, baptism now saves you-- not the removal of dirt from the flesh, but an appeal to God for a good conscience-- through the resurrection of Jesus Christ,
Negatively
"not the removal of dirt from the flesh,"
BUT
Positively
"an appeal to God for a good conscience-- through the resurrection of Jesus Christ,"

Now ladies and gentlemen, I want you to listen very closely to me. It is not just getting wet. It is not just being immersed in water, but it is possessing a saving, obedient faith. It is in that faith and in that act that I am appealing to God for a good conscience. Why would I be appealing to him for that which I already have? If my soul has already been cleansed by the blood of Jesus, why would I continue to appeal to God for a good conscience in baptism? I should already have one. He says, "baptism doth also now save us." Now, you know, folks can come up with all sorts of quibbles and we can try to go to these passages and say, well, the passage says that but it doesn't really mean that, but the Scriptures mean what they say. I recognize that the majority of denominational theology and religious theology says, "Yes, it says baptism saves us, but really baptism does not save us." None of that being considered will change one iota of this verse. Now we are all here because we profess that we love Christ and we want to serve God, and we are both saying we believe in the Bible, and we believe the Bible is the word of God. This is what the Scripture says, "Baptism doth also now save us." Baptism now saves you. It is not just getting wet. It is not just the removal of the dirt of the flesh, but it is an appeal to God for a good conscience, through the resurrection of Jesus Christ. That is what the Lord says. That is what the Scripture says. That is what the Bible says.

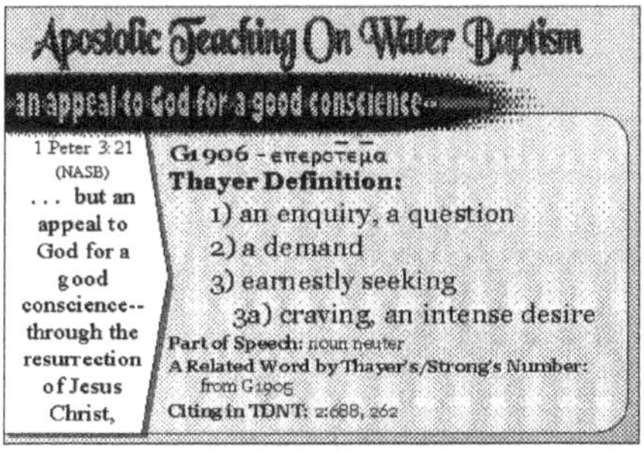
Apostolic Teaching On Water Baptism
an appeal to God for a good conscience--
1 Peter 3:21 (NASB)
. . . but an appeal to God for a good conscience-- through the resurrection of Jesus Christ,
G1906 - επεροτεμα
Thayer Definition:
1) an enquiry, a question
2) a demand
3) earnestly seeking
3a) craving, an intense desire
Part of Speech: noun neuter
A Related Word by Thayer's/Strong's Number: from G1905
Citing in TDNT: 2:688, 262

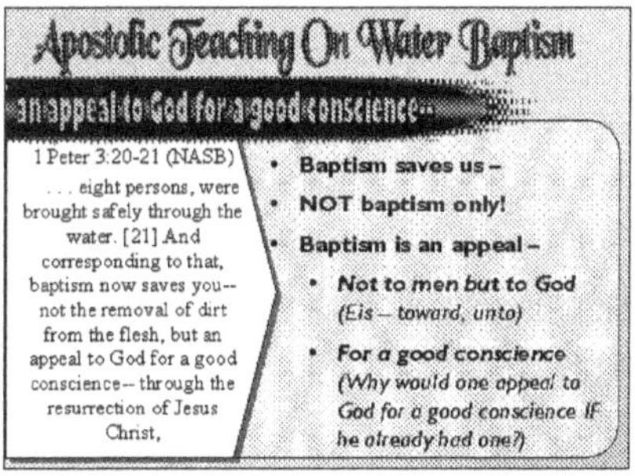
Apostolic Teaching On Water Baptism
an appeal to God for a good conscience--
1 Peter 3:20-21 (NASB)
. . . eight persons, were brought safely through the water. [21] And corresponding to that, baptism now saves you-- not the removal of dirt from the flesh, but an appeal to God for a good conscience-- through the resurrection of Jesus Christ,
Baptism saves us –
NOT baptism only!
Baptism is an appeal –
Not to men but to God
(Eis – toward, unto)
For a good conscience
(Why would one appeal to God for a good conscience IF he already had one?)

Negatively, it is not the removal of dirt from the flesh. Positively, it is an appeal to God for a good conscience through the resurrection of Jesus Christ. It is an inquiry, a question, a demand. It is an earnest seeking, a craving, and an intense desire. That is what the word of God says. Peter does not say baptism alone saves. I do not believe that baptism by itself saves the sinner. Baptism is an appeal, not to men, but to God.

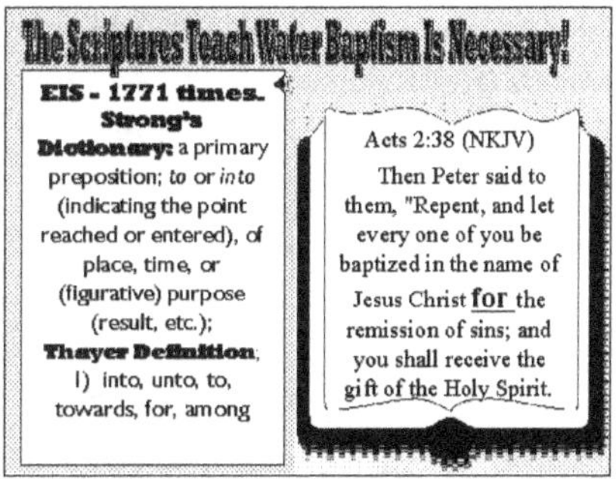
The Scriptures Teach Water Baptism Is Necessary!
EIS - 1771 times.
Strong's Dictionary: a primary preposition; to or into (indicating the point reached or entered), of place, time, or (figurative) purpose (result, etc.);
Thayer Definition:
1) into, unto, to, towards, for, among
Acts 2:38 (NKJV)
Then Peter said to them, "Repent, and let every one of you be baptized in the name of Jesus Christ for the remission of sins; and you shall receive the gift of the Holy Spirit.

Turn your Bibles to Acts 2:38. Mr. Cook introduced this passage and I would like to deal with his argument on the verse. We read about the day of Pentecost and Jesus is being preached, and Mr. Cook says, as he looks at this passage, that these people were forgiven of their past sins prior to asking the question, "What shall we do?" Acts 2:37 states: "Now when they heard this they were pricked in their heart and they said unto Peter and the rest of the Apostles, 'Men and brethren, what shall we do?'" They were asking what shall we do about the sin of crucifying the Son of God. He goes to this text and he plugs in his interpretation due to his theology. "And Peter said unto them, 'Repent and be baptized, every one of you, in the name of Jesus Christ, for the remission of sins, and you shall receive the gift of the Holy Ghost.'" Are we really to believe that the sinner receives the forgiveness of their sins prior to repentance and baptism when we read this verse? I think that is what we have been told. Ladies and gentlemen, you have read the Bible. You have looked at these Scriptures. You know better than that argument. Now then, "Repent and be baptized, every one of you, in the name of Jesus Christ, for the remission of your sins." You know the term *eis* is used at least 1,771 times in the New Testament. Out of those 1,771 times where the term "for" or *eis* is used, Mr. Cook has given us two cases in which the word "for" doesn't mean in order to, according to him, and even the two cases that he gives us, **even the two cases he gives us**, his interpretation fails the test. The term is defined by biblical scholars as "into, unto, to, towards, for, among." Now he mentioned to us Matthew 3:11, "I indeed baptize you with water unto repentance. But He who is coming after me is mightier than I, whose sandals I am not worthy to carry. He will baptize you with the Holy Spirit and fire." I understand Mr. Cook's point to be that this idea of "I indeed baptize you with water unto repentance" should be understood as "because of" repentance. However, the truth is that it should not. To define the term "because of" would render it oppositional to the very meaning of the word *eis*. John was pointing their hearts and minds to the one to come. We never see this statement after Acts the 2nd chapter. He is pointing them forward to a new life, to a reformed life. While it is true, it may be said that they were repenting because of the things he had to say, that is not the point of the passage.

In Matthew 12:41 we read that the Ninevites repented unto or into the benefits of Jonah's preaching, or in order to comply with Jonah's preaching. We cannot redefine the terms to suit our beliefs. Matthew 26:28 introduces the term "for" in three different ways and I want you to notice how it is used. Jesus says, "For this is my blood of the new covenant which is shed for many for the remission of sins." Now, does *eis* mean "because of" there too? Are we to believe that we have Jesus shedding his blood because of the forgiveness of sins or in order to the forgiveness of sins? We all know the answer to that question. Now you know what is interesting, is that the phrase, "for the remission of sins" in Matthew 26:28, is the same phrase that we have in Acts 2:38. We read Matthew 26:28 and we all understand that what that means is that Jesus shed his blood in order to, so that the forgiveness of sins would be provided. But for some reason, when we come to Acts the 2nd chapter and verse 38, the phrase, "for the remission of sins," does not mean what it meant over there in Matthew 26:28. Now we are trying to harmonize everything God has told us, we are trying to keep the words in their appropriate place, we are trying to look at the definitions and we are trying to understand what the Scriptures have to say to us.

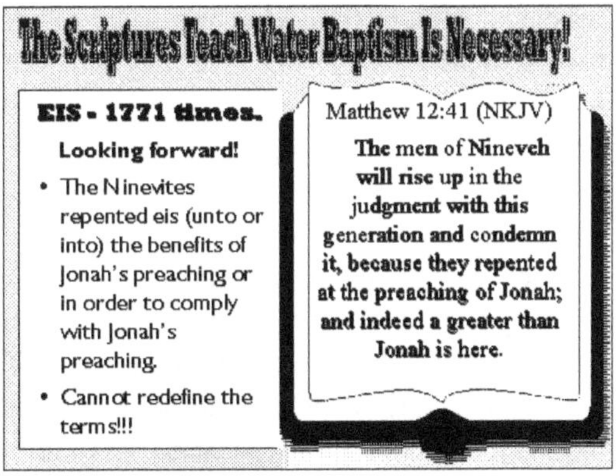
The Scriptures Teach Water Baptism Is Necessary!
EIS - 1771 times.
Looking forward!
• The Ninevites repented eis (unto or into) the benefits of Jonah's preaching or in order to comply with Jonah's preaching.
• Cannot redefine the terms!!!
Matthew 12:41 (NKJV)
The men of Nineveh will rise up in the judgment with this generation and condemn it, because they repented at the preaching of Jonah; and indeed a greater than Jonah is here.

The Scriptures Teach Water Baptism Is Necessary!
EIS - 1771 times.
Looking forward!
• To define the term "Because of" would render it oppositional to the very meaning of the word 'EIS'
• John was pointing their hearts and minds to the ONE to come.
Matthew 3:11 (NKJV)
I indeed baptize you with water unto repentance, but He who is coming after me is mightier than I, whose sandals I am not worthy to carry. He will baptize you with the Holy Spirit and fire. (cf. Acts 19:4)

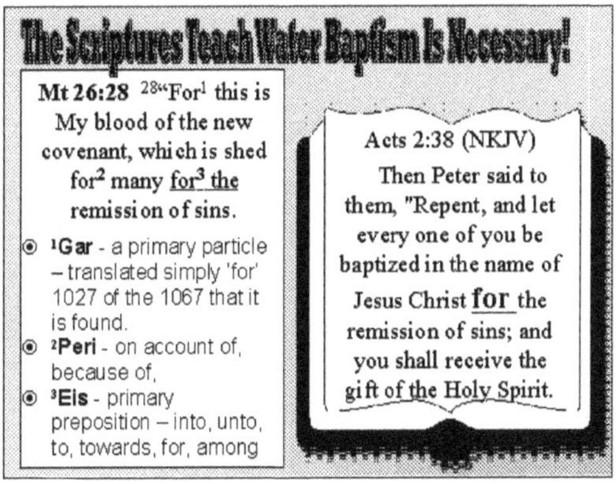
The Scriptures Teach Water Baptism Is Necessary!
Mt 26:28 28"For1 this is My blood of the new covenant, which is shed for2 many for3 the remission of sins.
1Gar - a primary particle – translated simply 'for' 1027 of the 1067 that it is found.
2Peri - on account of, because of,
3Eis - primary preposition – into, unto, to, towards, for, among
Acts 2:38 (NKJV)
Then Peter said to them, "Repent, and let every one of you be baptized in the name of Jesus Christ for the remission of sins; and you shall receive the gift of the Holy Spirit.

Friends, this is just not as hard as some have made it. Could it be that some folks simply do not want to accept what the Lord says, and therefore attempt to structure a theology that denies what the Bible teaches? Are we going to stay with our theology rather than stay with the Scriptures? You think for a minute, here these people are on the day of Pentecost and Mr. Cook has told us that when they said, "What shall we do," they were already clean from the standpoint of having their sins washed away. Is that what the word of God says? Or were they saying, "What shall we do?" because they had been convicted of their sin? They recognized that they had crucified the Lord of glory and the Son of God! That is why they asked, "What shall we do?" As a result, they were told, "Repent and be baptized every one of you, in the name of Jesus Christ, for the remission of your sins."

Such did not mean that they were earning or meriting their salvation, but they were simply obeying the Lord. Obedience to the gospel does not nullify grace. Mr. Cook told us that sanctification is by grace. We cannot earn sanctification and yet I think he tells us that is where baptism is going to go. He understands those principles. Being saved by grace through a faith that obeys God does not earn salvation. Therefore, when somebody gets up here and says, "Oh, now, you're talking about a works system, and you're trying to earn your salvation," that is just not so. That is a misrepresentation. It is a matter of what does the Lord say? 1 Peter 3:21 says, "Baptism doth also now save us." We are not just taking a bath, it is not the putting away of the filth of the flesh, but the answer of a good conscience, or the appeal of a good conscience toward God by the resurrection of Jesus Christ. Acts 22:16: "Arise and be baptized, washing away thy sins, calling on the name of the Lord" and friend, again, when you go home tonight and you lay your head on your pillow, it's not going to be about what Mr. Cook said, or what I've said. It is going to be about what this book teaches. Thank you very much.

Thursday Night

Second Negative

Gene Cook

I am pleased to be with you again for my final speech of the evening. I just want to say by way of introduction to this final speech, that I cannot respond to everything in a 30-minute period. I want to remind Mr. Reeves that this is the debate format that he chose, not I. I also want to remind Mr. Reeves that the reason why I had to spend the first part of my 30 minutes, rather than responding to his arguments, was because I had to clear up some things because of all the mischaracterizations that have taken place on Monday and Tuesday night. I will say this though, that in light of that, everything that I have said has been in the context of a response in this debate. Therefore, everything I said tonight was a response to what either Mr. Reeves said tonight, or he had said previously on Monday or Tuesday.

Getting back to the subject at hand, I would like to begin with this chart please. Now in Acts chapter 10, verse 44, we read, "while Peter was still speaking these words the Holy Spirit fell upon him, or rather fell upon all those who heard the word, and those of the circumcision who believed were astonished, as many as came with Peter, because the gift of the Holy Spirit had been poured out on the Gentiles also. For they heard them speaking with tongues and magnifying God. Then Peter answered, can anyone forbid water that these should not be baptized, who have received the Holy Spirit just as we have. And he commanded them to be baptized in the name of the Lord." Then they asked him to stay on for a few days. Was Cornelius a

Water Baptism & The New Birth
Let Scripture Explain Scripture
REGENERATION
John 3:5 (NKJV)
Jesus answered, "Most assuredly, I say to you, unless one is born of water and the Spirit, he cannot enter the kingdom of God.
Titus 3:5 (NKJV)
He saved us, through the washing of regeneration and renewing of the Holy Spirit,

regenerated man when he was baptized by the Holy Spirit? Well tonight, we heard Mr. Reeves say no, he was not. What does the Scripture say? Can I please call upon your chart (#73)? On chart (#73), we see here that Mr. Reeves makes an argument and he says that, he asks these rhetorical questions, was Cornelius saved while he was praying, when the angel appeared to him, when Peter began to speak, when the Holy Spirit came, or when he obeyed the command. He said no, he was not saved until he obeyed the command. However, is this not the same argument that he used for Abraham? I mean, in other words, he has totally flipped his argument.

When I showed you that Abraham was justified in Acts, I am sorry, in Genesis chapter 15, he came up and argued that there were certain things going on in the life of Abraham in chapter 12 that caused him to believe that Abraham was a justified man. What was that chart number Terry? Number 166 please. See this? He says Genesis 12:14 corresponds with Hebrews 11:8, Genesis 13:4, he says there were several things going on here that caused him to believe that Abraham was a justified man. Then he comes back and uses a completely different argument with Cornelius. Do you see that? Do you see that all these evidences of faith are taking place in the life of Cornelius, in fact more so, he received the gift of the Holy Spirit, than we see in the early chapters, mainly 12, 13, and 14 in the book of Genesis. I find that ironic that he would use this argument when he argued so vehemently against it. Now the question is, was Cornelius saved? Was he a regenerated man? Concerning Abraham, once again, I believe that the Father was drawing him. I do not believe he was regenerated until Genesis 15, or that he was actually justified until Genesis 15, and if I have time tonight, I will explain that. Acts 11:13, chart #35 please. Now this is Peter recounting the things that had happened there on that day as Cornelius, a Gentile, was praying to God and had a vision. Peter had a vision and Cornelius had a vision, and through this vision, they were brought together by the work of the Holy Spirit. Then as Peter began to preach to him, something happened. Peter relays this story in Acts 11:13, and he reports how he had seen the angel standing in the house and saying, "send to Joppa and have Simon, who is also called Peter, brought here, and he will speak words to you by which you will be saved, you and your household. And as I began to speak, the Holy Spirit fell upon him, just as it did upon us at the beginning and I remembered the word of the Lord which he used to say, John baptized with water but you will be baptized by the Holy Spirit."

What is happening here? Peter is preaching the gospel. Notice he is preaching the words by which you will be saved and he receives the Spirit, prior to his water baptism. Prior to his water baptism. Can the New Covenant gift of the Holy Spirit be given prior to justification? I mean, just from a common sense perspective, would we imagine that the New Covenant gift, that intimate fellowship that Jesus talked about in John 14 and in John 16, when he said, "I will send you a Comforter." He was speaking of the Holy Spirit. The Spirit had not yet been given because Jesus had not been ascended up on high, but when he had been ascended up on high, he gave the gift of the Holy Spirit. We see it first in Acts chapter 2. We are told that this is a baptism of the Holy Spirit. Are we to believe that people receive the comforter, the helper, the anointing, and they are not even Christians yet? I do not think so.

What does it say on chart #36 concerning Acts 15 verses 6-9? Now here we have the account of the Jerusalem Council, where all the Gentiles are now coming into the church, and they are not sure what is going on and so the leaders, the Apostles, are called together to go to Jerusalem and to discuss this issue of the Gentiles coming in. I mean, do they need to adhere to the Law of Moses? Should they be circumcised? All these are questions that were arising in their mind. Therefore, this event, the Jerusalem Council was centered on the fact that Gentiles were now coming into the church. In addition, it says in verse 6, "the Apostles and the elders came together to look into this matter. After there had been much debate, Peter stood up and said, brethren, you know that in the early days, God made a choice among you, that by my mouth the Gentiles would hear the word of the Gospel and believe." Sure enough, it happened, just as God had told them it would. The Gentiles would hear the word of the Gospel and believe through Peter, and verse 8, "and God who knows the heart, testified to them, giving them the Holy Spirit just as He also did to us, and He made no distinction between us and them, cleansing their hearts by faith." It is not as confusing as some would like to make it. We are saved from beginning to end by faith. We are told that on the cross, Jesus had the authority to forgive sins and pronounce somebody saved. Amen. But it was not just on the cross. It was on the day of Pentecost. It was throughout the book of Acts, all the way till Christ's second coming. Christ has the authority, the sole authority, to grant repentance and to regenerate. And so he does. Here we are told in verse 9, we are given divine commentary on Cornelius, divine commentary, commentary by the Holy Spirit. I love it when the Bible comments on the Bible because you know that the interpretation is true. What does it say? That he made no distinction between us and them, cleansing their hearts by faith. Now let me ask you a question. He made a big deal that the thief on the cross died and all of this took place before the Great Commission. After the Great Commission, were the Apostles re-baptized? No, they were not. They only had the baptism of John. There is no record, even in tradition, there is no record that any of the Apostles that were baptized, that took part in the ministry of John were re-baptized.

So why does Peter here say that the same thing that happened to us, now happened to Cornelius? You follow my reasoning here? It says in verse 9 that he made no distinction between us and them, cleansing their hearts by faith. Peter is saying our hearts were cleansed by faith. We did not submit to baptism in the name of the Father, Son, and the Holy Spirit. I mean, he is not saying that here but essentially, we know that he did not. So how was he made righteous? By faith. He had his heart cleansed by faith just as Cornelius did. Was Cornelius a regenerated man when he was baptized by the Holy Spirit? I will let you decide.

Concerning Acts 22:16, it refers to water baptism. No doubt. It says now, why do you delay, get up and be baptized, wash away your sins, calling upon the name of the Lord. This, I explained on Tuesday night, is another case where the sign and the thing signified are used interchangeably. Example, in case you were not here on Tuesday, John 1:36, "and he looked at Jesus as he walked," this is John the Baptist, "he looked at Jesus as he walked and he said, Behold the Lamb of God." Now if we were having a debate about the Lamb of God, Mr. Reeves, hypothetically speaking, if I can use an analogy here would get up and say, no, the Bible says that Jesus was the Lamb, and so Jesus must have four legs and a tail. I found out that lambs do have tails. The only lamb I have ever seen is in the zoo and I really did not pay much attention. However, my point is this. Look, Jesus Christ was the lamb because the lamb in the Old Testament was the typology that was pointing forward to the antitype, Jesus Christ, so much so that the two could be used interchangeably, that Jesus could be called the Lamb, and surely, he is. This is illustrated not only in the ministry of John the Baptist, but also in the book of Revelation. He is the Lamb. We know what that means. He is not the lamb meaning, "baa," like that. No. He is the Lamb because he has been the sacrificial Lamb of God. So much so that the type, the lamb itself, that little sheep, was pointing forward to Jesus Christ, the day that he would come.

Now let us look at the next chart. John 3:5 and let me demonstrate to you why this is not water baptism. By the way, the Roman Catholic Church also uses this as a proof text. It says in John 3:4, "Nicodemus said to Him, how can a man be born when he is old? He cannot enter a second time into his mother's womb and be born, can he? And Jesus answered, truly, truly I say to you, unless one is born of water and the Spirit, he cannot enter into the kingdom of God. That which is born of the flesh is flesh, and that which is born of the Spirit is Spirit, do not be amazed that I said to you, you must be born again. The wind blows where it wishes and you hear the sound of it, but you do not know where it comes from and where it is going. So is everyone who is born of the Spirit. Nicodemus said to Him, how can these things be and Jesus answered and said to him, are you a teacher of Israel and you do not understand these things?" Now why would Jesus say that last part? Are you a teacher of Israel and you do not understand these things? If Jesus here is talking about water baptism, if Jesus is talking about baptism of regeneration, what, in the Old Testament, which is the transcript that Nicodemus would use as a teacher of Israel, if he is a teacher of Israel, obviously he is using the Old Testament Scriptures. What in the Old Testament was it that Nicodemus should have been familiar with to tip him off on what Jesus was saying?

Remember, he says you must be born again, and Nicodemus says what am I going to do—crawl inside my mother's womb? I mean I am an old man. Jesus said, no, you must be born of water and the Spirit. Then he rebukes him, next chart please, in verse, on verse 9, he rebukes him and says, "Can these things be?" Jesus answered and said to him, are you a teacher of Israel and do not understand these things? Notice in this verse, there is no mention of baptism. Yet, Mr. Reeves says he understands the verses that refer to water baptism by their context. There is no mention of water baptism here. Jesus rebukes Nicodemus in verse 9. What was it that Nicodemus should have known? What was it that Nicodemus, as a teacher of Israel, should have been familiar with, in order to understand the things that Jesus was saying? Because Jesus gives us the impression that he is not teaching anything new here.

Well, I believe he is referring to Ezekiel 36 and verse 25. It says in verse 25, "then I will sprinkle clean water on you and you will be clean. I will cleanse you from all your filthiness and from your idols, moreover, I will give you a new heart, and put a new spirit within you, and I will remove the heart of stone from your flesh and I will give you a heart of flesh. I will put my spirit within you and cause you to walk in my statutes and you will be careful to observe my ordinances." Notice it is God who causes us to walk in his statutes. Is that clear? God causes us. If we are obedient to God, it is because of the power of the Spirit working through us in our lives, causing us to be obedient to God's ordinances. Now, look closely here, it says in verse

25, "but I will sprinkle clean water on you." What clean water is he talking about? There was no baptism in the Old Testament, not in the New Testament sense, there was a washing that took place with the priest, and there was a washing that took place for those who were Gentile proselytes.

In verse 5, Jesus says something very similar of John chapter 3. "Truly, truly I say to you, unless one is born of water and of the Spirit"—of water and of Spirit. Can you put up chart #167 please? Of water and of Spirit. Notice Ezekiel says, "I will sprinkle clean water on you and I will put my Spirit in you." Jesus says you must be born of water, *kai* even Spirit. Titus says in Titus 3:5 and 6, "he saved us not on the basis of deeds which we have done, but according to His mercy, by the washing of regeneration, washing of regeneration, and renewing by the Holy Spirit." You see, all of these, these three verses fit together. The thing that he is missing over here is Ezekiel chapter 36, because Ezekiel chapter 36 is talking about that New Covenant time when God would interact with his people in a completely new way. In fact, the writer of Hebrews alludes to this New Covenant language of Ezekiel 36 in reference to the New Covenant, that God, he takes our heart of stone, and he gives us a heart of flesh. He does this by his Holy Spirit. In John 7:38, the Holy Spirit is also reference to his water. Jesus says, "If any man come to me, out of his belly will flow rivers of living water."

John goes on to say, he was speaking of the Holy Spirit. However, the Holy Spirit had not yet been given because he had not ascended. He had not yet been glorified. Therefore, it is very common for the work of the Spirit to be used with the metaphor with water. Why? Because it is the work of the Spirit, through regeneration that cleanses our hearts by faith. That is exactly what Peter said about Cornelius and about himself, that he has done for him what he has done for us. He has cleansed our hearts by faith. Let us look at #42 Terry. I am sorry, not #42. Yes, #42, 42. Romans chapter 8, verse 5. Now, there was a lot of talk. He said, how could he say that a man must be regenerated? How can he say that in Acts 2:38, these men were pricked to the heart, these men were pricked to the heart and as a result, that meant they were regenerated. Where does it say that in the text? Well, in the text, it does not. However, when you go over to the epistles, it most certainly does. Romans 8:5, for those who are according to the flesh, set their minds on things of the flesh, but those who are according to the Spirit, the things of the Spirit." Notice, Paul is contrasting two different types of people: the man who is according to the flesh, and the man who is according to the Spirit. And then he says in verse 6, "for the mind set on the flesh is death, but the mind set on the Spirit is life and peace, because the mind set on the flesh is hostile toward God, for it does not even subject itself to the law of God, for it is not even able to do so, and those who are in the flesh cannot please God." Notice this, verse 8. "Those who are in the flesh cannot please God." Now the reason why I bring that to your attention is that one of the questions that I asked Mr. Reeves was, if somebody comes in faith to the waters of baptism, is that something that pleases God? He affirmed that. He said yes that is. Notice here, there is a contrast between the man that is in the flesh and the man who is in the Spirit, and he says that the man who is in the flesh, he cannot please God. Well, how do we know if a man is in the Spirit or a man is in the flesh? Well, thankfully, Paul tells us in the next verse. "However, you are not in the flesh, but in the Spirit if indeed the Spirit of God dwells in you. But if anyone does not have the Spirit of Christ, he does not belong to Him."

I hope you understand, and I think you do, my argument from this passage. The reason why I know that in Acts 2:38, when it says that those men were pricked in their heart and now they had a desire to please God, "What shall we do?" The reason why I know is because I compare Romans with Acts and I understand my theology of Acts through Romans that God makes an emphatic statement here, that no man who does not have his Spirit abiding in him, no man can please God. It is that simple. It is that clear. This is why I have been arguing all along that regeneration is unconditional. It has to be unconditional. It has to be unconditional because there is no way that we could ever receive the Spirit of God or we could ever be regenerated, more precisely, if this verse is true. Think about this. How could we be regenerated, how could we make a step toward God, if the Bible says that there is nothing that we can do to please God? The Bible also says that nobody seeks after God.

When I understand my salvation before God, I am not making this stuff up. I mean as many caricatures have been made about Calvinism, I believe this, not because I was raised in it, in fact I was not raised in it. I believe it because it is something that has been deduced from my study of God's word. This verse also, as I mentioned, destroys the notion of false, destroys the false notion of baptismal regeneration. How about verse 44? Verse 44, I am going to argue that Galatians 3:27 is not water baptism. It is not water baptism. Once again, I ask Mr. Reeves, how do you know if a verse is speaking about baptism of the Spirit or baptism of the water, or some other baptism? He said contextually. I agree. Galatians 3:27, "for all of you who were baptized into Christ have clothed yourselves with Christ." Look in the same chapter, Galatians 3:2. "This is the only thing I want to find out from you. Did you receive the Spirit by the works of the Law, or by hearing with faith? Are you so foolish having begun by the Spirit that you are now being perfected in the flesh?" Galatians 3:14, "in order that in Christ Jesus the blessing of Abraham might come to the Gentiles so that we would receive the promise of the Spirit through faith." The whole context of Galatians chapter 3 is the Spirit, the baptism of the Spirit. So now I'm supposed to believe that, based on everything Paul has taught me about beginning in the Spirit, I didn't really begin in the Spirit but the Spirit began in me when I jumped in the water? No, my friends. That is contrary, so contrary to the word of God. Are we reading the same Bible? I mean, if I had, and I am sure the same could be said for him, if we had more time, we could cite verses upon verses upon verses. We are trying to stick to the meat of the argument here.

Chart #46 please. 1 Peter 3:21 I believe, is speaking of water baptism. 1 Peter 3:21, "there is also an antitype which now saves you, baptism, not the removal of filth from the flesh, but the answer of God, or rather the answer of a good conscience toward God through the resurrection of Jesus Christ." Now something interesting has happened here, and I do not know if you noticed it. For whatever reasons, it seems it has been my perception; let me put it this way, it has been my perception, that Mr. Reeves prefers the New King James version, and the King James Version itself. That is my perception, I could be wrong. I have not asked him that question but when he puts up this verse, when he puts up 1 Peter 3:21 notice it is a new standard. Why is that? He puts up 1 Peter 3:21 in the New American Standard because contrary to the King James, and contrary to the New King James, it seems to support his argument. However, if you go back into the original language, you will find, actually, that the New King James and the King James provide a more literal translation.

That is why I posted the New King James here. The New King James says that this is not the removal of filth of the flesh, but the answer of a good conscience toward God. He wanted to make a big argument about how can we appeal for a good conscience. I would agree. We cannot. We cannot. However, baptism is an appeal or an answer of a good conscience, not *for* a good conscience, but *of* a good conscience. You can check that out in the King James Version. You can check it out in the New King James version. It is there. I believe it is a superior translation. You can go back to the original text and look. Which, it just fit with everything that I have been trying to tell you. Now here is another example, I believe, in 1 Peter 3:21, where the sign and the thing being signified are being spoken of interchangeably.

Christian baptism now saves us. Not literally, once again. I do not believe that this is a literal verse any more than I do the example of Jesus Christ being a literal lamb. What I am saying is this language of baptism is used interchangeably with the thing that it represents.

Now, let me ask you a question. We are told in this verse that baptism is the antitype of what happened with Noah. Some translations say, and now corresponding to the ark. Therefore, you have the story of Noah and then you have Christian baptism now. In addition, we are told that there is a correspondence, that they reference one another. Moreover, in like manner, just as Noah was saved through the water and the ark, so we are saved through water baptism. However, let me ask you a question. Does the Bible pronounce Noah as being a righteous man before or after he gets in the ark? Before. God pronounces in the word of God that he is a righteous man, that he is upright, that he is a righteous preacher, and that his message is firm. It represents God and God is pleased to use him. So if this is the antitype and Noah is saved before he gets on the ark, not saved from drowning of course, but he's saved by God, he's a righteous man we're told. Obviously, God's hand of protection was upon him. That is supposed to correspond to what Peter means here. It is not too much of a stretch to say so. If that is what Peter means and if Noah was a justified sinner before he got on the ark, so it is with us.

We are justified by faith. Our hearts are cleansed by faith and our baptism is a pledge from a good conscience. It is a pledge. Now what must I do? What tell me, what I need to do? Notice when that question is asked, you will never find anywhere the answer: "and you need to be born again." The Apostles do not say that in the book of Acts. What do they say? Be baptized, because they understand that this question is prompted by a changed heart, by a heart that is now been changed in opposition to God and his word. It has now been changed to the disposition of wanting to please God. It does so by the Holy Spirit working through that individual and sanctification.

By the way, if I can, you know, I have been rather portrayed as somebody, as somebody who does not think very highly of babies or something. Or my doctrine is uh, you know, anti baby. Let me just show you here that in this verse, you know, God saved eight people. Eight people. The rest of them drowned. Every single human being drowned with the exception of those eight people. God is a God of wrath and if people are not accounted righteous, and given the imputed righteousness of God, then the judgment of God will fall on them, not only in this life, but in the judgment to come.

I just want to appeal to you in my final moments. In a debate format, you always have one guy who speaks last, and as much as I'm sure Bruce would like to get up and respond to the things that I have said right now, I know, I know what he's feeling, because I felt the same way the last two nights that we debated. That is just the way the format is. That is just the way the nature of debate is. Once again, I want to concur with Mr. Reeves on this one thing. It is not about what Gene Cook says. It is not about what Bruce Reeves says. It is about what the word of God says. You are going to have to be persuaded and convicted in your own heart that you are standing on the truth. That is just between you and God. I want to appeal to you because the enemy of our soul is so clever in devising doctrines that will somehow either cause us to think of ourselves more highly than we should; or rather than place the (inaudible) of salvation on God, we, we are prone to place it on men because we are sinful individuals. And I just want to encourage you to go back and study these things for yourself, because if I'm right, if I'm right, and I believe with all of my heart that I am, there's going to be many people who are surprised on the day of judgment. I would hate for one of the listeners, somebody who sat within the distance of my voice proclaiming God's word, to be found among those that were cast out. May God bless you until we study together again.

Friday Night

Third Affirmative

Bruce Reeves

Good evening Ladies and Gentlemen, it is a pleasure to be with you. I certainly appreciate the fact that you are here and I want to join with the statements that were made regarding your presence and your conduct throughout this discussion. Many of you have been here every night, I appreciate that, and I know Mr. Cook does as well. I would feel remiss this evening if I did not take just a brief opportunity from a personal standpoint to express appreciation to Mr. Cook for his willingness to engage us in this particular discussion on this most vital and important issue, to the men who have aided me, brother Keith Sharp who has moderated for me, brother Don McClain who has aided me in the use of my charts and to all those who have aided me in the study of God's word. I have certainly enjoyed this time of study and discussion. I also want to express a special appreciation to my wife for her patience with me in my preparation for this debate. She has been very sacrificial because she recognizes the importance of what we are doing.

The proposition that has been read in your hearing is a very simple one. It was defined last night. I am affirming, "The Scriptures teach that water baptism is essential in order for the alien sinner to obtain the forgiveness of his past sins." Of course, Mr. Cook is denying this particular proposition.

I want to get right to his questions as I begin my discussion with you. He says in his first question, "On your chart, #256, in the last quote, you misquoted me again. I never said that Abraham was saved or exercised saving faith. Are you willing to retract that statement?" My answer to Mr. Cook would be, please explain to this audience when you believe Abraham had saving faith. Number two, "What should Nicodemus have known according to John 3:10. 'Jesus answered and said to him, are you the teacher of Israel and do not know these things'?" The answer is the spiritual nature of the new birth. Number three, "How was Cornelius' heart cleansed according to Acts 15:9, '...and He made no distinction between us and them, cleansing their hearts by faith.'" The answer to this question is that his heart was cleansed by faith. Number four, "What would God's word have to explicitly state to convince you that justification before God is by faith alone?" Well, it would have to **not** say that it is **not** by faith alone. And I might also respond to that question by asking Mr. Cook, what would it take to convince you that it is not by faith alone, when we understand James 2:24 says so? Number five, "Do you believe that men are predestined by God unto adoption as sons?" Yes.

I want to move on to some different things. There were so many things that I wanted to share with you from last night that I didn't have the opportunity to respond to, and there were some other things that I simply didn't get to.

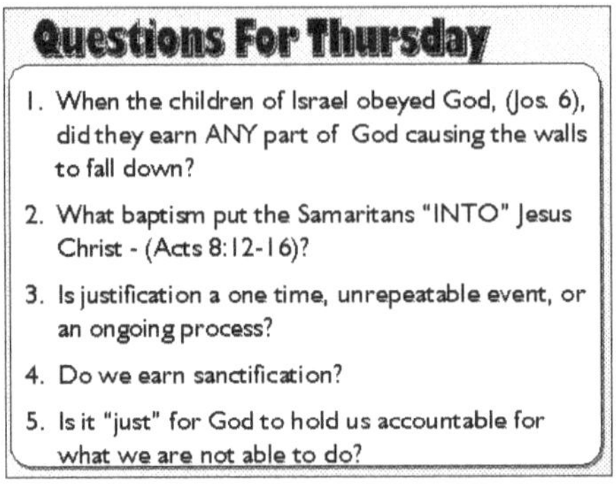
Questions For Thursday
1. When the children of Israel obeyed God, (Jos. 6), did they earn ANY part of God causing the walls to fall down?
2. What baptism put the Samaritans "INTO" Jesus Christ - (Acts 8:12-16)?
3. Is justification a one time, unrepeatable event, or an ongoing process?
4. Do we earn sanctification?
5. Is it "just" for God to hold us accountable for what we are not able to do?

Mr. Cook has properly defined our difference in this debate as being between the idea of faith only, or faith alone, and faith plus obedience so far as what is necessary for justification. I asked him last night, "When the children of Israel obeyed God in Joshua 6, did they earn any part of God causing the walls to fall down?" He said "no." Therefore, the children of Israel obeying God did not earn the falling down of those walls. We have been talking about baptism. Mr. Cook has told us that water baptism does not earn the benefit of the sacrifice of Jesus Christ and now he is saying to us that, when the children of Israel obeyed God, they were not earning any part of God causing the walls to fall down. That has been my position throughout this debate, that is, that obeying God does not earn salvation. You have heard a lot about this idea that I was teaching a works salvation, or that we earn salvation. However, even by Mr. Cook's

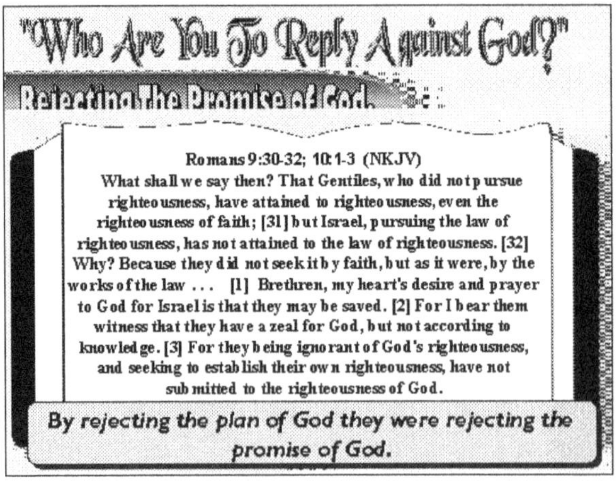
"Who Are You To Reply Against God?"
Rejecting The Promise of God.
Romans 9:30-32; 10:1-3 (NKJV)
What shall we say then? That Gentiles, who did not pursue righteousness, have attained to righteousness, even the righteousness of faith; [31] but Israel, pursuing the law of righteousness, has not attained to the law of righteousness. [32] Why? Because they did not seek it by faith, but as it were, by the works of the law ... [1] Brethren, my heart's desire and prayer to God for Israel is that they may be saved. [2] For I bear them witness that they have a zeal for God, but not according to knowledge. [3] For they being ignorant of God's righteousness, and seeking to establish their own righteousness, have not submitted to the righteousness of God.
By rejecting the plan of God they were rejecting the promise of God.

own admissions in his answer to this particular question, I think he should recognize better than that notion.

I want you to turn with me to the book of Romans as we think about this idea of faith. As we have looked in the book of Romans, we have noticed the kind of faith that saves us, the kind of faith that justifies us. Let us look at several passages together.

Let us read Romans 1:5, and the point I want to make to you is, as we see the word "faith" in the book of Romans, what you will notice, is it is a comprehensive term. It is inclusive of obedience to the Lord. Therefore, when Paul says we are saved by faith and not by works, the term works does not refer to obedience to the gospel of Jesus Christ. In Romans 1:5, "By whom we have received grace and apostleship for obedience to the faith, among all nations for His name." That is the focus of the book of Romans! We turn to Romans chapter 16 and in verse 26 and the Scripture would say to us there, "But now is made manifest and by the Scriptures of the prophets, according to the commandment of the everlasting God, made known to all nations." "Made known to all nations" for what? "For the obedience of faith." That is the meaning of the book of Romans.

We now turn our Bibles back to Romans the 6th chapter, and this is a very important point. In Romans the 6th chapter you will notice in verse 16, "Know ye not, that to whom you yield yourselves servants to obey, his servants ye are to whom you obey; whether of sin unto death, or of obedience unto righteousness." The word for *righteousness* there is the same word for justification. He said obedience leads to righteousness. Baptism is simply a part of that obedience.

Now turn to Romans chapter 10. It seems that Mr. Cook has been telling us in Romans the 10th chapter that this righteousness of God has reference to the imputed personal righteousness of Jesus. That is simply not the case. In fact, as you look at Romans the 10th chapter you must recognize that Romans is about the obedience of faith. When we talk about a saving faith, when we talk about a justifying faith, we are not talking about faith only. We are talking about a faith that obeys God. In Romans the 10th chapter Paul wrote, "Brethren my heart's desire and prayer to God for Israel is that they might be saved, for I bear them record that they have a zeal of God, but not according to knowledge." There are many people who believe religious philosophies and theologies and are zealous about those things, but they are simply not according to the truth. Verse 3, "For they being ignorant of God's righteousness and going about to establish their own righteousness, have not submitted themselves unto the righteousness of God." Friends, if the righteousness of God in this passage refers to the imputation of the personal righteousness of Jesus, what sense would this verse make? How would one submit to the imputation of the personal righteousness of Christ? That does not even make sense.

The fact is that the righteousness of God in this passage refers to those who submit to the conditions of the gospel of Jesus Christ. Romans 10:17 says, "So then faith comes by hearing and hearing by the word of God."

Mr. Cook has told us something else in this discussion. I asked him last night, "Is it just for God to hold us accountable for what we are not able to do?" He said "Yes." So it is just, he says to us, for God to hold somebody accountable for what they do not have the ability to do. He talked about Pelagius. Well I do not care what Pelagius said or anybody else, but I do care about what the Bible says. Mr. Cook's concept is that God will hold us accountable for that which we do not have the ability to do. The idea is that, if we are on the elect list, God miraculously enables us to meet certain conditions. If we are not on the elect list, even though God says, "Come," we cannot come. Now I want to think with you about the light that that puts God in. His idea is that we cannot seek God without this miraculous operation of the Holy Spirit, he even used Romans 8 which we will talk about in a little while, to try to say that water baptism is not essential. Think about that concept. Imagine for a minute that somebody's holding a piece of candy out in front of a small child, but the child is tied up to a tree. They say, "Come get this piece of candy," but they know the child cannot come and get the piece of candy. Yet they are holding it out in front of them. We say, "Come," but they cannot come. Is that just for God to hold a person in that situation responsible for that which they do not have the ability to do? That is the god of Reformed theology. That is the god of Calvinism. That is the god that has been presented to you this week.

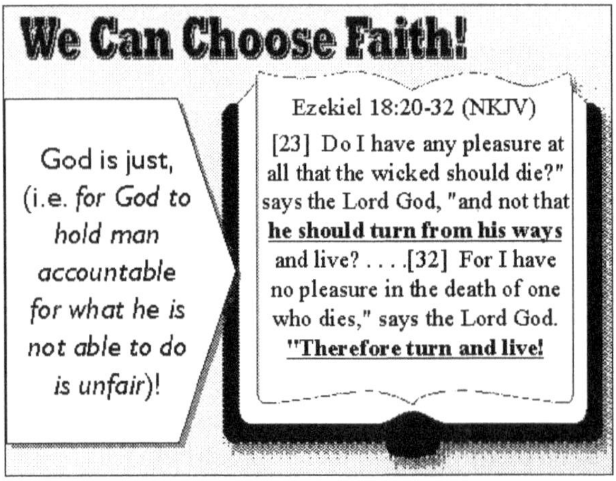
We Can Choose Faith!
God is just, (i.e. *for God to hold man accountable for what he is not able to do is unfair*)!
Ezekiel 18:20-32 (NKJV)
[23] Do I have any pleasure at all that the wicked should die?" says the Lord God, "and not that **he should turn from his ways** and live? . . . .[32] For I have no pleasure in the death of one who dies," says the Lord God. **"Therefore turn and live!**

Ezekiel 18 clearly indicates that such is not the case. God says, "I have no pleasure," I have no pleasure at all "that the wicked should die."

"'Do I have any pleasure at all that the wicked should die,' says the Lord God? 'And not that he should turn from his ways and live, for I have no pleasure in the death of the one who dies,' says the Lord God, 'Therefore, turn and live.'"

We have heard that regeneration is unconditional and that the non-elect cannot come, yet God holds them responsible for not coming, but they do not have the ability to come. Now, that is the light that God has been put in this week. It is almost as if, if you do not have it, you cannot get it. If you get it, you cannot lose it. If you lose it, you never had it. You can and you cannot. You will and you will not. You shall and you shall not. That seems to be what we have been told this week.

I want to talk some about the things we have heard and some of the problems we are having regarding Mr. Cook's denial of water baptism. We have looked at several passages that clearly affirm that water baptism is essential. We have looked at passages that talk about the fact that baptism puts us into Christ. The way that Mr. Cook has dealt with many of these passages, at least when we looked at Romans chapter 6, Colossians chapter 2, and Galatians chapter 3, is that he has told us the actual baptism that puts one into Christ, is Holy Spirit baptism. He goes to a passage, and he now redefines the terms by unnecessarily assuming secondary definitions. He asked me, "How do you determine what baptism is being discussed?" We understand it to be literal, unless the context demands otherwise.

You know, if this is the way that we are going to approach Scripture, if this is the way we are going to look at God's word, we are just going to take the secondary definition when a particular verse does not say what we want it to say, then this can get ridiculous after a while. Mark 16:16 says, "He that believeth and is baptized shall be saved." That is what that passage says to us. If I wanted to take the secondary definitions in this passage, I could actually turn that into something absurd. We could say, because belief can be an opinion, and because baptism is defined by Webster as sprinkling, even though the Bible doesn't define it that way, and because saved in Webster is defined as pickled in one of the secondary definitions, we could say that he that has an opinion and is sprinkled, shall be pickled. That is not what the passage is teaching. We cannot just assume secondary definitions.

Now turn in your Bibles to Mark 16:16. The Bible says there, "Go ye into all the world and preach the gospel to every creature. He that believeth and is baptized shall be saved, but he that believeth not shall be condemned." Mr. Cook asked me last night about a person who dies on his way to the baptistry. Well, first, he is trying to put me into the position of being a judge and that is not my role. I am to preach the gospel. Secondly, the gospel is not changed by a hypothetical. I want to ask Mr. Cook a question, "What about that elect man who is on his way to hear the gospel and would have believed but he dies before he gets there?" What about him? We have to be careful that we are not going to reason ourselves right outside of the gospel.

I want you now to turn to Acts the 2nd chapter, and verse 38. There were some arguments made about this verse that surprised me from Mr. Cook, in fact, disappointed me somewhat. The gospel is preached and in verse 36 we read, "Therefore let all the house of Israel know assuredly, that God has made that same Jesus, whom you have crucified, both Lord and Christ. Now when they heard this, they were pricked in their hearts and they said unto Peter and the rest of the apostles, 'Men and brethren, what shall we do?'" So Mr. Cook's argument has been, that by the time they are asking "Men and brethren what shall we do," they have already been regenerated. They are unconditionally regenerated and the very question they are asking is supposedly evidence of such according to Mr. Cook. His argument is that there was this miraculous quickening, that is, they were pricked and then they heard. That is not what the Bible says. The Bible says they heard, they heard the word of God, and they were pricked and then they asked the question. Now ladies and gentlemen, that is eisegesis because Mr. Cook is putting something in a passage that was not already there. Romans 10:17 says, "Faith comes by hearing and hearing by the word of God."

We have talked about Acts the 8th chapter and I have shown that Acts 8 makes it clear that Holy Spirit baptism is not the baptism that put the Samaritans into Christ, it's not the baptism that puts us into Jesus, and one of the things that Mr. Cook told us was that there was a difference between regeneration and Holy Spirit baptism. The Samaritans had been regenerated but had not received Holy Spirit baptism according to Mr. Cook. We know the Samaritans were saved and in Christ in verse 12 and Mr. Cook agrees with me about that point. Yet we know they had only been baptized in the name of Jesus Christ. Now that is water baptism and they were in Christ up in verse 12. A miraculous measure of the Holy Spirit had not fallen upon them, thus the passages in the epistles are clearly teaching us that water baptism is essential.

Now I want you to think about something. If the baptism that these epistles are talking about is Holy Spirit baptism and if water baptism is so closely connected to the idea of Holy Spirit baptism, thus Holy Spirit baptism is the baptism in Romans 6, Colossians 2, and Galatians 3:26 and 27. Yet we are told that it was regeneration that put the Samaritans into Christ, it would seem we have a contradiction. Which is it? Is it the regenerative measure or is it Holy Spirit baptism that puts one into Christ? Why does this happen? Because the teaching in this context destroys Mr. Cook's theology and proves that water baptism is the baptism that puts us into Christ.

What Put The Samaritans Into Christ?

One enters Christ through "baptism"

Romans 6:3-6; I Corinthians 12:13; Galatians 3:26,27

- The Samaritans were saved and "**in Christ**" in Acts 8:12. Yet, they had **only** been baptized in the name of Jesus Christ – (i.e. water baptism, Acts 10:47,48)
- They had received no miraculous measure of the Holy Spirit! (thus no Holy Spirit baptism had occurred!) – (Acts 8:15-17)
- Water baptism is the baptism of Romans 6:3-6; Galatians 3:27; & I Corinthians 12:13 which PUTS one INTO Christ!

Please turn your Bibles to Acts the 10th chapter with me. This was an argument that came up last night. I want to study with you about Cornelius. You know, Cornelius was a unique and non-repeatable event. The only two times that we can read about someone being described as receiving Holy Spirit baptism would be the Apostles on the day of Pentecost and Cornelius, and in both cases they spoke in tongues. Mr. Cook's argument regarding Cornelius was that the Holy Spirit falling on him proved he had already been regenerated prior to water baptism; therefore, water baptism was not essential. Now this is interesting because when we talk about the epistles, we were told water baptism and Holy Spirit baptism were just so closely identified with each other that to speak of one, was to speak of the other. However, Mr. Cook understands that in Acts 10 they can be separated, i.e. we can see them distinctively.

I want to mention to you that Cornelius knew some things about the Lord, i.e. he was not a raw pagan that did not know anything. In verse 2, we read that he feared and worshiped God. We would like to know tonight when it is that Mr. Cook thinks Cornelius was regenerated. We find that the word that God sent to the children of Israel regarding the peace of Christ had been heard by Cornelius. He also knew that Jesus was Lord of all and he knew about the works of Jesus. What did he not know? He had not been told what he must do in order to become a Christian. He had not been told that the Gentiles could be accepted by God. He was told, according to the word of God, what he needed to do in order to be regenerated or born again. He was told, "He will tell you what you must do." Peter was told that Cornelius had been "divinely instructed to hear words from you." Cornelius was told, "When he comes he will speak to you" and "He will tell you words by which you and your household will be saved."

Now Mr. Cook's argument has been and was last night, that because the Holy Spirit fell upon Cornelius before he was water baptized, that he was saved or justified before he was water baptized. I want to say that,

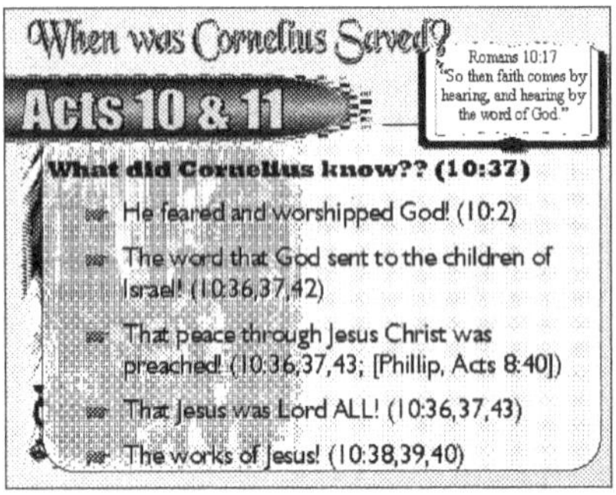
When was Cornelius Saved?
Acts 10 & 11
Romans 10:17
"So then faith comes by hearing, and hearing by the word of God."
What did Cornelius know?? (10:37)
He feared and worshipped God! (10:2)
The word that God sent to the children of Israel! (10:36,37,42)
That peace through Jesus Christ was preached! (10:36,37,43; [Phillip, Acts 8:40])
That Jesus was Lord ALL! (10:36,37,43)
The works of Jesus! (10:38,39,40)

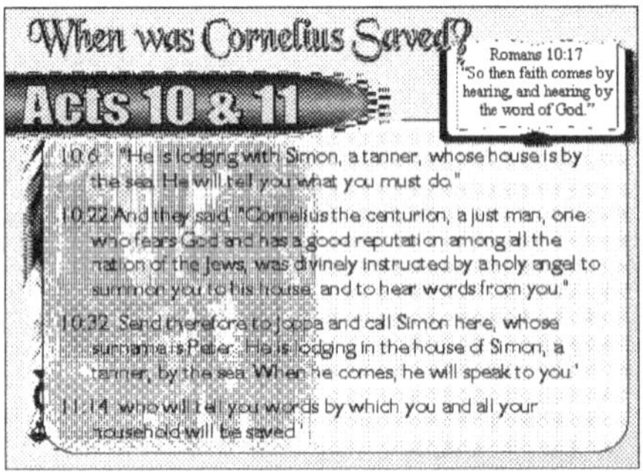
When was Cornelius Saved?
Acts 10 & 11
Romans 10:17
"So then faith comes by hearing, and hearing by the word of God."
10:6 "He is lodging with Simon, a tanner, whose house is by the sea. He will tell you what you must do."
10:22 And they said, "Cornelius the centurion, a just man, one who fears God and has a good reputation among all the nation of the Jews, was divinely instructed by a holy angel to summon you to his house, and to hear words from you."
10:32 Send therefore to Joppa and call Simon here, whose surname is Peter. He is lodging in the house of Simon, a tanner, by the sea. When he comes, he will speak to you.'
11:14 who will tell you words by which you and all your household will be saved.'

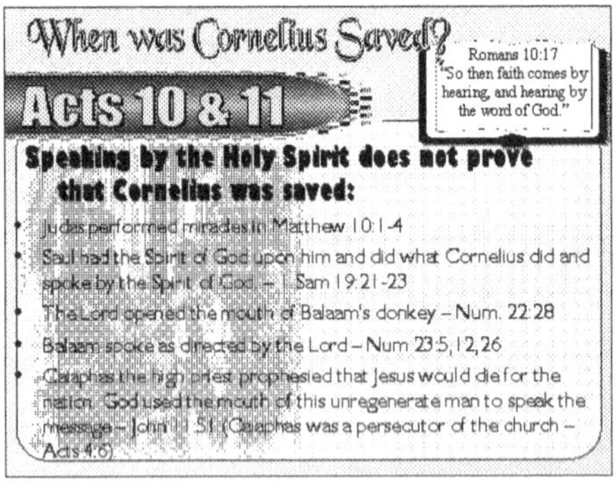
When was Cornelius Saved?
Acts 10 & 11
Romans 10:17
"So then faith comes by hearing, and hearing by the word of God."
Speaking by the Holy Spirit does not prove that Cornelius was saved:
Judas performed miracles in Matthew 10:1-4
Saul had the Spirit of God upon him and did what Cornelius did and spoke by the Spirit of God. – 1 Sam 19:21-23
The Lord opened the mouth of Balaam's donkey – Num. 22:28
Balaam spoke as directed by the Lord – Num 23:5,12,26
Caiaphas the high priest prophesied that Jesus would die for the nation. God used the mouth of this unregenerate man to speak the message – John 11:51 (Caiaphas was a persecutor of the church – Acts 4:6)

that just is not so! In Matthew the 10th chapter, we read about Judas. Now, certainly I would disagree with Mr. Cook about his view of what he would call the security of the believer. I think the believer has security, but not the kind that he would think of, i.e. the idea of once saved, always saved. Look at Matthew 10:1: "When he had called unto Him His twelve disciples, He gave them power against unclean spirits, to cast them out, and to heal all manner of sickness and all manner of disease." Judas had that power, friends. Down in verses 2, 3, and 4, you will see Judas Iscariot, who betrayed Christ, had that power. Just because the Spirit is working in and through a man, does it mean he is saved Mr. Cook? Now, was Judas doing this by the power of the Spirit? If his idea of "once saved, always saved" is true and if you lose it, you never had it, we have a problem here because we know Judas was not saved according to Mr. Cook. On the other hand, it would disprove this notion that if the Spirit is working in and through somebody that must mean that they are saved. Which one will be given up? The argument on Cornelius or once saved always saved.

We heard about Acts chapter 15. It says, "Their hearts were purified by faith." Mr. Cook believes they were regenerated and then they were

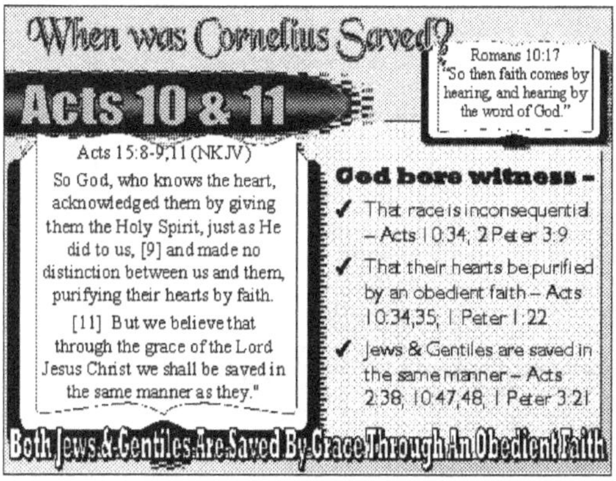
When was Cornelius Saved?
Acts 10 & 11
Romans 10:17
"So then faith comes by hearing, and hearing by the word of God."
Acts 15:8-9,11 (NKJV)
So God, who knows the heart, acknowledged them by giving them the Holy Spirit, just as He did to us, [9] and made no distinction between us and them, purifying their hearts by faith.
[11] But we believe that through the grace of the Lord Jesus Christ we shall be saved in the same manner as they."
God bore witness -
✓ That race is inconsequential – Acts 10:34; 2 Peter 3:9
✓ That their hearts be purified by an obedient faith – Acts 10:34,35; 1 Peter 1:22
✓ Jews & Gentiles are saved in the same manner – Acts 2:38; 10:47,48; 1 Peter 3:21
Both Jews & Gentiles Are Saved By Grace Through An Obedient Faith

given faith because of that regeneration. So really, their hearts were purified by this miraculous regeneration, rather than understanding, they exercised faith and then they were born again.

I want to go on to something else that has been mentioned. We talked about the lamb and whether or not the lamb had a tail. I think we got that straightened out (laughter). Mr. Cook has said that these verses that speak of baptism are speaking of water baptism, but that water baptism is merely a sign of salvation. He mentioned that Jesus is described as a Lamb, but we know he was not literally a Lamb and he cited John 1:36. John 1:29 says something very similar. So he has told us here, in Mark 16:16, baptism was just a sign of something else. He told us the same thing about Acts chapter 2 and verse 38, Acts chapter 22 and verse 16, and about 1 Peter chapter 3 and verse 21. There is a problem here and I want you to think about it. If the Lamb of God is the sign, does he literally take away the sins of the world? If that is the case, then baptism to him is a sign, and is literally involved in taking away sin. That in no way disproves that baptism is essential. Thank

Mr. Cook's Contradictions
The Sign And The Thing Signified
Mr. Cook Has Said That These Verses Are Speaking of Water Baptism
Mark 16:16 (NKJV)
He who believes and is baptized will be saved; but he who does not believe will be condemned.
John 1:29,36 (NKJV)
The next day John saw Jesus coming toward him, and said, "Behold! The Lamb of God who takes away the sin of the world!

Mr. Cook's Contradictions
The Sign And The Thing Signified
Mr. Cook Has Said That These Verses Are Speaking of Water Baptism
Acts 2:38 (NKJV)
Then Peter said to them, "Repent, and let every one of you be baptized in the name of Jesus Christ for the remission of sins; and you shall receive the gift of the Holy Spirit.
John 1:29,36 (NKJV)
The next day John saw Jesus coming toward him, and said, "Behold! The Lamb of God who takes away the sin of the world!

you, Mr. Cook, for that. Thank you. That is absolutely right.

I want you to turn to 1 Peter chapter 3 and verse 21. Now Mr. Cook made an accusation last night. He said, "Bruce has been using the New King James Version, and now he is using the New American Standard Bible." He got on to me about that as if I was trying to distort this passage. No, I use, in my Bible Study, the Old King James, the New King James and the

Mr. Cook's Contradictions
The Sign And The Thing Signified
Mr. Cook Has Said That These Verses Are Speaking of Water Baptism
Acts 22:16 (NKJV) And now why are you waiting? Arise and be baptized, and wash away your sins, calling on the name of the Lord.'
John 1:29,36 (NKJV) The next day John saw Jesus coming toward him, and said, "Behold! The Lamb of God who takes away the sin of the world!

Mr. Cook's Contradictions
The Sign And The Thing Signified
Mr. Cook Has Said That These Verses Are Speaking of Water Baptism
1 Pet 3:21 (NKJV) There is also an antitype which now saves us--baptism (not the removal of the filth of the flesh, but the answer of a good conscience toward God), through the resurrection of Jesus Christ,
John 1:29,36 (NKJV) The next day John saw Jesus coming toward him, and said, "Behold! The Lamb of God who takes away the sin of the world!

New American Standard. The important thing is to understand the meaning of the context. However, it is odd; I know he uses the New American Standard Version. Yet he said in his case, he preferred to use the New King James Version in reference to 1 Peter 3:21. Therefore, the very thing he is accusing me of, he was doing that very thing. On this chart, I put both the New King James version and the New American Standard Bible up.

He mentioned that this idea of appeal is not really the best translation. That is what I was told. However, you know, that just does not match up with the evidence. The fact is, that is exactly what the Bible is teaching in 1 Peter 3:21. Vine's *Dictionary*, in talking about this question, mentions that the term means "an interrogation, primarily a question or inquiry, denoting a demand or appeal. Some take the word to indicate that baptism affords a good conscience, an appeal against the accuser," and then he goes on to say this, "1 Peter 3:21 is not as in the Authorized Version an answer. It was used by the Greeks in a legal sense as a demand or appeal."

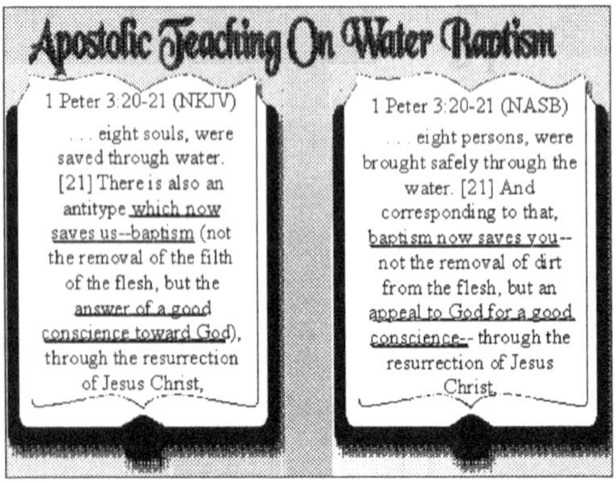
Apostolic Teaching On Water Baptism
1 Peter 3:20-21 (NKJV) . . . eight souls, were saved through water. [21] There is also an antitype which now saves us--baptism (not the removal of the filth of the flesh, but the answer of a good conscience toward God), through the resurrection of Jesus Christ,
1 Peter 3:20-21 (NASB) . . . eight persons, were brought safely through the water. [21] And corresponding to that, baptism now saves you--not the removal of dirt from the flesh, but an appeal to God for a good conscience--through the resurrection of Jesus Christ,

Now who is representing to you what the Bible teaches? My point was that "baptism doth also now save us." It is not just "the putting away of the filth of the flesh, but it is the appeal" or "answer of a good conscience toward God." Why would I be appealing for that if I already had it? It clearly affirms my position. J.H. Thayer says, "Which baptism now saves us. Not because in receiving it we have put away the filth of the flesh but because we have earnestly sought a conscience reconciled to God." That is exactly what

I was telling you. Arndt & Gingrich, "Baptism is an appeal to God for a clear conscience." It is not just Bruce Reeves. It is not just members of the church of Christ. Kittle's *Theological Dictionary*: "Baptism does not confer physical cleansing but saves as a request for forgiveness." Charles B. Williams, he was a Baptist, a Baptist scholar. He said, "Baptism is the craving for a clear conscience toward God." That was the point that I was making to you. Thayer says, "It's an inquiry, a question," that kind of thing.

Now, I want to move on. Mr. Cook brought up the babies again and he was talking about 1 Peter 3:21 and said, "You have heard a lot of things regarding my doctrine about the babies" and he mentioned that you have eight saved, and all these other people perished, and I took from that, that he was saying that it was within the nature of God, not only to condemn physically this vast majority of people, which would have included infants, but also that he would do so spiritually and

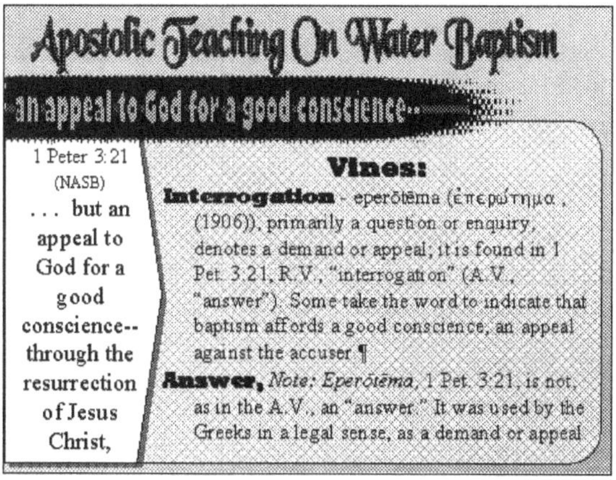
Apostolic Teaching On Water Baptism
an appeal to God for a good conscience--
1 Peter 3:21 (NASB)
. . . but an appeal to God for a good conscience--through the resurrection of Jesus Christ,
Vines:
Interrogation - eperōtēma (ἐπερώτημα, (1906)), primarily a question or enquiry, denotes a demand or appeal; it is found in 1 Pet. 3:21, R.V., "interrogation" (A.V., "answer"). Some take the word to indicate that baptism affords a good conscience, an appeal against the accuser ¶
Answer, *Note: Eperōtēma*, 1 Pet. 3:21, is not, as in the A.V., an "answer." It was used by the Greeks in a legal sense, as a demand or appeal

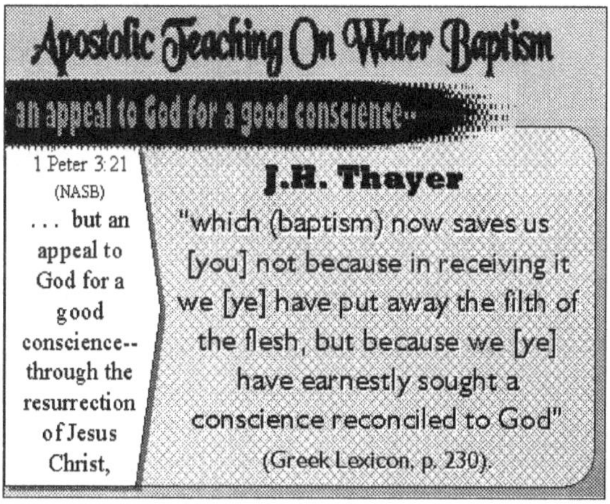
Apostolic Teaching On Water Baptism
an appeal to God for a good conscience--
1 Peter 3:21 (NASB)
. . . but an appeal to God for a good conscience--through the resurrection of Jesus Christ,
J.H. Thayer
"which (baptism) now saves us [you] not because in receiving it we [ye] have put away the filth of the flesh, but because we [ye] have earnestly sought a conscience reconciled to God"
(Greek Lexicon, p. 230).

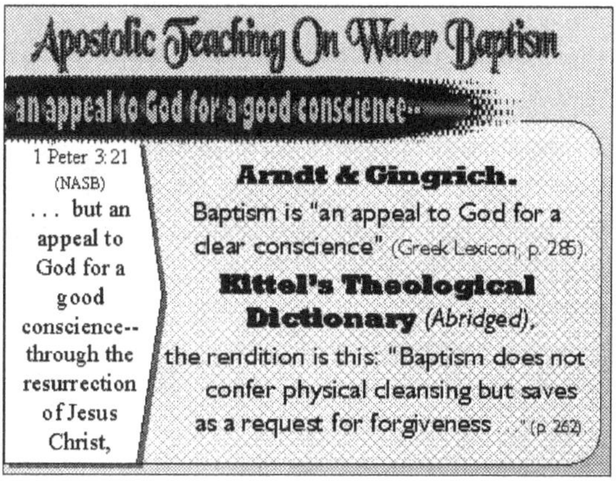
Apostolic Teaching On Water Baptism
an appeal to God for a good conscience--
1 Peter 3:21 (NASB)
. . . but an appeal to God for a good conscience--through the resurrection of Jesus Christ,
Arndt & Gingrich.
Baptism is "an appeal to God for a clear conscience" (Greek Lexicon, p. 285).
Kittel's Theological Dictionary (Abridged),
the rendition is this: "Baptism does not confer physical cleansing but saves as a request for forgiveness . . ." (p. 262)

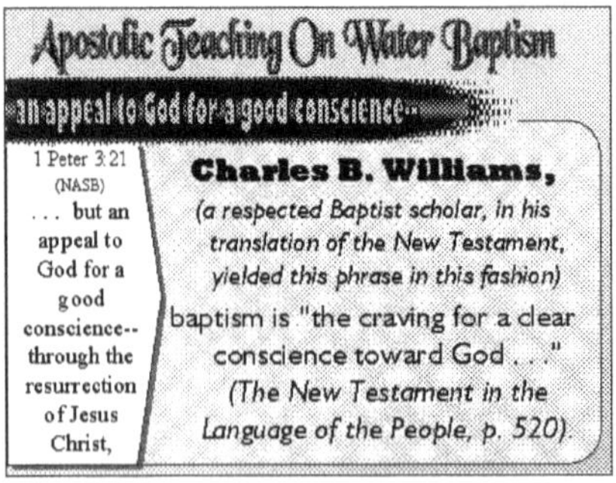
Apostolic Teaching On Water Baptism
an appeal to God for a good conscience--
1 Peter 3:21 (NASB)
. . . but an appeal to God for a good conscience--through the resurrection of Jesus Christ,
Charles B. Williams,
(a respected Baptist scholar, in his translation of the New Testament, yielded this phrase in this fashion)
baptism is "the craving for a clear conscience toward God . . ."
(The New Testament in the Language of the People, p. 520).

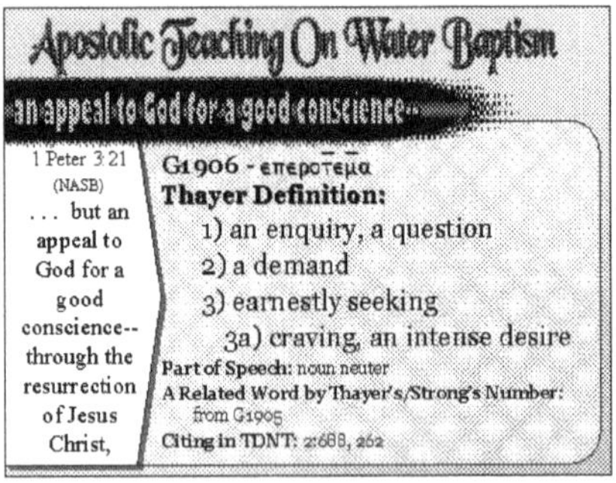
Apostolic Teaching On Water Baptism
an appeal to God for a good conscience--
1 Peter 3:21 (NASB)
. . . but an appeal to God for a good conscience--through the resurrection of Jesus Christ,
G1906 - επεροτεμα
Thayer Definition:
1) an enquiry, a question
2) a demand
3) earnestly seeking
3a) craving, an intense desire
Part of Speech: noun neuter
A Related Word by Thayer's/Strong's Number: from G1905
Citing in TDNT: 2:688, 262

that those non-elect babies would be condemned and that is the consequence of his position. I want you to understand what he really believes. This is the consequence of the doctrine. Listen to me, this theology is dark. If you want to talk about depravity, it is a depraved doctrine, in that it is teaching us that unconditionally we have one little baby that is non-elect and the other one is elect. One dies and goes to heaven and the other dies and goes to hell. Play the quote: "Non-elect infants who die in their infancy will spend eternity in Hell. I would answer true to that question. You have to be elect in order to be saved. If this question is false, then we should perform abortion, because abortion is the greatest evangelistic act that has ever taken place since the time that Jesus walked the face of the earth. Because every one of those children are going straight to heaven, according to Mr. Brown's theology."

The Nature of God
" 'Non elect infants who die in their infancy will spend eternity in hell' – I would answer true to that question, you have to be elect in order to be saved. If this question is false, then we should perform abortion, because abortion is the greatest evangelistic act that has ever taken place since the time that Jesus walked the face of the earth, because everyone of those children are going straight to heaven according to Mr. Brown's theology"
(David P. Brown & Gene Cook, Jr. Debate, Feb 16, 2000)

Let us understand why Mr. Cook takes that position and why those who believe Reformed Theology take that

The Nature of God
Which is Lacking: Power or Love?
If some men are unconditionally elected -
Then God does not will to save the LARGE majority

position. It is because of his view of sovereignty. I believe in the sovereignty of God, but not Reformed Theology's view of sovereignty. I want you to understand exactly what is being argued here and why we are being taught some of these things. Mr. Cook has said, (Quote is played): "God is sovereign; the devil is God's devil. He does what God allows him to do. He does what God commands him to do and no more and no less." The devil is God's devil. The devil, and he said that is right. The devil is God's devil. He does no more and no less than what God commanded him to do. It would be one thing to talk about God allowing it, whatever vicious thing we can imagine, whatever sinful, horrible, unbelievable thing that has ever happened—Gene Cook says the devil did it and God commanded him to do it. So, actually, when the devil was doing that, he was fulfilling the **will of God**! Those are the consequences of this doctrine, that is exactly what we have been told, and that is what he said about 1 Peter chapter 3 and verse 21.

He mentioned several things regarding John 3:5. He argued that in John 3:5 and Titus 3:5, that the word "and" means "even as." No standard translation renders it that way and if you will look at this chart, you will notice it broken down. John 3:5: "Born of the water and the Spirit," Titus 3:5: "Washing of regeneration and the renewing of the Holy Spirit," and Ephesians 5:26: "Washing of water by the word." You will clearly see we are talking about water baptism. Why does Mr. Cook want to redefine the terms? Why is it? Because they do not fit his theology.

Water Baptism & The New Birth
Let Scripture Explain Scripture
REGENERATION
John 3:5
Titus 3:5
Ephes. 5:26
born of water
washing of regeneration
washing of water
and the Spirit
and renewing of the Holy Spirit
by the word,

He mentioned Romans chapter 8 and he talked about being filled with the Spirit. What does that mean? Romans 8:14 says we are "led by the Spirit." Romans 8:2 talks about "the law of the Spirit of life in Christ Jesus," i.e. the gospel of Jesus Christ. It is through submission to the gospel of Christ that I have hope.

In John 1:12 we read that we have "power to become the sons of God, even to them that believe on His name." Who is it that exercises that power? Who is it that exercises that right? It is the one who is baptized into Christ on the condition of his faith according to Galatians chapter 3 and verses 26 and 27.

Mr. Cook told us that Romans 6 and Colossians 2 describe a burial in the Holy Spirit. You know, I am wondering, if I am buried in the Holy Spirit, am I raised up from the Holy Spirit? The same thing by which he gets the sinner, he loses the sinner. He says you have to be buried in the Holy Spirit. If that burial is talking about burial in the Holy Spirit, then when someone is raised up, he is raised up out of the Spirit. The fact is

Children of God By Faith In Christ
Who Has The Right To Become Children of God?
John 1:12 (NKJV)
But as many as received Him, to them He gave the right to become children of God, to those who believe in His name:
Gal. 3:26-27 (NKJV)
For you are all sons of God through faith in Christ Jesus. [27] For as many of you as were baptized into Christ have put on Christ.

that this passage is talking about water baptism. I have faith, and I am baptized into Jesus Christ. I am baptized **into** Jesus Christ and that harmonizes with all of the other things that we see in the Scripture.

That answers, for the most part, his speech last night and it is simply not so. It is simply not so. Now you are going to hear many theological terms and you are going to hear a lot of redefining of terms, and you are going to see all that, and I want you to pay very close attention. I want you to pay very close attention to what Mr. Cook is going to say as he attempts to negate this proposition. Thank you very much. Listen very attentively to Gene Cook.

Third Negative

Gene Cook

It is a pleasure to be with you once again tonight. I do appreciate your patience in this discussion that we are having here and I hope it has been beneficial to you. Sometimes it is very valuable to see two sides of an issue rather than one and so I am very much in favor of this type of medium. I want to begin by answering the questions that have been submitted to me by Mr. Reeves. The first question is "In Colossians 2:11-12, what is the element into which one is buried?" I would say his death. Through baptism, we are united to Christ in his death. Number two: "What Scripture would you use to prove that water baptism is a burial?" Romans 6 and Colossians 2:11-12. Now his argument is going to be that, I thought you said that is not water baptism. That is right. It is not water baptism, it is a baptism of the, it is the baptizing work of the Holy Spirit, but it uses the same language. That has been my position all along, that the language can be used interchangeably. It is not referring to water baptism but it does use the same, the same terminology, baptism, which points us back from water baptism when we see that language concerning water baptism. Number three: "Since you stated last night that the word "and" meant "even as" in John 3:5, what standard translations would you use to substantiate such a claim?" Terry if you'll escape that and bring up the Bible program there, because I just got this question before the debate began, didn't have time to put it up on a chart. If you will shrink up first, or enlarge James right there in the bottom of the screen, James 3:9. Reading from the King James Version: "Therefore we bless God even the Father." See that word even in there. That is the word *kai*. That same word is used in John chapter 3 verse 5.

Now can you bring up Thayer's definition please, by shrinking that down and it is over there on the lower left hand corner. Thayer's definition—definition Roman numeral number two and scroll down a little bit on that please. Okay. See that B added to words designating the cause; it marks something, which follows of necessity from that which has been previously said. Therefore, when we say "God even the Father," it is not saying two different things. It is saying that God, even our Father, or God is our Father. Therefore, it is totally legitimate what I have stated last night in my discussion. Okay, I am done with that Bible program there.

Question number four: "Did I understand you to say last night that neither water baptism nor Holy Spirit baptism put the Samaritans into Christ?" Yes you did. I am glad you understood me to say that because I have been saying all along that what puts us into Christ is saving faith in the gospel, or saving faith in Jesus Christ himself. He wants to know when Cornelius was regenerated. When Cornelius believed God, it was reckoned to him as righteousness, just as it was with Abraham. There is one plan of salvation from beginning to end. In fact, the Scripture says that the gospel was preached before Jesus Christ, did you know that? The gospel was preached beforehand to Abraham. That is why Abraham was a justified man, because he believed the gospel. That is the fifth question. "At what point was Cornelius regenerated?" When he believed the gospel. When did that happen? Before the apostles got there or after the apostles got there? When he believed the gospel. There were—remember it is my position that there are regenerated men in the Old Testament. I belabored the point by showing you that men had their hearts circumcised in the Old Testament and according to the book of Deuteronomy; we know that God promised to circumcise their hearts, and the hearts of their children. Well, what does Paul tell us in Romans chapter 2 verse 20? That, that circumcision of the heart is by the Spirit of God, it is the work of the Spirit. I see no confusion here.

Let me begin with my presentation. The reason why we have such a sharp difference of opinion on what these verses mean, I believe, is that we preach a different gospel. Now listen to this very carefully. "I'm amazed that you are so quickly deserting him who called you by the grace of Christ for a different gospel." That means that there are different gospels. There are different gospels, and from what I have heard, his gospel is the same gospel of the Mormon Church. It is the same gospel of the Oneness Pentecostals, it is the same gospel of the Jehovah's Witnesses, and it is, what does the *Book of Mormon* say? "We are saved by grace after all that we can do." Faith and works. It is the gospel of the Roman Catholic church. The gospel that sets itself from all the gospels of men's imaginations, is the gospel of grace and you are about to hear what the gospel of grace is. This is the gospel by which you will be saved. If you reject this gospel, you will be judged, you will be damned, and you will spend eternity paying for your sins. He says that there is a different gospel, verse 7. "Which is really not another, only there are some that are disturbing you and want to distort the gospel of Christ. Even if we or an angel from heaven should preach to you a gospel contrary to that which we have preached to you, he is to be accursed. As we have said before, I say again. If any man is preaching you a gospel contrary to that which you have received, he is to be accursed." The word "accursed" there is the word *anathema*. It is the strongest word in Greek for condemnation. He says it twice. Anybody that preaches another gospel is anathema, is eternally condemned.

Now would it not be nice if the Bible defined for us what the true gospel consisted of? In other words, the Bible says that we are saved through faith in the gospel. What is the gospel? Galatians 3:27 says, "For all of you who were baptized into Christ have clothed yourselves with Christ." Galatians 3:2, "This is the only thing I want to find out from you. Did you receive the Spirit by the works of the law, or by the hearing of faith? Are you so foolish, having begun by the Spirit, you are now being perfected in the flesh?" That is a rhetorical question. Who would be foolish enough to begin in the Spirit and then try to perfect that work that is begun in the Spirit, by the flesh?

Baptism is distinct from the gospel of grace. Baptism is not part of the gospel. With all due respect, it sounds like a broken record. Baptism, baptism, baptism, baptism. It is like the idol of baptism. In fact, I wrote a book called "The Baptism Cult." It is a different church—the International Church of Christ. They say you have to be born again through baptism in their church. They would present the same arguments that we have heard tonight.

Well, baptism is distinct from the gospel according to the Bible. This is very important for you to know, because my opponent has been arguing that we are saved by water baptism. No, baptism is an obedience. It is an evangelical or a Christian obedience. We are saved, and once we are saved, we desire to be obedient. That is why when they were pricked in their heart they said, "What must I do to be saved?" That is why, when we become regenerated, we have a desire to walk with God and to do that which he commands. That is obedience.

Bruce wants to talk about the "obedience of faith." He wants to take that, turn it around, and say no, faith is obedience. It is all obedience. In 1 Corinthians 1:17 Paul says, "For Christ did not send me to baptize, but to preach the gospel, not with wisdom of words lest the cross of Christ be made of no effect." You see there, the gospel was distinct from baptism. If it was baptism that actually saved a person, don't you think that Paul would say, "God sent me to baptize," or at least, "God sent me to save people through preaching and baptism." No, he does not say that at all. Because he realizes that baptism is only a sign that points to a spiritual reality. Therefore, he makes a distinction between baptism and the gospel.

1 Corinthians 15. Paul is going to tell us what the gospel is in very clear terms. You do not have to have a Greek concordance. You do not have to have 150 charts to figure it out. It is very simple; in fact, it is so simple that even a child can understand it. He says in 1 Corinthians 15, verses 1 and 2, "Now I make known to you the gospel which I preached to you, which also you received, and in which also you stand by which also you are saved if you hold fast to the word which I preached to you, unless you believed in vain." Now, notice that this is the gospel that Paul preached to them. He's about to tell us the gospel that he preached to them. This is also the gospel that they received. He says, "which also you received." This is also the gospel, which causes them to stand, and it is the gospel by which they are saved. In verse 3, "I delivered to you as of first importance water baptism." Is that what it says? No, that is not what it says at all. In fact, you can search in vain and you will not find one drop of water in 1 Corinthians 15, verse 3. "For I delivered to you as of first importance, what I also received, that Christ died for our sins according to the Scriptures, and that He was buried, and He was raised on the third day, according to the Scriptures, and He appeared to Cephas and then the twelve, and after that He appeared to more than 500 brethren at one time, most of whom remain until now. But some have fallen asleep. And then he appeared to James and to all the apostles and last of all, as to one untimely born, He appeared to me also."

This is the gospel: having faith, having belief that comes from the heart, in the death, burial, and resurrection of Jesus Christ. The word "gospel" is the word for good news. This is the good news. There is no good news in Mr. Reeves' gospel. Let me tell you why. If there were good news in Mr. Reeves' gospel, then Christ would not have needed to die. Why is that? Because in the Old Testament God gave men instruction. He told men where to sacrifice. He gave them his law. Right? In the New Covenant, what does he do? Do you think he turns around and says, OK, well let us try it over again? Get baptized, there is the first commandment. Then, here are the laws; you have to keep these. As long as you keep these you will be justified, but the moment you break them, we are back to square one. Is that good news? No. That is the same condemnation and slavery of the Old Testament. Because man cannot keep it. Man cannot—and let me tell you why you need the imputed righteousness of Jesus Christ. It is not enough to just have your sins forgiven. Because sin is a transgression of God's law. What about the positive commands of God's law? You see, Christ keeps for me, as I receive his imputed righteousness; Christ also keeps for me the positive commands of the law.

The law says you shall love the Lord God with all your heart, with all your soul, with all your mind and with all your strength. That is a positive command. Have you done that? Have you done that today? Have you done that every minute of every hour? Have you done that every second of every hour—can you say that you love God with all of your heart, with all of your soul, with all of your strength? What about loving your neighbor as yourself? You are driving home and you see two Mormon missionaries riding down the sidewalk, and you do not stop. Can you really say that you love them as yourself? If you did not stop, I mean, if that were you on that Mormon missionary bicycle, would you want somebody to stop if you were on your way to Hell? This is why we need the imputed—this is why Christ has become my righteousness. His death takes away my sins but his life marks me as God's own child, and as a result, I am accounted as righteousness. I will stand on the Day of Judgment, not because of my own good works, not because of my obedience, but because of the righteousness of Christ. I will stand on the day of judgment, because his righteousness has become my righteousness, and because he has clothed me in a white garment. I did not clothe myself. I cannot stand before God in my own filthy righteousness, as Isaiah calls it.

In Acts chapter 3, verse 12 through 26, Peter is preaching there. This is shortly after Pentecost. Peter is preaching there and he does not refer to baptism but links forgiveness of sins to repentance in Acts 3:19 where it says, "Repent therefore, and be converted that your sins may be blotted out so that times of refreshing may come from the presence of the Lord." If baptism was necessary for the forgiveness of sins, and Peter has a new audience, why did he not tell them? The answer is quite simple; because it is not. We saw last night, and he brought this up again and I am glad he did. In Acts 15:8-9, he agreed that they had had their hearts cleansed by faith, just as it said. This is speaking of Cornelius. Cornelius had his heart cleansed by faith. In Romans 10:17, "So then faith comes by hearing, and hearing by the word of God." Hearing is regeneration. A dead man cannot hear if the Bible says that his condition is one of deafness. A blind man cannot see, a dead man cannot get up and walk. Yet those are all metaphors for those that are outside of the body of Christ. We are said to be deaf, dumb, blind, miserable, naked, and there is even more that I have forgot.

Therefore, we are going to come in here and we are going to get the chart in front of us and, ok, baptism, obeying all that God commands, yeah, I think I can do that. You cannot. How do I know? Because your father is my father, Adam. Our first father is Adam. In addition, you as well as I have inherited a sinful nature with Adam. Let me tell you something. You do not need to teach a child to lie; you need to teach him to tell the truth. You do not need to teach a child to be selfish with his toys, you teach him to share. I know, I have had, well, I am in the process still of raising them. I have four children. The Bible confirms to me that we are cut out of the same cloth. We are sinners before God. The only way to rectify that problem is if God makes us perfect. Jesus said, "Be therefore perfect, even as your Father in Heaven is perfect." Are you perfect? Well, Mr. Reeves said that in order to maintain your justification, you had to do all that God commands. Jesus commanded you to be perfect. I am only perfect because I possess the righteousness of Jesus Christ. I am only God's son because he has brought me into his family.

Listen to what the Bible says on it. Romans chapter 10, verses 5-13. "For Moses writes that the man who practices righteousness, which is based on the law, shall live by that righteousness. But the righteousness based on faith speaks as follows: do not say in your heart, who will ascend into heaven, that is to bring Christ down, or who will descend into the abyss, that is to bring Christ up from the dead. What does it say? The word is near you, it is in your mouth and in your heart that is the word of faith, which we are preaching, that if you confess with your mouth Jesus as Lord, and believe in your heart that God raised Him from the dead, you will be saved. For with the heart a person believes, resulting in righteousness, and with the mouth he confesses, resulting in salvation."

I want you to notice something very interesting about this verse. The bottom part of it, Paul changes the order. He begins by saying that if you believe in your heart, or rather if you confess with your mouth, verse 9, if you confess with your mouth and then you believe in your heart, you will be saved. Then he goes on to explain exactly what he means by that. He says, "For with the heart a person believes, resulting in" what? Righteousness. Righteousness. Righteousness. With the heart, man believes unto righteousness and then as a result, all acts of obedience, including the confession of Jesus Christ as Lord, come from that heart. The heart is the source that drives man's motivations. That is why he goes on to say "and with the mouth he confesses, resulting in salvation."

Last night he said, Mr. Reeves said, "Gene has got up here and told us that he doesn't know who is elect and who is not elect." Well, that is only half-true. We know those who are elect by their fruits. I was, when I made that statement, referring to people who are not saved, people who are not Christians, and people who do not believe the gospel of God's grace. Therefore, in that sense, those that are among the unsaved, we do not know who they are; we do not know who the elect are. However, those who have the fruits that accompany salvation, we most surely know who they are, and he says, "Well, how does he know he's a Christian?" How does he know? Because I have believed the gospel and now, I desire to obey God. Romans 8:15, "For you have not received a spirit of slavery leading to fear again, but you have received the spirit of adoption as sons, by which we cry out, Abba Father. The Spirit himself testifies with our spirit that we are the children of God." That is how I know I am of the elect, because the Spirit of God testifies with my spirit that I am his.

Ephesians 1:5 says, "He predestined us to adoption as sons, through Jesus Christ Himself, according to the kind intention of His will, to the praise and glory of His grace which he freely bestowed on us in the beloved." Now, both of these verses speak of adoption. In other words, in order to be a child of God you are not born into the family of God naturally. That is the testimony of Scripture from beginning to end. It is not apt to the flesh. In other words, God does not have any grandchildren. In order to be counted as God's child, you must be adopted. Adoption, what is it? Adoption is a process whereby those who were without parents, without father or mother, are taken by somebody, and received into their home and given the privileges and the benefits of the father or the head of that new home. That is what adoption is. Maybe somebody here has been adopted. I have two very close friends who were adopted. In addition, if you told them that adoption in the Bible means you being obedient, they would laugh at you. Because they were not adopted that way and that is not what adoption means. We seem to forget that Adam has alienated us from God. We—throughout this whole debate, Mr. Reeves forgets the concept that Adam stands as a representative for mankind before God. Therefore, when he says can God hold you accountable for something you cannot do, I mean, would God tie us, or should we tie a child to a tree and then hold some candy in front of him and hold him responsible for not taking the candy? Well, what is it that has tied him to the tree? His sin has tied him to the tree. The reason that you cannot obey God perfectly is because your sin, namely the sin of your father Adam, has tied you to the tree. He keeps bringing up that passage in Ezekiel that talks about God not transferring the guilt of the father or the sins of the fathers. You want to know the context of that passage? They are arguing with God. They are telling God, look God; this is not fair that you are not blessing us, that you are, in fact, cursing us because of the sin of our fathers. And he says, ok, you want to be judged for your own sin? From now on you will be. That is the context of that passage. They were just as guilty as their fathers were.

Not only am I God's but God wants me to know that I am his. In 1 John 4:13, John says, "by this we know that we abide in Him and He in us, because He has given us His Spirit." You have the Spirit of Christ. Do you know what that means? 1 John 5:13, "These things I have written that you who believe in the name of the Son of God, that you may know that you have eternal life."

Does the gospel that he is presenting, the gospel of obedience, that is what it is, pure and simple, he even said, it is faith and works. Well, if it is not all faith, then it is obedience. If it is not all faith, then it is not grace. Remember grace means unmerited favor. We are supposed to be saved by grace but he teaches that we are obedient to God and therefore because of our obedience, we maintain our justification. That does not sound like unmerited favor to me. Now concerning the walls of Jericho, did their obedience cause them to earn the walls falling down? No. It was not them that knocked them down, was it? God knocked them down. It is God who gives us his righteousness, it is God who regenerates us, and it is not us. It is God who gives us the gift of faith, it is God who gives us the gift of repentance, it is God who gives us Christ, and it is God who gives us all of his merits—his atoning sacrifice and his perfect life. It is mine by faith. Thank God. Thank God.

Because I would not stand here for one minute, if there was one millionth of a percent of my obedience involved in my salvation. I would blow it every day. I would blow it. Young men, you are flipping through on the remote, you know what is on cable these days. You stop on one of those videos, or channels that happen to pop up that has some girl that is half-clothed, did you just loose your justification? It is an offense to God that we would even think, mark this, it is an offense to a Holy God, that we would even think that we have the blessings of drawing boldly into his throne room based on what we have done or based on a response of my, it's a mockery. And that's why Paul said that those who come and preach another gospel, they are to be condemned, they are to be accursed, they are to be numbered out, they are to be pointed out as those who are leading men astray. What were those Galatians doing? They were saying it is not enough just to believe. One must believe and be circumcised. It has always been faith plus something else. Faith plus something else. That is the doctrine of demons. Faith plus something else. The apostle Paul said, "Have I become your enemy because I have told you the truth?" I do not have one single thing to gain from being here. I am packing up and going back to San Diego tomorrow, never to see you people again. If you did agree with my opinion after today you could not come to my church because it is too far. I tell you this because I care about your soul. If the Lord of Glory is convicting your hearts about some of these passages, you need to reconcile that with him. In addition, you need to do it quickly. John says in John 5:24, "Truly, truly I say unto you, he that heareth my word and believes Him who sent me, has eternal life and does not come to judgment, but he has passed out of death into life." Praise God. How long is eternal life? How long is eternal life? It is forever is it not? So how can we have a doctrine that teaches that we gain eternal life and yet there are these interruptions in it? We have eternal life and then we do not have eternal life and we have eternal life, and then we do not have eternal life. Eternal life is forever and he says if you believe you have passed over from condemnation to life. You have eternal life.

Not only does God want me to know that I am his, but think about this. Isaiah 49:15 says, "Can a woman forget her nursing child, and have no compassion on the son of her womb?" He asks a rhetorical question that any mother would be able to identify. No, a woman cannot forget her nursing child. Yet he goes on to say, "Even these may forget, even the most wicked of women might forget, but I will not forget you. Behold I have enscribed you on the palms of my hands." We have children, both of us, and we love our children. Do you love your children based on their obedience? When your children disobey, do they cease to be your children? I do not think so. But if we adhere to the doctrine, the gospel that this man is preaching, then essentially, what you are saying is that you have a greater love than the Father, who loves his child one day, and then cuts him off the next day because his child has now sinned. Then loves him and receives him again because he has now repented, and he is now justified again, and so he is in good standing with father. Now he has done something else and now he no longer belongs to Papa. That is not the God of the Bible. It is just not. Think about it.

Friday Night

Fourth Affirmative

Bruce Reeves

Well, this is the last time that I will have the opportunity to speak to you in the affirmation of this proposition. It has been enjoyable to be with you and I will pray that we will continue to look into the Scriptures and make sure that everything that we say is in accordance with God's will.

I want to address something that we just heard or perhaps it is a lack of what we heard. Why did Mr. Cook not address the argumentation that I offered this evening? The proposition is clear. There is the proposition behind me. It reads, *"The Scriptures teach that water baptism is essential in order for the alien sinner to obtain the forgiveness of his past sins."* Why did he not deal with the argumentation that I offered this evening in affirmation of the proposition? You know, ladies and gentlemen, Monday night, Mr. Cook chided me about the responsibilities of the negative. He chided me and he said, "You know Bruce, the negative has certain responsibilities and that is to follow the affirmative, to follow the affirmation." You all who were here Monday night, I am sure that you remember that statement. What baptism passages did we hear this evening from Mr. Cook? What baptism passages did we hear? I examined several passages regarding the necessity of baptism. We studied those passages. What did we hear? Now, I would have been happy to sign a proposition about once saved, always saved, or the Calvinistic view of the perseverance of the saints, but those are not the propositions that we signed. I would have been happy to talk about the imputation of the personal righteousness of Christ to the believer and a host of other things but they are not under consideration this evening. Now, I mean this in all kindness, but I really think, after what I heard Monday night, when I was attempting to follow Mr. Cook, and Tuesday night as well, that perhaps he ought to take his own advice. That would have been profitable in our study and that is something that you need to ask. I suppose that I ought to feel good about the speech this evening. It must have been an excellent speech because he did not say anything about the arguments that I made.

Would you please turn your Bibles to Ezekiel the 18th chapter? Mr. Cook made a passing remark about this text and this is extremely important for us to consider. You need to understand the background in the doctrinal reason why he is denying that water baptism is essential. Ezekiel chapter 18 and verse 20, "The soul who sins shall die. The son shall not bear the guilt of the father; neither shall the father bear the guilt of the son. The righteousness of the righteous shall be upon himself and the wickedness of the wicked shall be upon himself." Now, friends, I think, in order for you to be able to grasp and to understand the consequences of the doctrine Mr. Cook has taught this week and in this debate you need to recognize that the doctrine reflects greatly upon the nature of God, the nature of man and the nature of saving faith. I gave you an illustration of a small child who was tied up to a tree and somebody is holding a piece of candy out and saying, "Come and get it," but the child does not have the ability to come and get it.

However, I do not know that I gave you the fullness of that particular illustration that would connect to what my opponent really is arguing and what the doctrine that he is arguing for really teaches. I want you to imagine that little child, perhaps that infant we will say for the sake of some of the things that we have seen and heard. That little child is being spanked vehemently, vehemently by a parent and tears are rolling down that child's face, for something, that child was not able to control. Now then, that does not compare with eternal punishment in hell. Mr. Cook's position is that we have a little baby, a little child, and were that child to die, if he is on the non-elect list there is nothing that could be done to save that child. Now he did not have anything to do with being on the non-elect list. He did not do anything to deserve being on the non-elect list. God is going to send him to hell because he foreordained before the world began that he should be sent to hell. The other infant, who is on the elect list, God has foreordained that he should go to heaven. Now that is the difficulty Mr. Cook is in this evening. How do we reconcile that picture of God with what we read in the Scriptures?

There are hosts of passages that you might consider with me. How do we reconcile those things? You know we looked at this chart, God's will, God's love, and God's desire. We hear Jesus saying, "Oh Jerusalem, Jerusalem, the one who kills the prophets and stones those who are sent to her, how often I wanted to gather your children together as a hen gathers her chicks under he wings, but you were not willing." We have been told that God wants them to be saved but he has not willed for them to be saved, but Peter said, "God is not willing that any should perish, but that all should come to repentance."

Now certainly, not all people will be saved, because not all people choose faith. They have dashed the cup of God's salvation. They have dashed the cup of his redemption, but it is not because God foreordained that particular individuals would be on the elect list and other particular individuals would be on the lost list. That is why we have heard argumentation that regeneration is unconditional. We have heard him say this very evening that the devil is God's devil, he does no more and no less than what God commanded, commanded him to do. No more and no less than what God commanded him, **commanded him to do!** Is that the doctrine of the Scriptures?

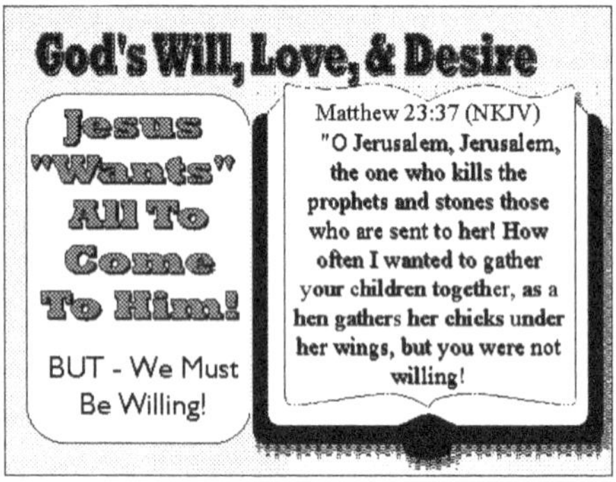
God's Will, Love, & Desire
Jesus "Wants" All To Come To Him!
BUT - We Must Be Willing!
Matthew 23:37 (NKJV)
"O Jerusalem, Jerusalem, the one who kills the prophets and stones those who are sent to her! How often I wanted to gather your children together, as a hen gathers her chicks under her wings, but you were not willing!

Let us continue looking at Ezekiel 18 and verse 20: "The soul who sins shall die. The son shall not bear the guilt of the father, nor the father bear the guilt of the son. The righteousness of the righteous shall be upon himself, and the wickedness of the wicked shall be upon himself. But if a wicked man turns from all his sins, which he has committed, keeps all my statutes, and does what is lawful and right, he shall surely live. He shall not die. None of the transgressions which he has committed shall be remembered against him because of the righteousness which he has done, he shall live."

Look at verse 23: "Do I have any pleasure at all that the wicked should die, says the Lord God, and not that he should turn from his ways and live." On one hand the Scripture says God did not have any pleasure in the death of the wicked, but on the other hand, we are told by Reformed Theology, and we are told by my opponent this evening that God willed that particular individuals should be lost. He did not want, but he willed. He foreordained before the world ever began. How do you reconcile that concept of election and that concept of salvation and condemnation with this passage? He says in verse 24, "But when a righteous man turns from all his righteousness and commits iniquity and does according to all the abominations that the wicked man does, shall he live? All the righteousness, which he has done, shall not be remembered because of the unfaithfulness of which he is guilty and the sin, which he has committed. Because of them he shall die."

Mr. Cook made a very impassioned plea. I think it was last night, I do not know if this was his exact wording, but it was the idea of yo-yo religion. It was the idea that you are in and you are out, and he indicated tonight that if you could fall from grace, which Galatians 5:4 says you may, and if you could leave the Lord after you had been in fellowship with him because of your own unfaithfulness, there's such insecurity in that concept. He mentioned that the way he knows that he is elect is because he bears fruit. How does he know that God has not commanded the devil at some point, to cause him to leave the Lord one of these days? Have there ever been people that thought they were elect but were not? When we see somebody and they seem to be bearing fruit, and yet later, they have left the Lord and then our religious friends tell us, "Well, they never were really saved to begin with."

He talked about perfection. I do not teach that we are perfect because we never make a mistake. Hebrews 10:14 tells you how we have been made perfect, i.e. through the offering of Christ. By the way, Romans 4 does not mention the personal righteousness of Christ being imputed to the believer. It mentions forgiveness and in verse 14 of Hebrews 10 we read, "For by one offering He hath perfected forever them that are sanctified."

I want you to turn to Galatians chapter 3. He mentioned that as an argument. Notice Galatians 3:14, Mr. Cook's position is that the Spirit regenerates a man and then a man is miraculously given faith. However, in this passage that is not the pattern that we have, "That the blessing of Abraham might come on the Gentiles through Jesus Christ, that we might receive the promise of the Spirit through faith." We receive "the promise of the Spirit **through faith**."

He mentioned Acts chapter 3 and verse 19 and he said something that interested me. He asked, "Why wasn't baptism mentioned there?" I want you to look at two passages with me. I want you to look at Acts chapter 2 and verse 38 and then I want you to look at Acts chapter 3 and verse 19.

Please note the parallel nature of these passages. In Acts chapter 2 and verse 38, the Scripture says, "Repent and be baptized in the name of Jesus Christ for the remission of sins, and you shall receive the gift of the Holy Spirit." Then in Acts 3:19, he says, "Repent and be converted that your sins may be blotted out, so that the times of refreshing may come from the presence of the Lord." Now notice both passages

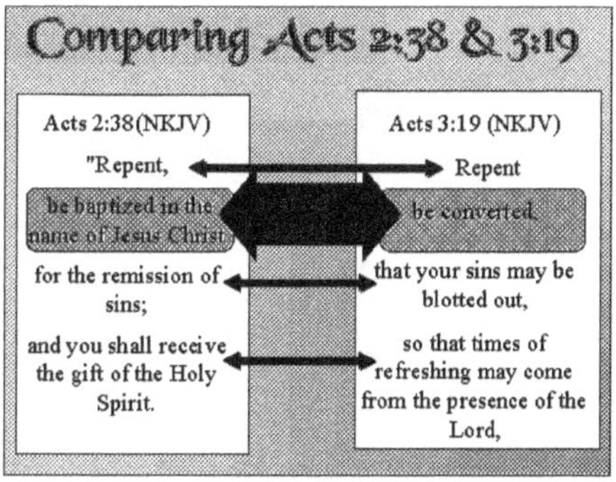
Comparing Acts 2:38 & 3:19
Acts 2:38(NKJV)
Acts 3:19 (NKJV)
"Repent,
Repent
be baptized in the name of Jesus Christ
be converted,
for the remission of sins;
that your sins may be blotted out,
and you shall receive the gift of the Holy Spirit.
so that times of refreshing may come from the presence of the Lord,

mention repentance. We have in Acts 2:38 the phrase, "Be baptized in the name of Christ," but in Acts 3:19 the term "converted" is employed. In order to be converted to the Lord, I must be baptized by the authority of Jesus Christ. That is not the only thing that I do. I am not working my way to heaven. I am simply accessing the working of God and that is what Colossians 2 says about it. Look at the harmony of the two passages: "For the remission of sins" and "That your sins may be blotted out." Even the last portion of both verses is similar: "And you shall receive the gift of the Holy Spirit" and "So that the times of refreshing shall come from the presence of the Lord." There is no contradiction here. All that does is prove that water baptism is part of conversion to Jesus Christ. We have to harmonize what God has said in his word and Mr. Cook knows that very well.

Now I want to show you a case of Scripture being taken out of context. Mr. Cook made the argument that baptism is not part of the gospel and he cited 1 Corinthians 1:17 as a supporting passage.

He went on to argue that even obedience to commands is not part of the gospel. Let us deal with 1 Corinthians chapter 1 and verse 17. You need to look at the context just a little bit. In 1 Corinthians chapter 1 and verse 13 he says, "Was Christ divided, was Paul crucified for you, or were you baptized in the name of Paul?" So Paul says, in order for you truly to have a right to belong to me, then I would have had to die for you and you would have had to have been baptized by my authority. He goes on to say in verse 15 the reason he was thankful he had not baptized more people was "Lest they should say that I have baptized in my own name," i.e. by my own authority. Now then, we go down to verse 17, "For Christ sent me not to baptize." He did not send Paul to baptize in his own name but to preach

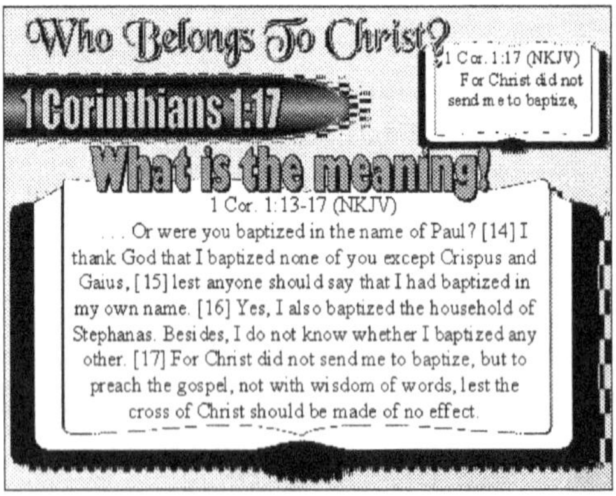
Who Belongs To Christ?
1 Cor. 1:17 (NKJV) For Christ did not send me to baptize,
1 Corinthians 1:17
What is the meaning!
1 Cor. 1:13-17 (NKJV)
. . . Or were you baptized in the name of Paul? [14] I thank God that I baptized none of you except Crispus and Gaius, [15] lest anyone should say that I had baptized in my own name. [16] Yes, I also baptized the household of Stephanas. Besides, I do not know whether I baptized any other. [17] For Christ did not send me to baptize, but to preach the gospel, not with wisdom of words, lest the cross of Christ should be made of no effect.

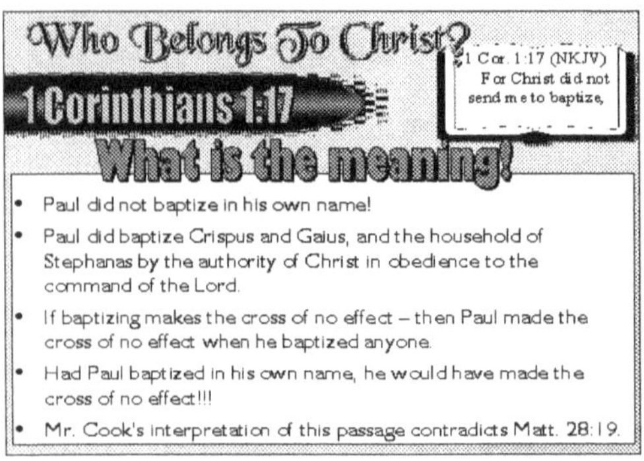
Who Belongs To Christ?
1 Cor. 1:17 (NKJV) For Christ did not send me to baptize,
1 Corinthians 1:17
What is the meaning!
• Paul did not baptize in his own name!
• Paul did baptize Crispus and Gaius, and the household of Stephanas by the authority of Christ in obedience to the command of the Lord.
• If baptizing makes the cross of no effect – then Paul made the cross of no effect when he baptized anyone.
• Had Paul baptized in his own name, he would have made the cross of no effect!!!
• Mr. Cook's interpretation of this passage contradicts Matt. 28:19.

the gospel, "Not with the wisdom of words, lest the cross of Christ should be made of none effect." Paul did not baptize in his own name. Paul did baptize Crispus and Gaius and the household of Stephanas by the authority of Christ in obedience to the command of the Lord. If baptizing makes the cross of no effect, then Paul made the cross of no effect when he baptized anybody. Had Paul baptized in his own name, he would have made the cross of no effect. Ladies and gentlemen, did Christ send the apostles to baptize? Matthew 28:19 says he did! To say, "Well, this says he wasn't sent to baptize at all" would not be true because we know that in the Great Commission in Matthew 28:19 that they were sent to baptize. Paul's point is, "I was not sent to baptize in my own name."

I want you to turn to Acts chapter 15 very quickly. In Acts chapter 15 and in verse 7 we read of hearts being purified by faith. You can note in verse 7 that Peter rose up and said unto them, "Men and brethren, you know how that a good while ago, God made a choice among us that the Gentiles, by my mouth, should hear the word of the gospel and believe." Contextually, to whom is Peter referring? He is talking about the Gentiles. He is talking about Cornelius. He is talking about those who have been cleansed by faith. I agree, if we are going to be saved, we are going to be saved by faith. You need to notice something else. Turn to Acts chapter 10. When were the people Peter is talking about forgiven? When were they cleansed? In Acts chapter 10 and verse 47: "Can any man forbid water that these should not be baptized, which have received the Holy Ghost as well as we? And he commanded them to be baptized in the name of the Lord, then prayed they him to tarry certain days."

He also brought up Romans chapter 8 and Romans chapter 10. Mr. Cook mentioned how the Spirit is to dwell in us. I agree that the Spirit dwells in us, the question is how? Look at verse 14. "For as many as are led by the Spirit of God, they are the sons of God." Now look at verse 2, "For the law of the Spirit of Life in Christ Jesus has made me free from the law of sin and death." Friends, that is talking about the gospel of Jesus Christ. I am walking in the Spirit when I am led by the Spirit and when I obey the teaching of the Holy Spirit.

Let us go to Romans 10:9, "That if thou shall confess with thy mouth the Lord Jesus and shall believe in thine heart that God has raised Him from the dead, thou shall be saved. For with the heart man believeth unto righteousness and with the mouth confession is made unto salvation." Absolutely! Now notice the rest of this text. How do I receive faith? It is through the preaching of the word of God. Romans 10:17, "So then faith cometh by hearing and hearing by the word of God." Now look at Romans 10:3, "For they being ignorant of God's righteousness and going about to establish their own righteousness, have not **submitted** themselves unto the righteousness of God." Obedience to the gospel of the Lord Jesus Christ is absolutely necessary.

Now, concerning my questions, I asked Mr. Cook, "Did I understand you to say last night that neither water baptism nor Holy Spirit baptism puts a man into Christ?" He said "Neither." He has given up the idea of Holy Spirit baptism putting somebody into Christ, if that is his answer regarding the conversion of the Samaritans in Acts the 8th chapter.

Now, shut that projector off Don. This is simply a matter of what the Lord says. What does the Lord say? What does the Bible teach us? Now, I am interested, if unconditional election were true, if it has been foreordained before the world began that certain individuals are elect and certain individuals are non-elect, then why is Mr. Cook in this debate? Why is he here? He talks about how you need to change and how you need to do this or you need to do that. If it is unconditional, if you are non-elect and there is nothing you can do about it, and that is what we have been told this week, why try to persuade you? There is nothing you can do about it. If you are elect, it is not going to matter what you do because regeneration is unconditional. That is what he has told us this week. Why preach? Why try to persuade people if what they do and the decisions they make have nothing to do with whether they are born again? That just does not make any sense and yet he is doing that. He is doing that.

Now what does the Lord say? We are going to look at the Scriptures tonight. Mark chapter 16 and verse 16. Let us think about what the Bible says, not what Reformed Theology says. I want to share with you the gospel of Jesus Christ. It is true, there is nothing you can do to deserve or earn salvation, but that does not mean that obedience to the gospel is not necessary. We have been told that faith is not obedience. We have been told that commands are not part of the gospel of Jesus Christ and yet, we know better. In fact, back in Romans the 10th chapter, before I get to Mark 16, you will notice in that context that, that is simply not the case. Romans 10:16 says, "But they have not all obeyed the gospel." We were told obeying a command, that is not part of the gospel. This says you obey the gospel. You obey the gospel!

Let us think about what is said to us in Scripture. In Mark chapter 16 and in verse 16 Jesus says, "Go ye into all the world and preach the gospel to every creature. He that believeth and is baptized shall be saved. But he that believeth not shall be condemned." We can turn on to the day of Pentecost and look at Acts the 2nd chapter and verse 38, "And they asked, 'What shall we do?'" "What shall we do?" They had crucified the Son of God. They were pricked in their hearts. They said, "What shall we do?" They were told, "Repent and be baptized, every one of you in the name of Jesus Christ, for the remission of your sins." We have looked at these passages this week. We have studied them. What convincing evidence have you heard or have I heard that denies these passages?

In Acts the 22nd chapter and verse 16, Saul of Tarsus was told, "Arise and be baptized, washing away thy sins, calling on the name of the Lord." We turn our Bibles to Romans the 6th chapter. In Romans 6:3, "Know ye not that so many of us as were baptized into Jesus Christ, were baptized into His death. Therefore, we are buried with Him by baptism into death that like as Christ was raised up from the dead by the glory of the Father; even so, we also should walk in newness of life. For if we have been planted or united together in the likeness of His death, we shall be also in the likeness of His resurrection: knowing this, that our old man is crucified with Him, that the body of sin might be destroyed and henceforth we should not serve sin, for he that is dead is free from sin." I am baptized into a relationship with Jesus Christ in which I can enjoy the benefits of his death.

Do you remember when I showed you John chapter 1 and verse 12 and it says that those who believe have the power or right to become the sons of God? They have the power or the right to become the sons of God. In Galatians the 3rd chapter and verse 26, we read that we are all the children of God by faith. That is right. He says you are presently the children of God by faith. Why? "For as many of you as have been baptized into Christ have put on Christ." Those are the children of Abraham according to the new covenant. So John 1:12 says, "You have the power to become. . . ." You are not already—you have the power to become saved and Galatians 3:26-27 tells you when you are baptized conditioned on your faith in Christ, you put on Christ.

I want you to turn to Colossians the 2nd chapter and notice this passage. I want to be clear about this point; the circumcision that is made without hands is not the water baptism itself. We have heard a lot about working your way to heaven, and Bruce is teaching a works system. I have denied that. I have spent time in Romans. I have shown you the meaning of the verses. Look at Colossians the 2nd chapter. In Colossians chapter 2 and in verse 11: "In whom also ye are circumcised with a circumcision made without hands." What is that? That is God "putting off the body of the sins of the flesh by the circumcision of Christ," but when does that happen? When we are "buried with him in baptism, wherein also ye are risen with him through the faith of the operation of God who has raised him from the dead, and you being dead in your sins in the uncircumcision of your flesh, having been quickened together with him, having forgiven you all trespasses." It is by the Lord's power, it is by his ability that those sins are cut away, but in the context, when does that happen? It happens when I, by faith, am buried with him in baptism. Did you hear what he said tonight? We asked him about these passages and even though he says baptism in these passages is really talking about Holy Spirit baptism, he can still use them to talk about water baptism. Does the word "baptism" in these verses mean two entirely different things at the same time? Do not let him tell you that Holy Spirit baptism and water baptism cannot be differentiated in this context. Think about what the Bible says. Think about the Scriptures. We have looked at 1 Peter 3:21, "Baptism doth also now save us, not the putting away of the filth of the flesh but the answer of a good conscience toward God by the resurrection of Jesus Christ."

I want you to think about those walls of Jericho. Mr. Cook made some statements and I want to deal with those at this time. I want you to listen very closely to me in the remaining time that I have. Just as there were these walls, you tonight, may be outside of the body of Christ. It may be that you have walls around your heart and those walls are not literal walls, but the wall of sin. The fact that God has required certain conditions of you being born again, does not mean it is not by grace. In fact, we find out regarding the walls of Jericho, that God gave them the city. Those walls fell by the power of God. I want you to notice Hebrews chapter 11. Hebrews chapter 11, we read that God gave them the city. God gave them the city. However, you know they had to exercise certain faith in order for that to happen.

"Salvation By Grace Through Faith"
The Walls of Jericho Fell By?
A) Grace Only?
?
B) Faith Only?
C) Works Only?
D
D) By Grace Through a Faith that obeyed?

In Hebrews chapter 11 and in verse 30, "By faith," we have heard about being saved by faith, "by faith the walls of Jericho fell down after they were encircled for seven days." They fell down by faith. Did they have to do what

God said? In all, they encircled those walls thirteen times. That is what I am telling you. Their faith obeying God did not earn their salvation. They simply accessed the power of God. God has a right to do that which He wishes. However, he always does that which is in harmony with his will. In addition, the fact that he said, "I'm going to knock these walls down," did not mean that they had earned such, yet they had to take action. Their faith obeyed just as James would say, "faith without works is dead." Tonight, while you may have the walls of sin around your heart, and you may be outside the body of Christ, Jesus Christ died for you. He shed his blood for you. He shed his blood for every one of us. We only receive the benefit of that blood when we render obedience to the gospel.

I am teaching you the grace of God. The Bible says, "The grace of God that brings salvation has appeared to all men, teaching us that denying ungodliness and worldly lusts, we should live soberly and righteously and godly in this present age." We are all going to appear before the Lord on the Day of Judgment. It is going to be based on God's word. It is not going to be based on human theology; it is not going to be based on what the majority of people say. It is going to be a matter of what God says and someone just getting up here and saying, "Oh no, that's a work system," is not going to change the truth.

What I am telling you is that salvation is by the grace of God but it is through faith that we are born again. This very evening, it may be, that you have not accessed and received the working of God and that working of God will come through obedience to the gospel. That is not you meriting salvation or earning it. It is simply you submitting to the conditions of the gospel. Remember Romans 10 and verse 3 and recognize that you submit to the righteousness of God by faith and that is the same God that loves everybody. No, we are not unconditionally regenerated or born again. We are born of the water and the Spirit. It is through obedience to the gospel. I will encourage you this evening; listen to Mr. Cook in his final speech. Think about the things that I have said to you. Remember the answer to the question is in the Bible. It is in the word of God, not just part of it, but all of it. Thank you for your attention.

Fourth Negative

Gene Cook

Ok, I am pleased to be in front of you one last time before we go home. We all have a lot to think about and Bruce was, I guess, a little bit disappointed that I did not address his arguments tonight. Well I believe I did address them. I addressed them from the standpoint of the gospel. My position all along has been that it is the gospel that saves us. It is not our good works; it is not our obedience, but the gospel that saves us. Therefore, to argue against the position of baptismal regeneration, it is perfectly legitimate to use a clear definition from the Scriptures as to what the gospel is. What is it that saves us and those are the passages that I went through so, I am sorry if I disappointed Mr. Reeves.

I do want to look at Romans chapter 9 for the remaining time that we have. The reason that I want—and let me say one other thing. I really did not hear any new arguments tonight.

Brother Sharp: Point of order, has this material been introduced?

Mr. Cook: Oh absolutely. You just heard Mr. Reeves make the argument that my version of God is a god who puts one baby on the baby list and another baby not on the baby list and I am going to show you from Romans chapter 9 that that is what the Scripture says.

(Brother Sharp attempts to talk with Mr. Cook's moderator.)

Mr. Cook: Is Romans 9 in the word of God?

Brother Sharp: I am going to speak to your moderator.

Gene Cook: I want you folks to pay close attention to what is going on here. Pay real close attention. I am about to read the word of God!

Brother Sharp: Please step away from the podium, Mr. Cook.

Gene Cook: My time is here. I did not even start yet actually.

Brother Sharp: The two debaters signed agreements. Now, he has a moderator. By the rules of honorable discussion, I am not going to discuss the rules with Mr. Cook. He has to step aside. I will discuss the rules with his moderator. Mr. McCartney is his moderator. He has to step to the podium, we will discuss this. We can discuss this aside where the audience cannot hear it.

Mr. Cook: That is not the rules of debate.

(Mr. McCartney and brother Sharp converse for a few minutes. Bruce Reeves and Keith Sharp converse briefly at brother Reeves' table)

Brother Sharp: On behalf of Mr. Reeves, I am registering our protest, that this is introduction of entirely new material when he's (Gene Cook) had the opportunity for four nights and seven speeches before now to introduce this material, and chose to introduce it at a time when Mr. Reeves cannot review it.

Mr. Cook:

Let me begin by saying that I would have loved a format that would have included a cross-examination. That is, an answering back and forth from both opponents. However, that was not the format preferred by Mr. Reeves. I agreed with the format that he preferred. On both Monday night and Tuesday night, he had the last word. I did not object, I did not complain, I did not warn you in advance, now he is going to have the last word. He has brought up almost every time he has stood at this pulpit; he has brought up the fact that I somehow have a god who chooses one baby over another. Has he not? He has brought up repeatedly that salvation or regeneration could not be by God's unmerited favor. It could not be unconditional, repeatedly. He has got up and said there is an elect list, he did it tonight. There is an elect list and there is a non-elect list, and you cannot be on it and if you are on it, you cannot get off it and I think that it is perfectly legitimate to respond to those charges from Romans chapter 9.

I did not understand for one moment in the rules of the debate that a verse had to be quoted in advance for to respond to something that is brought up. Why does he not want you to read Romans chapter 9? Why does he not want me to explain to you what Romans chapter 9 is? I suggest to you, because it is contrary to the version of God that he has laid out here before you. Let us look at Romans chapter 9, verse 6. "But it is not as though the word of God has failed, for they are not all Israel who descended from Israel. Neither are they all children because they were Abraham's descendants, but through Isaac your descendants will be named." That is, it is not the children of the flesh who are children of God, but the children of the promise who are regarded as descendants.

You see, there was this mindset in the Jewish mind that a child automatically inherited his Jewish identity and therefore he was in a covenant with God. Therefore, at this time, Paul is addressing the problem here. Why is it that most of the Jews are rejecting Christ? Why is it that they are not—if Jesus Christ is the Jewish Messiah—why is it that they have, for the most part, forsaken their Messiah? Paul answers that question here. And he says in verse 9, "For this is the word of promise, at this time I will come and Sarah shall have a son and not only this, but there was Rebecca also, when she had conceived twins by one man, our Father Isaac, for though the twins were not yet born and had not done anything good or bad, in order that God's purpose according to His choice, might stand not because of works but because of Him who calls." You want to talk about babies, fine. From the very first question that I received on Monday night, there was a question about elect babies. It is perfectly legitimate for me to raise this portion of Scripture to protect not only myself from the false accusation of worshiping a tyrant God, but to defend God's glory and God's honor. Listen to what God says. He says, "and not only this, but there was Rebecca also, when she had conceived twins by one man, for though the twins were not yet born. . . ." This is before the twins were born. They had not done anything good or bad according to verse 11. They had not done anything good or bad in order that God's purpose according to his choice might stand. Now you have heard repeatedly that it is your choice, your choice, your choice. What does God say?

He says I took two twins from the same father, from the same mother, in the same womb, and before they were ever born, God made a choice between them, so that his choice would stand, not yours, but his choice. What was that choice? It says in verse 12, "As it is written, the older will serve the younger, just as it is written. Jacob have I loved but Esau I hated." Did you get that? Jacob I have loved. And Esau I have hated. You say, "Well, that is unfair." How could God pick between two unborn children, between two beings that had not done anything good or bad, how could he choose one of them and neglect the other or pass over the other? How could he do that? That is unfair. That is unjust. Well, the Apostle Paul anticipates that this is the way that we would respond. In fact, he says in 14, "what should we say then? There is no injustice with God is there? May it never be." Paul anticipates that when you hear this you are going to say, "that's not fair." So when he stands over here and says his God is a monster, his God is not fair, his God sends little babies to Hell, his God is like somebody who spanks babies indefinitely while they are crying, and there's nothing that they could do about it, he is really arguing against the God of the Bible. He is really raising up his accusation, not at me as his debate opponent, but he is raising up his accusation at the God of the Bible and he is evidencing himself to be that, which he is, still an unregenerated enemy of God's gospel of grace.

Verse 15, "may it never be, for He says to Moses, "this is God speaking," I will have mercy on whom I will have mercy and I will have compassion on whom I have compassion, so then it does not depend on the man who wills or the man who runs, but the God who has mercy." All of the accusations against me that I have this warped view of God; they are simply derived from Scripture. I hope that even though you may disagree with me up to this point, you have found me to be a sensible man. I do not make things up when it comes to my understanding of God. I derive my understanding of who God is from his own revelation and therefore I submit myself to the word of God, even in those things that I find difficult to comprehend and understand. Why? Because it is God's word. Who am I to stand in judgment of God's word? What is God going to say? For the Scripture says to Pharaoh for this very purpose, "I raised you up to demonstrate my power in you, that my name might be proclaimed throughout the whole earth." So then, he has mercy on whom he desires, and he hardens whom he desires. Is that your God? Is that Mr. Reeves' God? You say, well how do I know Gene Cook isn't misinterpreting what this verse—I mean, you're probably thinking to yourself, well, I'd really like to hear Mr. Reeves explain what this means to us because I am sure Gene Cook is wrong. Well do not be so sure because if your response is in verse 19, then why does he still find fault for who resists his will? "How could God still find fault?" is the question that comes to the mind. The Apostle anticipates that question so much that he includes it in his discourse. When a human being hears this, his natural response is, "Well, then why does God find fault?" If everybody is doing what he or she have been made to do, and God is the one who hardens one and softens another, and God is the one who chooses one and rejects another, then how does God hold man responsible? That is the question.

Moreover, the way that I know that I have understood the text right is because when I preach this text the same questions come up. In fact, we have been hearing these objections all week long. How could that be? How could God still find fault? How can man resist his will? On the contrary, Paul says, "Who are you; oh man, to answer back to God? Will the thing molded say to the one who made it, why did you make me this way? Or does the potter have right over the clay to make from the same lump one vessel for honorable use, and another for common use?" Of course he does. Does the potter have right over the clay, to make one vessel for honorable use, and one vessel for ordinary use or common use? Well of course—if he is the potter, of course he does. Who would argue with that? Verse 22, "but if God, although willing to demonstrate His wrath and to make His power known endured with much patience the vessels of wrath prepared for destruction." I represent this God. I believe in this God. The God that I stand before, the

God whom I worship, is the God who is God. He is not on an equal with the devil. In fact, he made the devil. In addition, when the devil wanted to harm Job, he had to go get permission from God. He is God's devil. He is God's devil. He is not competing with God. Any power that he has been given to him was given to him by the Almighty. Any restrictions he has have been put upon him by the Almighty. He's God's devil.

Mr. Reeves asked the question, well if this is true, then why would he even come here? I mean if you took this audience here and, Mr. Cook you believe that there are those that are elect and there are those that are non-elect, then why do you bother? Why would you even come here? Because the Bible says that faith comes by hearing and hearing by the word of God, or the word of Christ. You see, I never said that obedience was not necessary. Obedience to the commands of God are very necessary, every one of them. Are they a prerequisite for justification? That is the question. That is the question that I have answered, not only in my previous presentations, but also tonight. Once I put up last night Romans chapter 8 where it showed the distinctions between the man who is in the flesh and the man who was in the spirit, the whole baptism issue is moot. Because it says that the man who is in the flesh, he is unable to please God. Yet Mr. Reeves even conceded himself, that baptism is something pleasing for those who are about to undergo water baptism and thus have their souls cleansed from sin. Yes, obedience is very necessary. Obedience to all that God commands, that is why I am here. God has commanded me to be his ambassador; God has commanded me to study his word to show myself approved.

God has commanded me to answer those with gentleness and respect concerning his word that they might have the same hope and that perhaps God may grant them repentance. 2 Timothy 2:24-26, because he tells us in 2 Timothy that man has been held captive by the devil to do his will. This is no laughing matter. What I am showing you here tonight is how the God of the Bible reveals himself. Now it is one thing for both of the participants of this debate to get up and to give their views. I give my view; he gives his view. Some of you agreed with him, some of you agree with me. I got up and made the charge that I believe from Scripture, and I believe this with all my heart that what we have heard from this side of the room is another gospel. Now, it is one thing to make that charge. I mean, he could say the same thing about me. I am sure he thinks that. Let me ask you a question. Which side of the room represents the God represented in chapter 9? Because you can walk out of here saying, "I still believe that I'm saved through water baptism." Well that is fine, but what about Romans chapter 9? He said it himself. We have to take all of God's Scripture, not just part of it. We have to take all of God's Scripture. Let us go back to Ezekiel chapter 18 for just a moment. Verse 2 gives us the context. Verse 1 and 2, "Then the word of the Lord came to me saying, what do you mean by using this proverb concerning the land of Israel? The fathers eat the sour grapes but the children's teeth are set on edge. As I live, declares the Lord, you are surely not going to use this proverb in Israel anymore." You see, what was happening was they had read Genesis where it says the sins of the fathers are visited on the second and the third generation. They had said that all the calamity and all the lack of prosperity that is coming upon us is not because of our sin but because of our fathers. Therefore, God answers from Heaven and he says, "Ok you want to be accountable for your own sin, that's fine, because even without the sin of your fathers, you are still guilty before God."

However, he says something interesting here that I heard Mr. Reeves read in verse 24. It says, "But when a righteous man turns away from his righteousness and commits iniquity and does according to all the abominations that a wicked man does, will he live? All the righteous deeds, which he has done, will not be remembered for his treachery, which he has committed, and his sin, which he has committed for them, he will die. Yet you say the way of the Lord is not right. Hear, oh house of Israel, is my way not right? It is your ways that are not right." Notice what he says, when a righteous man turns from his righteousness, and goes back and commits wickedness all of the righteousness that he had preformed before will be forgotten by God. If he wants to apply that verse, then he needs to be re-baptized every time he sins, because it says all of his righteousness is forgotten before God. This is not, once again, this is not good news. My desire was to come here, to stand before you, to answer the questions concerning baptism, to try to harmonize the Scriptures to try to demonstrate that if there was any hope of us being saved, it is all of Christ, and none of me. My hope lies in Jesus Christ and his righteousness and nothing less. Thank you very much.

Mr. McCartney: I would like to say that the reason Mr. Cook had the right, yea I even believe, the obligation to address Romans 9, is because of the many attacks, not only upon his person, but also upon his doctrine and theology. Mr. Cook came here to debate the topic of water baptism, whether is it essential to salvation or not, but from the get-go, from the very outset, his theology has been attacked. Instead of staying with the topic and the subject, all these questions about babies and everything else was brought up so, in my opinion, Mr. Cook had every right to address Romans 9 and tell what he really believes about a Holy God who is sovereign and has the right to do all his good pleasure. Thank you very much.

Brother Sharp: Thank you Mr. McCartney and Mr. Cook, Mr. Reeves. The audience has just been splendid. I do not think that we could have asked for a better audience. I appreciate that throughout this four-night debate two men passionately presented the things that they believe, that you have listened carefully, that you have considered the Scriptures.

The Truth About Romans 9

Bruce Reeves

Introduction

The text under consideration in this article forms the most contested territory in the debate over Calvinistic theology and its consequences concerning the character of God and man's salvation. In my debate with Gene Cook, Jr. we felt it necessary to establish the fact that the sinner was to meet God-ordained conditions in order to experience the new birth. It would be senseless to affirm baptism as a condition of one being born again prior to the establishment of the truth that there are conditions of regeneration. Although earlier on, we were looking forward to an exegesis of this text in the course of the discussion, Mr. Cook intentionally waited until his last speech to introduce his argumentation on this section of God's word. He clearly did this in order to prevent the other side from responding to his presentation. My moderator called a point of order, but Mr. Cook insisted on proceeding with his decision to present new argumentation and material. Our objection was not to this particular section of Scripture being discussed, for earlier in this discussion it would have been fair game, but to him presenting the argument in the last speech of the debate. He was clearly attempting to gain an unfair advantage in the debate by this maneuver, and this was very obvious to the audience. The following portion of this article will serve as a brief response to the Calvinistic interpretation of this text. We consider it both fair and worthwhile to the reader in light of the fact that Mr. Cook broke the rules of the debate (see debate rules).

The Calvinistic Reflection Upon God's Character Per Romans 9

Before we enter into an examination of the ninth chapter of Romans I feel it beneficial for us to consider the consequences of the Calvinistic interpretation of this context. At the forefront is the Calvinistic view that God does not love all men. Calvinists will speak of "common grace," i.e. the physical providence God pours upon all men, but at the end of the day their position denies that salvation is available to all. In fact their position not only denies the availability of salvation to all, but it affirms that God unconditionally decreed that the vast majority of mankind should be lost and there is nothing the "non-elect" can do about their eternal destiny. In the face of this, the Scriptures are replete with affirmations of God's redemptive love for all men (2 Pet. 3:9; John 3:16; 1 Tim. 2:4-6; Tit. 2:11-14). We recognize that many will be lost, but such is due to their refusal to accept what was available to them.

The phrase "sovereign grace" is thrown around a lot, but the truth is that according to this false theology God's grace is not even made available to the majority of human beings. For those individuals it is not grace at all! The Calvinistic position denies that God in his sovereignty decreed that all accountable men have the ability to either choose or reject salvation. In contrast it argues that God irresistibly gives some the ability to exercise faith, but refuses most. Additionally, it affirms that God yet holds men accountable for that which they do not have the ability to do. The consequence being that God condemns most men for not believing, although he determined that it would be impossible for them to believe. One is forced by the faulty logic of this to ask, "Is this the God of the Bible?" The emphatic answer is "NO!" Interestingly, Mr. Cook accused me of being an "unregenerated enemy of God grace" when, in fact, it is his doctrine that denies that God's grace is available to all of mankind. Note some of the quotations by Mr. Cook below in reference to his view of the character of God as he attempts to explain his theology:

> "Non elect infants who die in their infancy will spend eternity in hell"—I would answer true to that question, you have to be elect in order to be saved. If this question is false, then we should perform abortion, because abortion is the greatest evangelistic act that has ever taken place since the time that Jesus walked the face of the earth, because everyone of those children are going straight to heaven according to Mr. Brown's theology (David P. Brown & Gene Cook, Jr. Debate, Feb 16, 2000).

> You want to talk about babies? Fine. From the very first question I received on Monday night there was a question about elect babies. It is perfectly legitimate for me to not only protect myself from the accusation of worshipping a tyrant God but to defend God's glory and God's honor. . . .You have heard over and over again that it is your choice, your choice and what does God say? He says, "I took two twins from the same father, the same mother, the same womb and before they were ever born God made a choice between them so that his choice would stand, not yours, but his choice. . . .Jacob I have loved and Esau I have hated."

> Did you get that? Jacob I have loved but Esau I have hated. You say, "Well that is unfair? How could God pick between two unborn children? Between two beings that had not done anything good or bad? How could God choose one of them and neglect the other. . . .How could he do that? That is unfair, that is unjust…" (Reeves-Cook Debate, Gene Cook's 4th Negative, June 24, 2005).
>
> So when he (Bruce Reeves) stands over here and says, "His (Gene Cook, Jr.) God is a monster, his God is not fair, his God sends little babies to hell, his God spanks babies indefinitely and there is nothing they can do about it," he (Bruce Reeves) is really arguing against the God of the Bible. He is really raising up his accusation against not me as his debate opponent but he is raising up his accusation against the God of the Bible and he (Bruce Reeves) is evidencing himself to be what he is—still an unregenerated enemy of God's grace (Reeves-Cook Debate, Gene Cook's 4th Negative, June 24, 2005).
>
> You just got up and heard Mr. Reeves make the argument that my version of God is a God who puts one baby on the baby list and another baby not on the baby list and I'm going to show you from Romans chapter nine that that's what the Scripture says (Reeves-Cook Debate, Cook's fourth Negative, June 24, 2005).
>
> The devil is God's devil. He does what God allows him to do, he does what God commands him to do, no more and no less (Reeves-Cook Debate, Quote played from a sermon by Gene Cook, Reeves third affirmative June 24, 2005).
>
> Both evil and good come from God. . . .So what happens when you emphasize the will of man, then evil becomes only associated, there is no sense in which God decrees evil, there is no sense in which God wills evil and so evil is only from the heart of man and from the heart of Satan, . . .but we recognize as reformed Christians that those are secondary causes, that the first cause of evil is God, himself. . . .Man does not resist evil when he is fulfilling the decrees of God (Is God schizophrenic? "The Two Wills of God," Gene Cook—8/12/05).

Man does not have a libertarian choice in his salvation, "non-elect babies spend eternity in hell," "the devil does what God commands him to do," and "God is the first cause of evil"—these are the stated consequences of Calvinistic theology. We are told by R.C. Sproul, a well known Calvinist, that Romans 9 proves Calvinistic theology and disproves the non-Calvinist approach (R.C. Sproul, *Chosen By God* [Wheaton, Ill.: Tyndale House, 1986], 151). It is imperative therefore that we at least consider what this text is actually teaching.

Putting Romans 9 Back Into Context!

It is an exegetical mistake to isolate Romans 9 from the rest of the epistle. Actually, Romans 9-11 is recognized by most scholars as a single cohesive argument forming the climax of Romans 1-11. The term "faith" in this epistle is used comprehensively, i.e. it includes obedience to the gospel of Christ as a necessary element of being justified (Rom. 1:5; 6:16-17; 16:26). Paul contrasts two possible systems of justification: "the law of works" versus "the law of faith" (Rom. 3:27). The "law of works" refers to a system which would demand sinless law-keeping (Gal. 3:10-11), whereas, "the law of faith" refers to a system that offers forgiveness of sins on the basis of a submissive faith (Rom. 3:24). Understanding that all men have sinned, both Jew and Gentile must exercise faith in Christ in order to have hope of salvation (Rom. 3:9-23).

Several questions probably and consequently occurred to the mind of the Jewish reader: (1) "If God was going to provide salvation to the Gentiles, why did he ever choose the Jews to begin with?" (2) "Does God still love the Jews who have rejected the Christ?" If it is God's sovereign will unconditionally to damn specific persons then it is difficult to account for Paul's anguish over their loss and for his zealous effort to save some of them (Rom. 10:1; 11:14).

The Jews were chosen as the lineage through whom God would bring the Messiah into the world and by whom he would offer a blessing to both Jews and Gentiles (Gal. 3:14; Rom. 1:3; 9:5). *Paul is considering God's sovereign choice of nations, rather than particular individuals in this text.* This is a key point, and must not be missed. The most zealous opponents of God's offer of salvation to the Gentiles were the Jewish people. They did not want God to offer salvation to all men. Ironically, they wanted unconditional election for themselves based on physical lineage, which is the very thing Paul is denying in this context (Rom. 10:1-3; 11:22).

Calvinists appeal to Romans 9:10-13 for support of their theory that God does not as a part of his redemptive plan love all men and, thus, unconditionally chooses to elect and reprobate certain ones. Simply researching the original passages in the Old Testament which Paul is referencing would, on the surface, clear up the misunderstanding. Romans 9:12 references Genesis 25:23 which says, *"And the Lord said unto her, 'Two nations are in thy womb, and two manner of people shall be separated from thy bowels; and the one people shall be stronger than the other people; and the elder shall serve the younger.'"* Notice that the Scripture says, "two nations are in your womb." Israel came from Jacob, whereas, the Edomites came from

Esau. Esau never physically served Jacob, but the Edomites did serve the Israelites (1 Chron. 18:12, 13).

Romans 9:13 follows the same pattern that we have observed regarding national election. The statement: "Jacob have I loved, but Esau have I hated" does not refer to personal election as is obvious by its original occurrence. We find this statement in Malachi 1:2, 3 years after Jacob and Esau had died. Notice that the statement refers to the desolation of the Edomites. The Scripture says, *"I have loved you, saith the Lord. Yet ye say, 'Wherein hast thou loved us? Was not Esau Jacob's brother?' saith the Lord: 'Yet I loved Jacob and I hated Esau and laid his mountains and his heritage waste for the dragons of the wilderness.' Whereas Edom saith, 'We are impoverished.'"*

Romans 9:14 addresses the Jew who would attempt to call God into question for extending the invitation to the Gentile who would seek God by faith. The Jews were not in a position to challenge God's right to offer redemption to both Jews and Gentiles. Romans 9:15, 16 is not an example of Paul forging the doctrine of unconditional individual election but it is an example of the Lord's freedom to pour out his mercy and grace beyond the boundaries of Jewish ethnic identity.

There is no doubt that God hardens certain men, but the real question is how? The Scriptures teach us that God hardened Pharaoh's heart and Pharaoh hardened Pharaoh's heart. We see in Pharaoh a man already shaking his fist at Jehovah in defiance of truth. God simply put him into a position of leadership over the Egyptians so that he might demonstrate his power over a man that had bent his will on doing evil (Rom. 9:17; Exod. 10:17). Did God miraculously and directly manipulate his mind? Absolutely not! In Exodus 9:34 we read, "When Pharaoh saw that the rain and the hail and the thunder had ceased, he sinned yet more, and he hardened his heart, he and his servants." It was through God's miracles, wonders and signs that Pharaoh's heart was hardened. Today the gospel of Christ hardens some hearts because individuals have already developed insensibility to the truth of their own accord. Too, he gave Pharaoh a command that he did not want to keep ("Let my people go…"), and he refused to keep it. Today he gives the disobedient all sorts of commands that they do not want to keep, and they refuse to keep them.

Paul's usage of the "potter and the clay" illustration takes us back to Jeremiah 18 and once again if one would go back and read that text in its own context he would find that the passage is addressing God's dealings with nations and it also affirms conditional election. Jeremiah writes,

"Then the word of the LORD came to me, saying: 'O house of Israel, can I not do with you as this potter?' says the LORD. 'Look, as the clay is in the potter's hand, so are you in My hand, O house of Israel! The instant I speak concerning a nation and concerning a kingdom, to pluck up, to pull down, and to destroy it, if that nation against whom I have spoken turns from its evil, I will relent of the disaster that I thought to bring upon it. And the instant I speak concerning a nation and concerning a kingdom, to build and to plant it, if it does evil in My sight so that it does not obey My voice, then I will relent concerning the good with which I said I would benefit it. Now therefore, speak to the men of Judah and to the inhabitants of Jerusalem, saying, "Thus says the LORD: Behold, I am fashioning a disaster and devising a plan against you. Return now every one from his evil way, and make your ways and your doings good."'" This text destroys the Calvinistic interpretation from at least two perspectives. First of all, it is dealing with God's relationship with the "House of Israel." It teaches national election. Secondly, the Lord's manifestation of mercy does not deny, but rather demands the condition of an obedient faith. Paul's point is simple and it is that God had every right to bring the Messiah into the world through the Jewish lineage and, likewise, he had every right to sincerely extend the invitation of salvation to all men.

Conclusion

It is believed that the position taken in this short appendix harmonizes the biblical presentation of the character and nature of God, the scriptural teaching regarding the sincere invitation on the part of the Lord to "whosoever wills" (Rev. 22:17) and the scriptural affirmation of the free-will of man. Calvinists tend to shroud their dark theology by misinterpreting and misapplying this text which was originally written irrefutably to affirm that no group of people is in a position to deny God's sovereign right to invite all of mankind to come to the feast of salvation—which is the very thing that Calvinism does. May we always glorify God for the sovereign power of his love!

www.ingramcontent.com/pod-product-compliance
Lightning Source LLC
LaVergne TN
LVHW011230080426
835509LV00005B/423
9781584271666